Endorsements

It is a great honor and joy for me to endorse this awesome book called *The Wild Ones* by my dear friend Nate Johnston. Over the many years I have known Nate I've seen him walk through many seasons. Some were dark valleys; others were times of intense training as he faithfully served other ministries. God has developed him into a highly prophetic voice crying in the religious wilderness to the broken, discouraged, and wounded soldiers, and I am so grateful for the way God uses him. Within the pages of *The Wild Ones*, you will be challenged to think different, to approach things from another angle, to not be someone who lives in a sealed spiritual box but someone who can begin to live a limitless Christian life by the power of God's awesome grace. This book is not only the story of Nate's journey but it also has many spiritual gems within it to help you be part of the new breed in the earth that marches to the beat of a different drum. I highly recommend it and know that it will definitely impact your life

Revivalist Chris Harvey

We have had the privilege of journeying with Nate and Christy as they have navigated difficult situations, contended for breakthrough, and come through victorious and more in love with Jesus. Watching as they have maintained their integrity in the midst of trials and have continued to trust God despite what they saw in the natural has been a blessing, a joy, and an inspiration to people all over the world. Nate has hope that is not hollow, and it is this hope forged through fire that is now ministering to many. Open your heart and allow this book to inspire, encourage, and empower you to see God come through for you too!

Katherine Ruonala
Senior Leader, Glory City Church

Before the creation of the world, God looked across the generations and saw a group of Wild Ones whose hearts would burn for Him in a unique way. They'd follow wherever He led. They'd do whatever He asked. They wouldn't compromise or be distracted from what was true. Their shouts would carry the ring of His Presence. Their conviction would lead them toward the lost. And their determination to see the Son receive His full reward for His sacrifice would be their purest motivation. This group of Wild Ones needed a voice, someone to lead them in a way that no other voice has been able to speak to their unique season or call. It is in this hour that God has anointed Nate Johnston to shepherd a global migration of those who are moving outside of the ordinary and into this unique flow of the Spirit. This timely and anointed message is for each person who hears the Father beckoning, who hears the call of *The Wild Ones*.

Becky Thompson
National bestselling author and creator of
the Midnight Mom Devotional
www.beckythompson.com

Once in a while, you pick up a book that is more like a flaming sword that pierces your heart or a burning bush, fork-in-the-road encounter than just words on a page. This is that!

While reading this, our insides burned and resonated with the pioneering call in these pages to march into unchartered territory. This book is dripping with anointing that will ignite you, provoke you, and propel you forward into your unique and wild call.

We have known Nate and Christy Johnston for over a decade now, and know them to be of the highest character and integrity, true pioneers of revival, and pure hearted ministers of Jesus' love. They embody this message and we've watched them live it out. We unreservedly recommend them, and *The Wild Ones*, to you.

If you know you're branded by fire and called to not just roads less traveled, but to build the "less traveled" roads others will use to reach their destiny, this is required reading. *The Wild Ones* is a branding iron for the pioneer and a catalyst of courage to build what hasn't been seen before.

Ben and Jodie Hughes
Pour It Out Ministries
Revivalists, authors, TV hosts
www.pouritout.org

My friend Nate Johnston carries a pioneer spirit. I have known him and his wife, Christy, for many years and have admired the way they've positioned their lives, being led by God's prophetic instruction. Nate is not afraid to adventure through wilderness seasons, living on the cutting edge, knowing that staying on the front lines allows a person to witness the greatest victories! Through this book, you will glean from his life experiences in the prophetic realm and learn how to navigate the path that God has set before you. This guide is not for the faint of heart; it's for *The Wild Ones*!

Joshua Mills
Author, Power Portals and Creative Glory
www.joshuamills.com

If you've ever wondered where your place is or had to fight to find your voice, *The Wild Ones* will serve as a guide to you again and again. Nate doesn't write about ambiguous concepts or theories but from a lived experience of the call to the wild and unknown. This practical book will enable you to understand where and how God is positioning you for your destiny as you embrace the road less traveled. I have had the immense joy of watching my friends, Nate and Christy, answer the call of Jesus, and their pioneering spirit will provoke you to live out the authentic call God has placed on your life.

Sarah Cheesman
The Happy Prophet

Nate is a strong voice and advocate for the misfits, the Christian conundrums who feel they don't fit but yearn to find a place to belong. Artists and prophets, pioneers who innovate and create, taking new ground often uncomfortable for the church and misunderstood by the world.

The Wild Ones will impart true identity and open your eyes to a community of believers just like you. Get ready for the adventure. Your purpose and calling waits.

Fabiano Altamura
Dean, Bethel Conservatory of the Arts
Director and producer

From long ago God has invited His people to walk the "ancient paths, where the good way is" (Jer. 6:16), to sojourn in the Spirit until a resting place is found for the soul and a violent flame in the heart. I believe this dimension of relationship is opened to those who will take on the pilgrimage to discover what God is really like. It might surprise you how wild He truly is. Make no mistake, He is an all-consuming fire, and those who dare to truly walk with Him will catch His wild nature as well.

Nate Johnston is one of God's movers and shakers and his newest release, *The Wild Ones,* opens the gate for God's lions to be released into the earth. You will be challenged and stirred in your Spirit to say "yes" to a fresh invitation from the Lord. You're not a crazy person! No, you are chosen by God for such a time as this. Be emboldened by the Spirit as you read this well-written book.

Charlie Shamp
Destiny Encounters International
Vice president, Renaissance Coalition
Author, *Angels and Transfigured*

This book carries within it the fires of revival, and I believe that it will stir your heart to break free from the fear of man and step into new levels of freedom to be all that God has created you to be!

Aaron Damianopoulos
Lead pastor, Glory City Church, Brisbane

Nate Johnston's book, *The Wild Ones,* is a beautifully written guide for thousands of contemporary Christians who have refused to settle for the sleepy, shallow traditions of self-satisfied religious churches/organizations and instead have chosen to follow the Spirit of God through whatever difficult circumstances may be necessary to gain true unity with Jesus Christ. This is truly a book for our time, as our Father is doing everything He can to prepare a bride for His Son who is spotless, without wrinkle, and ready to stand with Jesus. Read this book and share what you learn because thousands of others need the wisdom it contains.

Joan Hunter
Author/evangelist

This is a book about permission. Permission to be who you were made to be. Permission to think differently and run with authentic passion. Nate has beautifully and transparently laid out his own story on these pages to help you understand the value and necessity of your unique voice in the kingdom. I believe you will be refreshed and reignited anew to fulfill the original, fiery mandate on your life as you read this book.

Roma Waterman
Founder, HeartSong Prophetic Alliance and HeartSong Creative
Academy Award-winning songwriter and author

We are truly in unprecedented times and now more than ever there is a cry in the earth for the unadulterated Word of the Lord to be released. My dear friend and brother Nate Johnston has been graced by God in our generation to awaken, equip, and cover this new emergence of prophetic voices coming forth. *The Wild Ones* is not only a must have but a clarion call to the hidden ones to arise. My life and calling has been marked over the years in a personal way through both Nate and Christy Johnston. This book is drenched in the presence and each page marked with the fire of God. Get ready to be changed forever!

Torrey Marcel Harper
Pastor and itinerant prophet
Habitation NYC
www.globalprayernyc.org

Nate Johnston is a friend and hard core prophetic encourager. He continues to speak to the prophetic potential in believers and stokes the fire of revival in their lives. This book, *The Wild Ones*, will fan the flame of reformation and prophetic destiny in your life!

Ryan LeStrange
Author of *Breaking Curses*
Founder of ATLHub, RLM, TRIBE Network, and owner,
LeStrange Global, LLC

I love the local church. It was in that place I found Jesus, encountered His presence for the first time, and found my place at God's great table. Passion, purpose, and presence were all evident as my heart found home and my spirit became alive with holy fire.

Nate's words in *Wild Ones* are like fuel for any embers in hearts that are waning, and a "calling home" to those who feel reduced to the edges of a church they don't identify with. Take heart. There's a place for YOU at the table. The world we find ourselves in today aches for a church who loves boldly and authentically and who is not afraid of being misunderstood.

I pray this book opens a doorway to the wildness for Jesus within you.

Darlene Zschech
Songwriter, worshiper, and author

THE

Wild Ones

THE

Wild Ones

THE PIONEER CALL
OF EMERGING VOICES
FROM THE WILDERNESS
TO THE FRONTLINES

NATE JOHNSTON

DESTINY IMAGE® PUBLISHERS, INC.
P.O. Box 310, Shippensburg, PA 17257-0310
"Promoting Inspired Lives."

This book and all other Destiny Image and Destiny Image Fiction books are available at Christian bookstores and distributors worldwide.

Cover design by Nate Johnston & Eileen Rockwell

For more information on foreign distributors, call 717-532-3040.

Reach us on the Internet: www.destinyimage.com.

ISBN 13 TP: 978-0-7684-5890-9

ISBN 13 eBook: 978-0-7684-5891-6

ISBN 13 HC: 978-0-7684-5893-0

ISBN 13 LP: 978-0-7684-5892-3

For Worldwide Distribution, Printed in the U.S.A.

1 2 3 4 5 6 7 8 / 25 24 23 22 21

Dedication

I DEDICATE THIS BOOK TO MY FAMILY:

To my wife Christy for being there with me every step of the way, through every trial, wilderness, and mountain top. For always championing me selflessly, reminding me who I am, and helping me birth the message I was created to share. You are my greatest role model and best friend. This book happened because you kept me true to the core message I carry and I will be forever grateful for not letting me settle for something less than that.

To my girls Charlotte, Sophie, and Ava, I wrote this book with you at the forefront of my mind because legacy is written in these pages and before anyone else this is written for you, to arm you and prepare you for a life less ordinary with Jesus. My prayer for you is that my ceiling will be your floor and that your own adventures with God will eclipse every one of my own. You have all stirred up the wild in me that I thought was lost – thank you.

To those who fanned my flame into my calling and took a chance on me in the early days, Sue & Terry Walker, Louis Vasiliou, Nick Vujicic, & Chris Harvey, and the true mother's and fathers in my life who poured into me – thank you!

To the other wild ones and misfits out there that encouraged me along the way and lifted up my arms – thank you. You know this road and you know this is the moment we shine. To our closest friends and people in our corner – thanks for always cheering me on.

Contents

Foreword

I resonate with the sound that comes forth from Nate Johnston. It feels like a pent-up roar that has been deeply held within for months, if not years. There is an ache, a cry, a longing for a generation to arise that is not tethered by moral failures of the past or by the excessive pride of successful obtainment. There is a desperation to shake off shame, self-limiting labels, and any definition other than what our Father says.

Nate is truly focused on what our Father has to say because he is focused on who our Father is. Relationship. Formation. Maturation. Process. These are all key components in becoming a true "Wild One." God knows we have seen some fake ones. They might act different, shout or sing with zeal, light up the night for a while, but can they handle the pressure? Will they stay the course and keep their hand on the plow when things get tough? The Body of Christ and the world are waiting to see those who are truly "set free" from the opinion of man and who live for the audience of One. These are the authentic "Wild Ones."

Some years ago, in the height of the Father's Blessing movement, the Holy Spirit spoke something to me that rocked my boat, shook my world, and became a defining moment in my life. I heard Jehovah Sneaky say, *"I am going to keep coming upon you with waves of My presence until I make you into a wild man."*

At that time, I needed to hear that word. I was willing to pay the price to become that word. Frankly, I was getting rather tired of being respectable Clark Kent, and I deeply longed to shed the garments of the fear of man and soar like a superman that I knew I was created to be. But I was caught in the thick woods of respectability and the fear of rejection, and I did not know the way out. But something inside of me longed to blaze my way out of that maze.

Then that liberating voice of the Father came to me and validated me. It's so interesting, like Nate, I had to be convinced that this word *wild* was accurate, appropriate, and appeared in Scripture. So, I too did my word studies. I found a measure of confirmation and relief in Psalm 92:10 where it speaks about being anointed with fresh oil like that of a wild ox. Fascinating. Not a domesticated tame ox, but a wild ox. When I saw that my new friend, Nate Johnston, was composing a book titled *The Wild Ones*, I thought, *I relate to that!*

As a writer, a coach in writing, and a mentor to a few, when I glanced at this manuscript, I was impressed with the structural skill. Not only does Nate carry revelation as a gift from the Holy Spirit as a prophet, but he is first a priestly worshiper unto God. But as I get to know him better, I am also observing some other rare commodities. It is a blueprint capacity to help the person get from point A to Z. It is one thing to point the way and say, "It's that way!" It's another dimension to point that way and say, "Let's go on the journey together."

So, with a fulness of joy and gladness of heart, I want to thank the Lord for this timely book on "the wild ones" by worshipping warrior and prophetic way maker, Nate Johnston. And may waves of God's presence continue to come upon each of you until He makes you into the very special unique creation He has ordained for you to be in Christ Jesus. Amen and amen!

With Gratitude,
James W. Goll
Founder of God Encounters Ministries
GOLL Ideation LLLC

An Invitation to the Adventure

When I was a kid, I was always off on adventures. I loved the outdoors, the rugged Australian bush, our prehistoric rainforests, and our white beaches. During the times when things were hard in my home and I was struggling to process life and mature, nature was always a place of escape and mystery for me. I found it to be a place of infinite possibilities and unexpected encounters. I was a dreamer, and nature was the landscape for imagining incredible stories of dangerous missions, lost treasure discoveries, and daring rescues.

In my teens, I used to love camping. I would go for days into the bush with few supplies, hoping to learn the art of survival in the wild. It often ended badly, but I loved the risk and thrill of being completely vulnerable to the elements and the ultimate test of problem-solving my way out of crazy situations.

One time stands out in my memory. My best friend and I decided to put our skills to the test and were dropped off into the wilderness by his dad. My friend's father said he would be back in five days. It was an unmapped part of the national forest, and we had limited water and food, but we were determined to put all our knowledge to the test as well as our mental aptitude. Within two days, we had ran out of water and started to dehydrate in the hot sun, and so without any cell phone reception, we pushed on further into the bush, wasting precious energy hoping to find a stream or creek or something—but it all was to no avail.

On the fourth day, we managed to find a hill with some tall trees, so we climbed them and managed to get hold of the State Emergency Service (SES) and notify them of our situation, but they never found us. On the fifth day, dehydrated, chased by wild bulls, sunburned, and suffering heat stroke, we made our way back to the starting location to be picked up. We went a different way there, however, and to our amazement, not ten minutes from the pickup was one of the most beautiful, flowing streams with the freshest water. We screamed, we yelled, we jumped up and down, and then we drank water until we were filled. Finally, we lay under a tree until we were picked up.

Now, I'd like to say that this trip was a once off, but it wasn't. Over the years, I would go on to have many more successful survival adventures as well as some failed ones with near death experiences. I eventually grew up. It's called having a wife who talks some sense into me.

That trip with my friend taught me that, no matter what I thought I knew about wilderness survival, I was no match for the unexpected terrain. Then I said *yes* to Jesus and the prophetic call, and I was yet again in deep waters, out of my depth with no map, no compass, or any way to know how to navigate this unique calling. I realized that yet again I was in a survival situation. Only this time, it was spiritual. I understood that I could try to navigate in my own strength and know-how but, ultimately, I wouldn't make it through without divine intervention. I needed a guide. I needed the Holy Spirit, and I know for certain that, without Him, I wouldn't be where I am today.

You see, this call is not for the faint of heart. It's not for the half-hearted pursuers of Jesus or the ones happy with three songs on a Sunday and a hallelujah. What if I told you that there will be never any greater risk you will take or purpose you will find than when you say *yes* to the *wild* path of fulfilling the prophetic call. It's a call to a lifestyle. A life of responding to the prophetic call can be the most incredible life and adventure you could ever imagine.

I have written a guide, a mudmap, of some of the terrain you will cross, the "bears" you will fight, and the "giants" you will find in your path to your destiny. I want to give you some keys and tools to walk it out. If I could write something and send it back in time to my twenty-five-year-old self, this book would be it. Every chapter and every topic would be like a lifeline to my younger self when I was stepping into the unknown. This book is for the prophetic pioneers out there, the forerunners, the renaissance creatives, and the reformers needing GPS navigation from obscurity into purpose. This book is for you.

Perhaps like me, you haven't quite ever fit the mold, and it resulted in your laying low or hiding out. I want you to know, though, that God has created you for a very powerful and unique reason. Maybe you know it, maybe you don't, but I pray that this book is an anointed guide that issues a clarion call to you to come out from obscurity. You have been in hiding for far too long.

This book is for the wild ones—the generation of pioneering, reformational, emerging voices that God is calling to the frontlines right now. This is for those who feel the rhythm of the Lion of the tribe of Judah beating in their spirits and His roar in their bellies. This is for those who are carrying the keys for the new day God is leading the Church into but don't yet know how to navigate it. This is for those who have been on the fringe for so long they don't know where to begin. Yes, this is for you. This is your prophetic survival guide for the unusual and yet wonderful adventure to which you have been called.

Just a heads up, you will hear me throughout this book refer to the *wild ones* as *pioneers, forerunners, reformers,* and *emerging prophetic voices* because, while many of those titles carry some similarities, at their core the wild ones are all called to be the hands and feet of today's reformation and the revival in the nations. And it's just as important to note that the wild ones all go through the wilderness journey to the frontlines.

I believe there is a heart cry of a generation ringing out right now. It's the heart cry of a remnant that are longing for the wild, for the real, for the "more" of the Lord. This remnant longs to break past every obstacle that stands in the way of their being unbridled for Jesus in every aspect of life. You may have thought your wilderness was your endgame, but it was just the beginning. It was the place that marked you for a lifestyle beyond the mediocrity of religion and called you into deep intimacy with the King of kings. It was where you sacrificed your appetite for the mundane and stale to obtain something rugged and unknown, yet extraordinary. Where you are heading isn't the wilderness anymore; in fact, I believe this season marks the beginning of the end of that season of isolation, but God wants to reawaken you to the wild nature of the Holy Spirit working in and through you. The Holy Spirit is stirring you. He is generating a rumble within your being. It's something you haven't experienced before, and it's meant to cause you to rise to the mighty call upon your life.

I wrote the following after experiencing my own "call to the wild season":

I can't fight it. My heart is wild. It doesn't long for pews and green rooms but altars and living room floors. You have branded me so deeply that I can't ever let go of this burning passion that seems to break out without permission. I can't play the game and talk the talk, but I can be a lover at Your feet and go where You take me. My heart is wild. My Lion King, You gave it to me. You forged me in the wilderness and called me to my post, anointed me with oil and filled me with the Holy Ghost. I'm not a rebel. I'm a son who doesn't see limits in his Father's house. I used to hide from the table, but now I set the feast. I used to cower to people's judgments, but now I'm bringing balm to the ones who rejected me. It's a changing of the guard and the unleashing of Kingdom power, the foolish things to confound the wise, and the trumpet call of a new hour. My heart is wild. I dream of forests and streams and adventures chasing Your voice, but also I'm a worshiper always looking for ways to simply love You, so it's not my will where I go. I'm happy with Your choice.

Are you ready to say *yes* to the wild adventure?

Lord, raise up your wild-hearted ones.

PART 1

The Call of the Wild

CHAPTER 1

The Call of the Wild

"You would not have called to me unless I had been calling to you," said the Lion. —C.S. Lewis

If you have picked up this book, I'm going to assume at least one, if not all, of the following four things are true:

- You are curious.
- You are searching for your purpose and calling.
- You were strangely drawn to the title as if its two words somehow sum up your life.
- You long to live wild and free in Jesus and not be held back anymore.

To be honest this wasn't the book I expected to write. For me it would have been so much easier to write some prophetic book on dreams and prophecy, and it would have helped people, but as my writing process began the Holy Spirit began to dig deep and revealed something He had his finger resting upon. This is truly *His* book for *this* hour for so many who have been search-ing, looking, and longing to make sense of their path and their purpose.

If this is you, then today your journey with the Holy Spirit begins. You are on your way toward embracing your calling as His *wild one*.

A STRATEGIC REMNANT

When I say the word *wild*, what is the first thing that comes to mind? Is it a wild animal in the jungle hunting its prey, or maybe you think of someone who is rebellious, radical, irresponsible, undignified, or heretical?

For the most part, the word *wild* in the Church has always had a negative connotation. We think of the guy, for example, who gets saved yet still wears his Megadeth shirt every Sunday or the girl who still smokes before and after church. Wild for us represents those who aren't pure or refined in any way. They are unruly, rough around the edges, and in desperate need of a Christian makeover. But what if I were to tell you that wild means something else entirely and that you were actually called to be a wild one for Jesus?

First, let's look at the dictionary definitions of wild.

- Occurring, growing, or living in a natural state; not domesticated, cultivated, or tamed.
- Not inhabited or farmed.
- Uncivilized, barbarous, and undomesticated.
- Lacking supervision or restraint.
- Disorderly; unruly.
- Characterized by a lack of moral restraint; dissolute or licentious.
- Lacking regular order or arrangement; disarranged.
- Full of, marked by, or suggestive of strong, uncontrolled emotion.
- Extravagant; fantastic and highly enthusiastic.
- Furiously disturbed or turbulent; stormy.
- Risky; imprudent and impatiently eager.
- Deviating greatly from an intended course.

- Having an equivalence or value determined by the cardholder's choice.

Some of these definitions highlight positive side of wild while others underscore the unruly or imprudent side of the word. Let's look at each definition, however, from a Kingdom perspective or how the Father sees them:

- **Occurring, growing, or living in a natural state**. People who are not tainted by any institution or system but are true to their original design.
- **Not domesticated, cultivated, or tamed, inhabited, or farmed**. People who are not made to fit a mold, who are not subdued, controlled, or expected to look like the rest.
- **Uncivilized, barbarous, and undomesticated**. Those who are rough around the edges and don't know the protocols, but neither are they infected by the religious and legalistic system.
- **Lacking supervision or restraint**. Those who need fathers, mothers, and godly leaders, but they aren't under submission to man but to God.
- **Disorderly; unruly**. People are the rule breakers of the Kingdom and often do things backwards or unlike anyone else would.
- **Characterized by a lack of moral restraint**. People who move not by sight or by what is around them but by the Spirit. They are often seen as being fleshy or arrogant, but when in submission to the Holy Spirit, they are a weapon.
- **Lacking regular order or arrangement; disarranged**. Those who don't operate by the normal standards or by regular protocols. They are led by the Spirit.
- **Full of, marked by, or suggestive of strong, uncontrolled emotion**. They are passionate, raw, real, fiery, and seen as radical.

- **Extravagant; fantastic and highly enthusiastic**. Those who are movements waiting to happen.
- **Furiously disturbed or turbulent; stormy**. People who are a "storm in a bucket," which is why the enemy is afraid of them.
- **Risky; imprudent and impatiently eager**. People who don't sit and waste time. They move!
- **Deviating greatly from an intended course**. They are pioneers of a new path.
- **Having an equivalence or value determined by the cardholder's choice**. God uses such people however He pleases and whenever He pleases.

Also, the Greek word for wild is *agrios*, and it is used a few times in the New Testament. It means "fierce and untamed." But why would God need us to be fierce and untamed?

WE'VE BEEN TAMED

What if God has always called us to be wild and unbridled for Him, but religion, which is the enemy's counterfeit, has lied to us to keep us checked, at bay, and tamed? What if God has always wanted us to be wildly in love with Him and radically in pursuit of Him?

Religion has successfully raised wimps and powerless, passionless, clones who often leave the seminary disillusioned and spiritually dead. From there churches and empires are created around theology and the philosophy of Christianity instead of the fiery gaze only found in encountering Christ in the secret place. Churches open their doors to the masses and lead them to programs and more ways to busy themselves in activities that are more like cages than launching pads and distractions rather than Kingdom effectivity. Yes, we have been tamed.

I had this revelation when I was eighteen. I was at a birthday party for a friend when a musician for a once globally known rock band started talking to me. He told me how he was at the peak of his career when he got saved. He said he was so in love with Jesus that he listened to people around him who told him to give away all his money and his home, stop wearing the same clothes, cut his hair, and start talking differently, so he did. With tears in his eyes, he said to me, "Nate, don't make the same mistake I did. Sell out to Jesus not to religion because it cost me everything." He wasn't talking about the money or the house. He was talking about losing his wildness. He was numb, emotionless, and living in deep regret.

We can't afford to be tamed by religion, but we must be the ones who push back against it and accept who we have been created to be.

HE ISN'T A TAME LION

In *The Chronicles of Narnia* series, the author and visionary C.S Lewis writes Jesus into his story as a Lion called Aslan. Aslan brings order and justice to a world under submission to and oppression by a witch. In *The Lion, the Witch and the Wardrobe*—the first published book of the Narnia series—there is an interesting conversation about Aslan:

> "Is—is he [Aslan] a man?" asked Lucy.
> "Aslan a man!" said Mr. Beaver sternly, "Certainly not. I tell you he is the King of the wood. . . . Aslan is a lion—the Lion, the great Lion."
> "Ooh!" said Susan. "I'd thought he was a man. Is he—quite safe? I shall feel rather nervous about meeting a lion."

> "That you will, dearie, and no mistake," said Mrs. Beaver. . . .
>
> "Then he isn't safe?" said Lucy.
>
> "Safe?" said Mr. Beaver. . . . "Who said anything about safe? 'Course he isn't safe. But he's good. He's the King, I tell you."[1]

Much later in the book, Mr. Beaver is remembered as having said this about Aslan:

> "He's wild, you know. Not like a tame lion."[2]

Jesus has been painted over the years as a God-Man who was almost void of passionate emotion or feeling, but that wasn't the case. Jesus wept with those who mourned, rebuked and told off His disciples, called the Pharisees "whitewashed tombs," and turned over the tables in the temple (Matt. 16:23; 21:12; 23:27; Luke 11:33–35)! How does that fit into the current, progressive, church narrative of loving and tolerating everything and being placid and apathetic? That's right, it doesn't.

Even the way Jesus chose His disciples reveals the heart of God. He chose fishermen, tax collectors, and thieves, and He dined with, stayed with, and ministered to the same types of people. God chose a wild man called John the Baptizer to prepare the way for His ministry, went into heathen towns to spark revival, and turned water in wine so people could drink more at a wedding. Is that what you would call wild? Is our Savior wild? Wild-hearted, yes! He may be the Spotless Lamb that was sacrificed for us on Calvary, but let's not forget He is the Lion of the tribe of Judah as well.

> *Then one of the elders said to me, "Stop weeping. Look! The mighty Lion of Judah's tribe, the root of David—he has conquered! He is the worthy one who can open the scroll and its seven seals." Then I saw a young Lamb standing before the throne, encircled by*

the four living creatures and the twenty-four elders.
He appeared to have been slaughtered but was now
alive! (Revelation 5:5–6 TPT).

WILD & FREE

We are made in God's image and bear His heart, marked with the fire of heaven. We are wild and free. We are the wild lovers of God. The wild ones of this hour are those who don't quite fit the mold. They are the pioneers, forerunners, and reformers who have been marked for a unique and special purpose but haven't always known or recognized it.

The wild ones are the misfits who haven't been able to fully identify with the church. They even have been rejected by the church yet carry keys to unlock what is coming. They are the worshipers rising with new songs and never before heard sounds, the creatives and artisans carrying revolutionary blueprints and plans to build and create Heaven on Earth. The wild ones are the prophetic voices who have been called to stand on the mountaintop and call in the next wave—the new voices rising to declare the Word of the Lord into the earth and establish it.

THE WAKE-UP CALL

I believe there is a clarion call going out across the earth right now for the wild ones who have been in hiding, for the ones who have been feeling inactive and tamed, or those who have been ready and waiting at the gate for their moment. The Holy Spirit is breathing life into dry bones and commissioning the decommissioned, and just like Jesus called Lazarus from the tomb He is calling you and I out of our tomb, out of our caves of defeat, out of our silence, and unravelling the bandages and grave clothes we have been wearing, standing us to our feet, giving us a new robe, and sending us into the earth as his messengers for the hour.

Then Jesus added, "Lazarus, our friend, has just fallen asleep. It's time that I go and awaken him" (John 11:11).

HERE IT BEGINS

If you have read this far and haven't called me a heretic or got offended, then you have done well. This is where it begins. This is the moment of recognition of the unique call upon your life to be a sold-out radical for Jesus no matter the cost. But despite what it may sound like so far, this book hasn't been written to make you rebellious but to stir up the passionate, on fire for God, wild one you have always been though hidden or kept under wraps up until now. This book has been written because you and I need to *get back* to our wild, to find our wild, and to embrace it as part of our calling.

This isn't a book about being wild for the sake of being wild. This is about embracing who you are called to be, moving past the obstacles, and finding your rightful place at the frontlines for this time in history. Are you ready?

PROPHETIC SURVIVAL KEY

Don't be tamed by religion but ask Holy Spirit to reacquaint you with the person He called you to be. Look at Jesus and the Father. You were made in the image of God.

CAMPFIRE PRAYER

Dear Father, You created me with a fire in my belly that cannot be contained. I can't explain it away, suppress it, or hide it any longer. Instead, I give it room to begin to develop into a full flame in my life. Lord, where I have been tamed, I ask that You would unbridle me again and lead me onto the path ordained for my life, in Jesus' name.

NOTES

1. C.S. Lewis, *The Lion, the Witch and the Wardrobe* (New York: HarperTrophy, 2000), 79–80.
2. C.S. Lewis, *The Lion, the Witch and the Wardrobe*, 182.

CHAPTER 2

A Different Drum

When the whole world is running towards a cliff,
he who is running in the opposite direction appears
to have lost his mind. —attributed to C.S. Lewis

He was as wild as you could get. Some called him crazy, but he wasn't born for the old wineskin. He was born to break out of it and be the bridge to the new thing God was doing. John the Baptizer, as he was known, did not just break out of the box, he was outright heretical, constantly challenging the religious system of his day. But was he a rebel? Maybe. But was he in error? No, he was following the divine blueprint for his life and had zero fear of man in doing so.

To the religious order of that time, John was a threat even though he was only preparing the way for the prophesied Savior who was to come, but what the Pharisees of that day didn't know yet was the wineskin was about to burst and many boxes were going to break open. They didn't know John was the pioneer and forerunner for the ministry of the prophesied Messiah they had been waiting for. He marched to the beat of a different drum—the drum of the Spirit that was leading him into new terrain where his people had never been before.

AN UNEXPECTED DEFINING WORD

When I was seventeen, a Pentecostal preacher named Jim Williams came to our church. Jim was a white-haired man of seventy, but he had the charisma and energy of a twenty-year-old, and everyone loved when he came because he was a real, "say it like it is," fair dinkum, Aussie preacher. When he spoke, it was undeniable that God was upon him. I sat on the second back row because he also did this thing where he would walk down the middle aisle and talk to the crowd. It felt as if he were staring right into your soul if you happened to be in his line of sight.

Toward the end of the service, Jim began calling people up and giving them words of knowledge. He called me up. I was happy about it because he had just given the two ladies before me amazing words of encouragement, so I expected that mine would be the same. "Worship singer guy," he said to me and then looked down for an awkwardly long time. Finally, he looked up with a very serious look in his eyes, poked me in the chest, and said, "Boy, you beat to a different drum." Jim continued to stare at me for another ten or more seconds and then moved on. What was I supposed to do with that, and what did it even mean?

THE DRUMBEAT CALL

I always knew I was out of the box and had a rebellious streak to boot, but until that moment, I didn't know it was something God put in me. I was always told I needed God to work on me because I was always asking questions and challenging the status quo. It took me a long time to realize I was made this way for a reason, and I'm not alone. There are others who are out of the box and appear to walk to the beat of a different drum. But why were we made this way? Why don't we feel like we fit in?

I thought it was personal, but it never was. I felt rejected for years because I just didn't fit in no matter what I did and what I compromised to be accepted. Whatever I did to be accepted didn't work, but just because I was rejected didn't mean God had rejected me. In fact, that was far from the truth. God had called and accepted me into a different regiment, a special force of sorts, to be the bridge from the old into the new. That was John the Baptist's mission, and I believe it's also yours—to be the new thing, to be a *voice* crying in the wilderness, preparing the way for Jesus and revealing Jesus to the world.

THE NEW IS THE THREAT

Church history has shown that we believers create monuments around certain "mountain top moments," as I like to call them, that we experience. Since the Church's beginnings in the book of Acts, people have encountered God and experienced various movements. Though these should have been celebrated among the Church, denominationalism has been the result of these "moments" that divided the Church instead of binding us together. We see this in revival history, especially where God moved in a notable way, and then the Church camped around that expression or value as if it were the only truth and thus rejected anything that looked different or subtly opposed it. This is where we have locked ourselves out from the wonder and adventure of exploring the infinite Kingdom and robbed ourselves of encountering the endless and multifaceted dimensions of God's nature and heart.

The new move of the Spirit will always shake everything up because it will cause us to have to get our feet out of the muddy areas we have become stuck in and experience God in a new way. This is exactly what John the Baptizer did, and this is what you and I have been called to do.

SHIPS WITH NO SAILS

The religious order of John's day was stuck—stuck in the mud of the old covenant laws. They were waiting for a Savior who was soon to be revealed, but because they were so stuck, they not only failed to recognize Jesus as their long-awaited Messiah when He came, but they failed to see the Spirit of God upon John as well. This is what Jesus spoke of regarding John:

> But I tell you, Elijah has already come, and they did not recognize him, but have done to him everything they wished. In the same way the Son of Man is going to suffer at their hands (Matthew 17:12).

Why couldn't they recognize John as being sent from God? And the greater question, why didn't they recognize Jesus? The answer here is that they became a people not led by the Spirit but by the laws. Their religious text had become their God over the Spirit who made the Scripture living, and in doing so, they were unable to recognize something from the Spirit when it presented itself. In essence, they became ships with no sails, vessels with nothing in place to capture the wind that could have taken them anywhere. They were truly stuck, and the Church has been stuck, too.

Enter the wild ones. In John 3:8, it says,

> The wind blows wherever it pleases. You hear its sound, but you cannot tell where it comes from or where it is going. So it is with everyone born of the Spirit.

What if your mandate was to lead others off the hamster wheel of religion and back onto the path of adventure with the Holy Spirit? What if you were called to model the Spirit-led life even when it made you look silly, rebellious, or arrogant? Romans 8:14

spells it out clearly, *"For those who are led by the Spirit of God are the children of God."*

Wow! So you aren't crazy or on the wrong track; you are being led by the Spirit! Well done!

PROTOTYPES OF PURPOSE

One of the most significant characteristics of John the Baptist's life that every pioneer and reformer can relate to is that he was on a very different path and trajectory than others. Have you ever felt that way? Have you ever said, "God, it would be so much easier just to go with the flow!" But no, it's like you are being towed by an imaginary rope in the *opposite* direction that others are going in. *Why is this?* you may be wondering. Just as John was the prototype for Jesus, you are the prototype of what is to come.

A prototype is someone or something that serves as a model or inspiration for those who come later. The prefix prot-, or proto-, comes from Greek and has the basic meaning of "first in time" or "first formed" and "original mold."

You see, what God has given you isn't second rate or defective just because it's how people perceive you based on what they know and have seen. You are actually the prototype for what is to come, the first of many!

IN TUNE WITH THE BEAT

Maybe like me you have always felt like you were following a different rhythm or tune, like there was just a different sound you were hearing but couldn't quite explain it. At its very core, the truth is God has hardwired you to be in tune with the beat of

His heart so that you can reveal it to others who have forgotten the sound. Here are a few signs you have been created to do this:

- You have an unusual sense of purpose in something not done before.
- You don't identify with the norm or feel called to the status quo.
- You feel like following the same road and pattern others have would be soul crushing,
- If you aren't doing something new and different, you feel complacent and apathetic.
- You see things others don't see, and you value things others don't see.

Do you feel like you walk to the beat of a different drum?

We have truly entered an era of history where God is awakening and stirring up a new breed of prophetic voices that were born as chaos specialists and way-makers for the Body of Christ to break through the greatest obstacles and lead us forward. But these voices have been in hiding, lost in the wilderness, and not knowing how crucial their role in this hour really is. But here God's reformers come, not shackled by the fear of man. They are walking out of their long season of obscurity and confusion with a fresh message, a power-packed anointing, and a heart to see Heaven touch down on Earth. These who were once the outcast, the out-of-the-box misfits, and the dreamers are being commissioned to restore and align the Church back to her rightful place and keep her eyes set on Jesus!

PROPHETIC SURVIVAL KEYS

You are a mold-breaker, not a conformist or a square peg meant to be cut down to fit a round hole. Your key is to **lean in**

to the beat of a different drum and not run from it. Be confident in how you have been made and do not allow insecurities to victimize you.

CAMPFIRE PRAYER

Father, I am beginning to see the fullness of my design and believe that I have been created perfectly and with a unique call that, while often misunderstood, has a powerful purpose in this era. Today, I shake off the many misconceptions people have of me and even I have had about myself. I embrace the true me that marches to the beat of a different drum as you have created me to do, in Jesus' name!

CHAPTER 3

There's something about being close to the Lord's heart that seems to keep at bay the taming nature of religion and all the external influences that daily try to take our wildness away. —Nate Johnston

It all started in the garden. Can you imagine the beauty and the rugged landscape that the garden of Eden was. Eden, which means "delight," was God's masterpiece, His dream, and man and woman were his tangible poetry that He placed within it. The garden would have been stunning, bursting with smells, tastes, and vibrant colors of plants, trees, and fruit. There would have been constant sounds of the wildlife everywhere you turned. It was the place of intimacy where God would walk in the garden with Adam and they would speak face-to-face, and this was God's original design until man chose to eat from the wrong tree and the garden was closed off. Instantly, everything changed. The enemy had tricked man and woman, and they were then suddenly aware of their sinful state, having the ability to choose life or death. Instead of face-to-face relationship with God, life became about rules and customs, sacrifices and atonements, and always reminded them that things weren't the same and they would never measure up again. Humanity lost the garden and lost their wild.

SMALL COMPROMISES

What is your wild? To me it's your purest form of identity in Christ. It's untainted by religion, where you're free to hear and receive from the Lord without restriction. It's your Holy Spirit receiver, your ability to pick up on His scent and know where He goes.

The greatest tragedy in the Christian world today is men and woman who began by encountering God in a powerful way and then slowly over time lost their wild, their zeal, their passion, their pursuit. It's where their belief system becomes linear and instructional instead of being exciting, adventurous, and full of wonder.

A line that always stood out to me was from Marvel's *Ironman 3* where Tony Stark says, "You start with something pure, something exciting. Then come the mistakes, the compromises."[1]

I have dealt with this many times in my life. In one season, I felt on fire for God, wanting to get more and more time in His presence than I was able. In another season, I wasn't as passionate, experiencing more difficulty in prayer . Have you been there? It's where we rest on our gifts and our ability to turn on a function outside of connection. If we continue to function without being connected to God in the garden or secret place, we inevitably crash and burn. Sometimes, that happens privately, but unfortunately, it can be happen publicly, creating quite the mess.

Far too many pastors and leaders I know come to me and tell me that they are burnt out and want to give up, or they tell me they are suddenly dealing with lust or some other temptation they didn't struggle with before. And they want to know why they are experiencing what they're experiencing. The answer is simple: At some stage, they compromised and traded their wild for the cage. When we lose our wild, we lose our passion, and when we lose our passion, we become numb, emotionless, and desirous of an escape from the harsh reality of the *Groundhog Day* world we live in.

This is true with our walk with God if we lose our very cornerstone of our existence—connection in the garden. We need it to live, to survive, and to thrive.

THE THREE GARDENS

One of the most powerful descriptions of the gospel I have ever heard was that the gospel is a story of a father who lost his children in the garden. So he bankrupted Heaven to get them back. I don't think there is any better description of the Father's heart than that, but He set something up so beautifully in how He orchestrated His rescue plan. Let me show you how:

- **Eden**—We were cut off in the garden of Eden, which means "delight," because we were created to enjoy God and for God to enjoy us. It was never meant to be living by a rule book but being fulfilled in a powerful relationship.

- **Gethsemane**—Jesus was sent to Earth, and on the night of His arrest, He stayed up all night, praying and interceding in the garden of Gethsemane, which means "oil press." This represented the crushing and wounding He would endure for us to reconnect to Him.

- **Garden Tomb**—It was a divine prophetic setup that Jesus' body was taken to an unused tomb owned by Joseph of Arimathea. The tomb was in a garden, of all places, representing the full circle redemption plan of God to bring us back to the place where it all began and all went wrong. While the garden tomb was unnamed, I believe it was no accident it was owned by Joseph, whose first name means double and whose surname (Arimathea) means high place, because the Father's mission was not just to take us back to the garden of delight but to give us double for our trouble and for us to ascend and be with Him in heavenly realms.

This is what Jesus accomplished on the cross. He fixed the sin issue and the access issue, and He reinstated us back where we belong. In essence, Jesus the Lion of Judah came to the earth to be sacrificed so that we would enter back again into Eden, where we find Him and find our roots.

THE BROKEN TABLE

In the movie version of *The Lion, the Witch and the Wardrobe*, the saddest scene is when Aslan the lion is tied down to a stone table (representing the cross of Calvary) and killed and de-maned.[2] After his assailants leave, there is a loud sound, and the scene suddenly shows the lion gone and the table split in two, representing the stone that was rolled away and the veil that was torn in the temple.

> *At that moment the curtain of the temple was torn in two from top to bottom. The earth shook, the rocks split* (Matthew 27:51).

The very next scene shows Aslan going to the witch's castle and breathing over each of the characters who have been turned into stone. Every time I watch this, I get goosebumps because what I see is our Savior who gave Himself selflessly to see us restored to who we really are. He could have left us out of the garden, and we couldn't blame Him for it. Man made that decision, but the Father decided to send His only Son so that we may have life again.

For here is the way God loved the world—he gave his only, unique Son as a gift. So now everyone who believes in him will never perish but experience everlasting life. God did not send his Son into the world to judge and condemn the world, but to be its Savior and rescue it! (John 3:16–17 TPT).

THE COUNTERFEIT

In the absence of the garden relationship, religion became the replacement, the place card, and the counterfeit. It was a means to an end that constantly reminded the people of Israel that they were falling drastically short of the mark, even with all the rules and rituals in place. But what we see today is a people who have been given access back to the garden, but they don't go there! They are still acting like they are bound! Jesus said this very thing to the Pharisees in Matthew 23:13.

But woe to you, scribes and Pharisees, hypocrites! For you shut the kingdom of heaven in people's faces. For you neither enter yourselves nor allow those who would enter to go in (ESV).

This is what religion does. It shuts the doors of the Kingdom of Heaven that people are called to walk through. It numbs people to the reality and endless resources that they have access to. Look what happened when John the Baptist came on the scene.

From the moment John stepped onto the scene until now, the realm of heaven's kingdom is bursting forth, and passionate people have taken hold of its power (Matthew 11:12 TPT).

Right now, God is awakening a people to be those who would forsake the trodden path of religion and go back to the garden, back to their origins, and back to where it all began—and dare to begin the quest of the wild!

WHY DO WE NEED TO GO BACK?

Aside from the points I have shared already, there are a few other major fruits of finding your wild roots again.

- It breaks all bondage to and all agreements with the demonic or religion.
- It ushers in freedom into your life you didn't have before.
- Creativity is rebirthed.
- Your voice is rebirthed.
- And your authority is activated.

Now the Lord God had formed out of the ground all the wild animals and all the birds in the sky. He brought them to the man to see what he would name them; and whatever the man called each living creature, that was its name (Genesis 2:19).

Coming back to your original design and purpose unlocks a level of creative birthing you just cannot access through religion or religious activity. It's just impossible.

SCHOOL OF THE SPIRIT NOT MAN

A year before we launched out into ministry, I had a few interesting spiritual warnings and encounters regarding protecting the anointing and the call of God on my life. (I'll share them in the next part of this book.) Staying surrendered and in submission to the Holy Spirit is a journey that requires constant taking stock and analysis of what I am following, what I am feasting on, what I am agreeing to, and with whom I'm running. We can't serve two masters. Jesus said it like this:

> No one can serve two masters. Either you will hate the one and love the other, or you will be devoted to the one and despise the other. You cannot serve both God and money (Matthew 6:24).

It's interesting that He uses money as the opposite of God in this verse because it's money and fame and power that often pull people away from God. That's what caused Adam and Eve to fall. Anyway, back to my warning.

I had a dream one night where I was preaching at a big church (at the time, this was not on my grid as I was a worshiper who prophesied a little). Signs and wonders were breaking out in the dream. I was giving accurate words of knowledge, and God was setting people free. At the end of the message, during the altar call, I saw a man in a long trench coat standing at the back of the building, and he was glaring at me with this strange look in his eyes. As I was praying for people, I looked up and saw him slowly wade through the crowd to get to me. I began to feel nervous yet kept praying for people. After I was done, I got my things, looked around, and couldn't see him anywhere, so I quickly moved toward the exit as fast as I could until I felt a hand grab my shoulder.

"Nate, that was an outstanding service!" The man said with genuine appreciation. "But . . . I would love to make you better. I think you need to be groomed and mentored by me to be the best you can be." He then put his arm over me like a wing, and I was standing there awkwardly as he then said, "You have raw anointing and passion, yet I'm afraid unless you are trained by me, you won't see what God has placed within you." Suddenly, a friend of our family, Aussie revivalist Tim Hall, appeared and pointed at me. He said, "Nate, get his hands off you! From this day forward you will be mentored by no one but the Holy Spirit!"

I can't even tell you how many times this warning has saved me over the years from foolishly almost coming under man's yoke—a yoke God never asked me to come under. I'm not against mentoring and people raising us. My wife, Christy, and I run a school, and it's powerful, but it can *never* be a substitute or replacement for our students' loyalty to Heaven and submission to the Holy Spirit. When you trade your freedom for unhealthy alignment, it only creates disastrous fruit, and eventually you become discouraged and disillusioned regarding your call.

So, stay wild, mighty ones. Don't let anything steal your wild heart. It's a gift and a weapon. Cherish it, protect it, and live wild for Jesus with it!

PROPHETIC SURVIVAL KEYS

Protect your calling, protect your anointing, and protect your legacy by not allowing man to make small modifications to you that, over time, steal from the purity of who you are. Guard these at all costs.

CAMPFIRE PRAYER

Dear Father, help me continue in this calling in the same purity and conviction I started with and not slowly suffocate by the seductive tamings of religion. Keep my passion raw and my hunger uncontainable. I want to stay wildly in love with You. If I have lost it, I ask for it back. Just keep my heart tethered to You and nothing and no one else in Jesus' name!

NOTES

1. *Iron Man 3*. Burbank, CA: Buena Vista Home Entertainment, 2013.

2. *The Chronicles of Narnia: The Lion, the Witch, and the Wardrobe.* Directed by Adam Adamson, screenplay by Ann Peacock et al., Walt Disney Pictures, 2005.

CHAPTER 4

Ambushed

My responsibility is to obey, to surrender my heart and to yield myself to the will of God. It is in the process of obedience that we gain understanding. You can't get the peace that passes understanding until you give up your right to understand. —Bill Johnson

I was ambushed. It was a Friday night service at Bethel Church in Redding, California, and we were visiting with friends, not sure what to expect. The atmosphere that night was electric, and my heart was beating fast. *What's going on?* I kept asking myself. I honestly was struggling to function normally and couldn't make sense of this growing burning in my chest. Then I realized what I needed to do for this feeling to stop—I had to rush down to the altar and give Jesus whatever it was that He was wanting. It didn't make sense because I was already saved; in fact, at the time, Christy and I were travelling full-time with a worldwide ministry, and I was the on-the-road pastor!

The only thing I knew was that I needed to say *yes* to God in a new way, whatever that even meant. As soon as the invitation for prayer and ministry time was announced, I rushed down to the altar and knelt as the worship team played. Then it happened. I felt as if rivers of water had hit me from every direction and were holding me under. As the heavy glory rested on me, God began to speak to me about a coming reformation and a people He was raising up for it. *Reformation? What?* I thought.

I had no idea what that word even meant, but for the next two weeks I couldn't stop dreaming and writing down the visions God showed me. I saw visions of people gathering in homes all around the world, people gathering in fields worshipping Jesus, and the church doors opening up to let Christians out. I saw things that the church was idolizing torn down, and I saw the new blueprint of what the church was heading into. I heard words, language, and themes that I had never heard before. This encounter rocked me deeply. It confronted my beliefs and activated something that would forever ruin me for the status quo or mundane. The course of my life had changed in a moment though I didn't ask for it.

Let's be honest. You didn't exactly choose to be a wild one either, right? It came to you. Woven into your DNA and marked over your life was this calling. Maybe you didn't see it right away or haven't quite known its purpose, but you have known for a long time that God has called you to a unique path that few take. All it takes is one moment where God suddenly flicks on the switch and activates what has always been there, and you just can't live or function the same way you did.

It's the detour to the road of least resistance and the breaking away from the norm. It's the divine design of a Father who created you for a unique role that you would fulfil but maybe haven't seen until now.

THE WILDERNESS KING

David didn't ask for it either. He wasn't hanging around the palace or trying to be noticed by Saul. David was raised in the wilderness, tending to his families flocks. That was his sole mission; to him, his mission had nothing to do with being groomed to be king. That wasn't on his radar or his father's, yet that is what God ordained for his life.

I often try to imagine the moment that the prophet Samuel rolled into town trying to find the next king whom God would choose for Israel. As Samuel arrived at Jesse's house, this is what took place:

> When they arrived, Samuel saw Eliab and thought, "Surely the Lord's anointed stands here before the Lord." But the Lord said to Samuel, "Do not consider his appearance or his height, for I have rejected him. The Lord does not look at the things people look at. People look at the outward appearance, but the Lord looks at the heart" (1 Samuel 16:6–7).
>
> So he asked Jesse, "Are these all the sons you have?" "There is still the youngest," Jesse answered. "He is tending the sheep." Samuel said, "Send for him; we will not sit down until he arrives." So he sent for him and had him brought in. He was glowing with health and had a fine appearance and handsome features. Then the Lord said, "Rise and anoint him; this is the one" (1 Samuel 16:11–12).

I find it interesting that God would choose someone like David to lead His people over someone who looked and sounded the part. Instead, God chose someone who had the right heart. What was He after? Someone who was wild at heart. Someone who had the Father's heart.

THE INTERRUPTION

Samuel was a miracle baby, born into a time when the Word of the Lord was rare and prophets no longer had visions. Why? Because they had lost their zeal and fire and wild pursuit of God's voice. Yet God granted Hannah her desire to have a child.

His name was Samuel, and she gave him to the priesthood to be raised by Eli.

Eli knew Samuel had a unique call, but it was one night's encounter that changed the course of Samuel's life. "Samuel," God called out. Samuel, thinking Eli had called him, ran into to Eli and said, "Yes, Eli?"

"I didn't call you, go back to sleep," Eli said.

"Samuel!" God called again, and Samuel ran into Eli again asking, "You called me?"

This happened a few more times before Eli said to Samuel, "Next time you hear that voice say, 'Yes, Lord'" (1 Sam. 3:1–10). So that's exactly what Samuel did, and the rest is history.

Right now, God is visiting people as they sleep, as they work, and as they do normal life. He is setting up divine ambushes that *awaken and activate* them to the reformational life for which they were created. As you continue your journey today, you need to know that, as unknown as your path has been behind you and as unsure as it feels ahead of you, you are not alone. In fact, your steps are more thought out than you realize, and God is taking you on this route for a very special reason. Let's press on!

POINTS OF NO RETURN

There are certain moments in our lives that become like points of no return. It's like when you experience that ambush, encounter, download, epiphany, or revelation, you shift internally to such a degree that, not only can you not go back to where you once were, but you are no longer the same person that you were. Have you ever experienced this in your life? Maybe it was that service you went to where the glory fell powerfully, or that moment in worship at home where the Holy Spirit spoke to you so clearly, or that strange and yet defining moment of clarity you had while driving your car. These moments become like portals or crossover points into a whole new way of life that you didn't orchestrate or anticipate.

My good friend Chris Harvey used to say, "It can often feel like you are sitting at the door of breakthrough praying and waiting for it to open, then suddenly in a moment you are there on the other side. You didn't open the door. You are just there, and you can't tell people the secret because you didn't have a part to play in it." Defining moments are not by your choosing, performing, or striving. They don't come by giving more, worshiping more, or trying to be more holy. They are sovereignly determined by God in the same way you were sovereignly appointed by God, and now you can't do anything to reverse it!

THE LEGACY SHIFT

As I was writing this, I felt the Holy Spirit wanted to say to you, "You can't go back!" Just because it seems scary and it's been such an unknown road, don't give up! I know you may have wrestled with this call for a long time, and I know that wrestle, but it will be worth it. I keep being reminded of Jacob who, after a life of much pain and toil—after trying to make something out of His life and trying so desperately to leave his reputation behind—came to a defining moment. There Jacob stood at the brook Jabbok, which means "emptying out, a pouring out" and represented a place of being completely emptied to move forward. Jacob sent all his family and possessions over to the other side of the brook, and there he waited alone. Then the passage says:

> *A man wrestled with him till daybreak. When the man saw that he could not overpower him, he touched the socket of Jacob's hip so that his hip was wrenched as he wrestled with the man. Then the man said, "Let*

me go, for it is daybreak." But Jacob replied, "I will not let you go unless you bless me." The man asked him, "What is your name?" "Jacob," he answered. Then the man said, "Your name will no longer be Jacob, but Israel, because you have struggled with God and with humans and have overcome" (Genesis 32:24–28).

Jacob was done with struggling, with not being able to outrun his past, with having to defend himself, and he was done with not seeing God's promises come to pass. So, he stood there and wrestled God until his destiny changed.

Ambushes are moments of surrender. It's where you are trying too hard to make things happen all the time and you just give up and lean into the Father. Prophetic voices can relate to Jacob's story because it's how we all feel in our journey. The road feels long, and the horizon just never seems to arrive, but your next destiny shifting moment is only ever just a breath away.

THE NEW TRAJECTORY

These moments are more than we realize they are. They are destiny changing moments that shift the course of our lives and futures. You walk away different, and people begin to notice. People will say, "What happened to you?" And you won't know what to say except, "Jesus," because you had nothing to do with what happened except that you emptied yourself and said *yes* to God.

God is ambushing people around the world who He has marked with the reformational call to the frontlines. He is stirring up faith, radical hope, and dropping ideas and solutions of His heart for them to run with. Right now, He is hovering over the earth, looking for those who will simply say, "Pick me. No matter what it costs, use me!" and He is setting them up for the most out-of-this-world ambushes that will change the pages of history.

Watch out, my friend, because you may just be inadvertently volunteering yourself for this life. Even now, feet are crossing over borderlines into new territories, shame and names are breaking off, and new names are being given. Assignments are being handed to you, and old activities are being left in the dust. This is your defining moment, I pray in Jesus' name.

SIGNS OF BEING AMBUSHED

I want to end this chapter with some language and definition to help you recognize your divine ambushes.

- Your feet have moved, but you didn't move them. It's the difference between when you buy an ice cream and someone brings one to you. You didn't make it happen. God did it.

- You recognize something has majorly shifted in your life. Things are just not the same as they were before. Ambushes are not always big thunder and lightning moments; they can often be quiet, or even seem insignificant until you realize something has shifted.

- Your eyes are suddenly opened. You aren't sure how, but you just see differently, and you seem to be the only one in the room seeing that way.

- Your conversation has changed. You just sound different and seem to be focused on something God given that you didn't before.

- You feel like a balloon that is about to burst. Non stop revelation seems to flow all the time.

- You feel ruined for the ordinary.

- You suddenly recognize areas of apathy around you that you didn't before, and It feels like you are a sellout if you go along with it.
- You are consumed with a new theme, idea, or revelation you didn't have before. You have found your global message.
- You feel suddenly activated and all systems are go.
- You can't stop prophesying and speaking what you see.

Have you experienced any of these?

PROPHETIC SURVIVAL KEYS

Surrender, surrender, surrender. Let go of the steering wheel and how you have decided its meant to go. Get hungry for Him and when he visits you say YES.

CAMPFIRE PRAYER

Dear Father I surrender to your plans for my life. I am done with feeling inactive or not living completely to the full extent of my calling, so today I ask you to visit me, and ambush me. Today I stop wrestling and fighting what You have called me to and ask you to reignite my heart and fresh joy to run with it in Jesus' name!

CHAPTER 5

Uncharted Pursuit

If you're not pursuing a dangerous quest with your life, well, then, you don't need a Guide. If you haven't found yourself in the midst of a ferocious war, then you won't need a seasoned Captain. —John Eldridge

I heard His voice, but I just didn't know it was Him. I felt the call, but I just didn't know who was calling me.

From a young age, I felt different like I was being pulled in a different direction than most. There were these subtle yet almost definable moments where I felt this intense tug but didn't quite understand what it was. Maybe you can relate. It was as if there was an invisible rope tethering me to something I knew nothing about, and I didn't want to let go. "Stop being a dreamer," my family would say. "Come back to Earth!" They would say this because, while the world was rushing all around me, in my heart and head I was in the forest, rock hopping in creeks and enjoying secret adventures. I was curious and creative, and I craved adventure in everything. If there was ever too much routine or monotony, I would get complacent very quickly. I loved the outdoors and the thrill of survival, risk, and discovering new things. It wasn't that I was a thrill-seeker. I was more a God-chaser, though I just didn't quite know it then. It was the pursuit of His voice that I was preoccupied with, but I just didn't have the words to explain it.

One of my very first encounters with God wasn't at church or in a youth service but simply in my dreams. I began having a recurring dream where I was lost in a forest, desperately seeking, craving to find someone I was missing. I would anxiously climb every mountain peak, but he was never there. I would sing out, cry out, and scream, but there was never any response until I was exhausted, and then I would climb back down and fall in a heap.

When I woke up, my heart was distressed. Who was I looking for? I would think. I didn't know, and I couldn't shake the question. There was a void that needed to be filled. Then about the fifth time I had this dream, I heard a voice call to me in the distance, "Nate!" I began running again frantically because I didn't want to miss it. I didn't want to miss this moment. Then I woke up. I realized I had this longing pursuit in me to find who it was my heart was chasing, and I needed to take this unusual road to encounter Him.

THE PLACE OF MEETING

While the rest of the Israelites were doing other things and chasing other passions, Joshua was following the lifestyle he saw Moses live. Most Israelites only went into the tent of congregation (tradition), but Joshua spent his time in the other tent, the tent of meeting (intimate encounter) that wasn't in the main dwelling area but set outside the village.

Joshua had a call to the wild. He had tasted of the presence and glory of God, and He just couldn't live any other way ever again. It changed his whole life! Many years later when he was sent among others to spy out the Promised Land, his unique calling and training was finally seen. Looking at the story in Numbers 13, we discover that the other spies basically said, "This land is full of giants, and we are like grasshoppers!"

But Joshua and his friend Caleb said, "Look at the fruit that is there! And the giants? We can take them. We were born for this!"

Joshua and Caleb's response demonstrate the reformational call at its core: hearing the voice of the Lord and walking different than most to do what God says. Reformation, at its very core, is the call to the wild—the call to pursue His voice, His heart, and His mission. It starts with a longing and ends with mighty exploits, and right now God is tugging on the hearts of so many around the world whom He is calling to this reformational life. He is calling us back to the simplicity of his voice *above* all else. Will you respond to the call today? Will you pick up only what you need for the journey and embark on this unique adventure with Jesus?

HUNGRY & DISSATISFIED

Unfortunately, this secret place path is one that not all take. If you ever see a Christian who is constantly dry and burned out, either they stopped being with Jesus in the secret place or never knew how. It was for this reason that Christy and I began our school back in 2016. We wanted to introduce a very head-knowledge-filled Bride to her first call: the priesthood. As the Bride of Christ, we have been called to be priests in the secret place, ministering to the Lord and having Him minister back to us.

> *"I will raise up for myself a faithful priest, who will do according to what is in my heart and mind. I will firmly establish his priestly house, and they will minister before my anointed one always"* (1 Samuel 2:35).

This is the priestly call and the rite of passage for any emerging voice who is serious about living a life unto the Lord. We don't live unto works, or to the Kingdom, but to the King. That's the standard.

Before we go any further in our story and journey together, I want to share a part of my story from many years earlier, the year Christy and I were married. It was April 2006, and we had just returned from our honeymoon when I found out that I had been successful in acquiring a job at Benny Hinn Ministries. Months earlier, I had applied for it. I remember my first day. I felt unequipped for what they were asking me to do, which was to pray for people over the phone. I would nervously pray from a prayer book like a script because, although I knew the Lord, I was yet to really encounter His Spirit in a powerful way. A few months later, I was working at a Benny Hinn Crusade in Auckland, New Zealand, when I witnessed the power and presence of God in a tangible way that would ruin my life forever. I stood at the back just crying as the love of God seemed to flow over and in me like a liquid. I had never experienced God quite to that level before, and I was hooked! I said, "Lord, I must have *all of You!*"

When I returned home, I was agitated, dissatisfied, and hungry, just unsure of what to do to meet the growing craving of my heart. Then a friend of mine introduced me to the testimony of Todd Bentley. I learned that Bentley had suffered an accident at work and was homebound for months. He would just rest in God's presence for hours upon hours until the glory of God would come. I didn't know if this would work for me, but I began "soaking," as it is now called, for hours upon hours a night, from until twelve or one in the morning.

For weeks, I pressed through distracting thoughts and feelings of discouragement as I thought it was all to no avail. I would pray and pray and cry out to God to come. I was exhausted! Then one night after a hard day, I lay down with nothing to say. I was spent and frankly over trying to hear God and all my efforts to engage with Him. Suddenly, a very heavy, weighty, presence flooded the room—so much so that I could barely move. Then

I heard Him speak to my heart so much louder than I had ever heard him, and I was undone!

This became a way of life for me, and I kept soaking every night and developing this deep connection with the Lord. Christy told me many years later that she would walk past me, seeing me soaking thinking, "Oh Lord, who have I married? He is crazy!" Interestingly, only a few short years later God began speaking to her in the same way. I didn't realize it back then, but that season was the very foundational season of many years to come where Christy and I really needed to know God intimately to navigate the new places He was taking us. It helped us navigate seasons of plenty, opposition, increase, displacement, and the unknown.

THE FATHER'S PURSUIT

I look back now, and I can see the pursuit of the Lord in my life even when I wasn't pursuing Him intentionally or even aware of His presence. I was ten years old when I first discovered the power of intimate worship. Our home was a tough place much of the time, my brother and I were raised by a step-father who was being healed of his own father wounds and a mother who was in the middle trying to keep the peace. The pain I felt was too much to handle, and so one night after it felt like a world war had broken out, I found myself downstairs screaming silently in the dark. I poured my heart out as if I were talking to someone. Then the strangest thing happened. It was like a tangible blanket of peace descended on me, and I heard a voice on the inside of me say, "It's going to be okay."

Those encounters became the place I learned to know the Lord's voice and learned the power of worship in crisis. In those years, I was so drawn to King David. I remember reading the story of David at Ziklag. After returning home, he and his men found all their possessions and family had been taken by the enemy.

It says that David and his men were greatly troubled and were considering stoning David. The end of 1 Samuel 30:6 says, *"But David strengthened himself in the Lord his God"* (ESV).

In original Hebrew text, it translates that David "encouraged" himself. How did David do that? He worshiped the Lord. It was his go-to, his response in trouble, his hiding place (Psalm 32:7). And what happened? It created room for God to speak a solution amid a troubling situation, and David and his men recovered *everything*!

THE SONGS FROM THE CAVE

I believe God is raising up a generation of worshipers like David to release the sound of the mighty flood of Heaven in this hour. These worshipers have been raised in the wilderness, equipped in the shadows, and anointed in the secret place for public exploits and victories that will lead the Body of Christ into her greatest years of outpouring and influence in the earth.

The thing about worshipers is they aren't disadvantaged by the dark. In fact, it's where they develop their song. The dark is where they are the strongest! Many have been hidden for so long, but it's now time to come out of hiding. And they are coming out in droves to raise up the name of Jesus throughout the earth. These worshipers cannot be bought or bribed, and they carry a conviction that terrifies the enemy, a shout so fierce it makes demons tremble, and a melody so powerful and sweet it ushers Heaven to Earth.

Over the next few years, we will see the greatest emergence of Davidic worshipers and creative pioneers we have ever seen. These will be a company of lovers who have laid down their lives for Jesus. They will lead the Church into the inner courts. Revival is already churning in the hearts of these hidden ones. They are incubating the songs of Heaven that will reach into the darkest of the darkest places and reach the ones who seem unreachable, as well as restore passion to the pulpit.

I believe God has been doing this in you. Maybe in your season of waiting you have felt as though you have been wasting away. Maybe many dreams are still on the shelf, unused and dormant, but the truth is you have not lost anything. You have not wasted anything. Open your mouth and let your song out, and you will discover the power and breakthrough that will come from lifting your voice in struggle and crisis. The wilderness was your worship, and your songs from the cave are going to be anthems sung on the rooftops. Breakthrough power is on your own tongue, and I pray today that you find your own song in this season—a song that will take you out of the "stuck" place you have been in for far too long and usher you into your greatest season of thriving and enabling for the fulfilling assignment God has prepared for you.

PROPHETIC SURVIVAL KEYS

The presence is your survival key. You won't go far without it, and you will burn up and dry up if it is not your daily go-to. He is waiting to be encountered. Get hungry for His presence and glory to crash into your life!

CAMPFIRE PRAYER

Dear Father, I give my life for Your glory, and as a worshiper at your throne, I pray like Moses, "If your Presence does not go with us, do not send us up from here" (Exodus 33:15). I must know Your presence and your glory, so today I pray make my life a habitation of Your presence in Jesus' name.

CHAPTER 6

Come away with me. Come away with me. It's never too late. It's not too late. It's not too late for you. I have a plan for you. I have a plan for you. It's gonna be wild. It's gonna be great. It's gonna be full of me. —Jesus Culture

These lyrics of the song "Come Away" by Jesus Culture are still on repeat in my spirit to this day. We had moved back to Australia after a busy ministry season in the USA, working full-time on the road with our friend Nick Vujicic. We were starting over again. We had sold everything to go to the States and found ourselves back in Australia with no jobs, cars, furniture, or home. In fact, we had to sell our house in Australia at a loss due to the rising interest rates we couldn't afford.

In debt, defeated, and with no direction forward, we felt like we failed or maybe we hadn't heard the Lord correctly. Yet we couldn't deny one thing. We both encountered God only eleven months earlier in a way that shifted something significantly, and we were all in for whatever was next. We could feel a strange pull as if God was leading us somewhere that we had no grid for, and to a degree we were okay with that. But what was He leading us into?

I remember one day sitting on the floor in an empty room of the house—which was bare of furniture except for a couch, bed, and fridge—we started renting, and I worshiped on my guitar until the presence of God was so strong and I was a mess. Then I began to sing "Come Away," but I felt as though the Lord was singing the song to me, inviting me to trust Him with something. "Yes, Lord, I'll go," I said in reply.

In the years to come and two church seasons later (more on that in the chapters to come), the pull only became stronger, and I didn't know where it was leading except by describing that:

- I had a discontent for the norm.
- I had an inability to enjoy what we were doing.
- I had a feeling of being misplaced or in the wrong environment.
- I felt like a square peg in a round hole.
- I felt as if there was something else I was meant to be doing, yet that made no sense.
- I was on the wrong road or path.
- I had the unusual sense that I was neglecting something very important.
- I felt suddenly separate from others, as if I were going in a different direction.

For years, I had experienced these strong feelings and convictions but didn't know that I was tied to an invisible rope that was eventually going to lead me to a place where God would bring to fruition what He had started in me. What was this place He was leading me into?

It was my wilderness.

THE TWO WILDERNESSES

Elijah was a prophet who was used by God to do some major purifying of Israel. King Ahab had married a woman called

Jezebel. She was an evil priestess. Together, they worshiped other Gods, sacrificed babies, committed very sinful acts, and tried to kill anyone left who served the true God. One hundred prophets were actually in hiding because of her. They were afraid for their lives.

Enter Elijah. He confronted this evil, brought a drought upon the land, and defied Ahab, Jezebel, and their evil regime. The progressive Christians of today would have told Elijah to love and serve Ahab and not be political. To God and to Elijah, this was about good versus evil, and God was done with the mockery. But there are two events in Elijah's life that reveal two distinctions of the wildernesses many of us experience in our journey.

Wilderness 1: The Escape Room

Elijah ran into the wilderness as a response of fear. He feared for his life, and so he escaped to a place. In essence, he was led into further torment and no longer wanted to live.

> *Then Jezebel sent a messenger to Elijah, saying, "So let the gods do to me, and more also, if I do not make your life as the life of one of them by tomorrow about this time." And when he saw that, he arose and ran for his life, and went to Beersheba, which belongs to Judah, and left his servant there. But he himself went a day's journey into the wilderness, and came and sat down under a broom tree. And he prayed that he might die, and said, "It is enough! Now, Lord, take my life, for I am no better than my fathers!"* (1 Kings 19:2–4 NKJV).

This is the wilderness many of us face where we are constantly bullied by the enemy. It starts with a fear, trauma, hurt, or woundedness, and it becomes a place that feels impossible to leave. We can even begin to find our identity in that place. It is where the enemy has us backed into a corner, and he convinces us that God sent us there to be developed; however, it's a place of punishment not development.

Wilderness 2: The Preparation & Setup

God called Elijah into a wilderness for a time of refreshing, refueling, and preparation for what was next.

> *Then the word of the Lord came to Elijah: "Leave here, turn eastward and hide in the Kerith Ravine, east of the Jordan. You will drink from the brook, and I have directed the ravens to supply you with food there." So he did what the Lord had told him. He went to the Kerith Ravine, east of the Jordan, and stayed there. The ravens brought him bread and meat in the morning and bread and meat in the evening, and he drank from the brook* (1 Kings 17:2–6).

The interesting thing to note was that in this wilderness Elijah was fed by ravens— supernatural supply—and in his very next mission, he was sent to a widow who was dying from lack of food. Elijah performed not only a supply miracle for her, but he also raised her dead son. Without the wilderness, he wouldn't have been equipped for the miracle. This is the wilderness that we are all called to in some point in our lives, and we often revisit.

I'VE BEEN IN THE WRONG WILDERNESS!

You may be beginning to think, *Have I been in the wrong wilderness*? Let's look at a few of the differences between the wilderness the enemy tries to lead you into compared to the one God does.

The God-led wilderness:

- Declutters you, delivers you, separates you.
- Cuts ties and bondages, and removes blockages.
- Takes you through the refiner's fire.
- Purifies your heart and motives.
- Makes Jesus your only source of affirmation and value.
- Is a place of encounter.
- Restores your wild.
- Reveals your purpose.
- Births your purpose.
- Sets you up for the days to come.
- Fast-tracks and upgrades you.
- Develops you into a warrior.
- Promotes you and launches you.
- Increases the anointing upon your life.
- Upskills you (like David with the bear and lion).
- Puts a new song/new message/new language on your tongue.
- Restores and empowers you.
- Brings you back to the original design.
- Reforms your heart and brings about personal revival.

Therefore I am now going to allure her; I will lead her into the wilderness and speak tenderly to her. There I will give her back her vineyards, and will make the Valley of Achor a door of hope. There she will respond as in the days of her youth, as in the day she came up out of Egypt (Hosea 2:14–15).

The enemy-led wilderness:

- Places you in bondage to fear—fear of the future, fear of being a voice, and fear of man.

- Is a distraction to prevent you from stepping into your calling.
- Derails and takes you off course.
- Is a place of discouragement and defeat where you lose your passion and purpose.
- Makes you question your promise, your assignment, and everything you have heard God say.
- Comes with torment and bullying.
- Strips you of your passion and fire.
- Causes you to doubt yourself and your worth.
- Will make you feel abandoned by God.

Can you identify with any of these? Which wilderness have you been in? Have you experienced some of both? Wilderness seasons are definitely uncomfortable, but when I hear people talking about their wilderness as if they have been demonized, then I know that the enemy has been trying to hijack something God has been doing. Refuse to let the enemy bait you into his counterfeit wilderness season because, if you aren't aware of it, then chances are you may never know how to break free and leave.

THE STRATEGY

God gave me a strategy for this. He said, "The wilderness is My terrain, not satan's!" In Matthew 4:1 it says, *"Afterward, the Holy Spirit led Jesus into the wilderness to experience the ordeal of testing by the accuser"* (TPT).

The enemy probably felt as if he was in charge of this situation and was going to break Jesus down, but he wasn't the one who led Jesus there. The Holy Spirit was!

So, your strategy is to take back your wilderness from the enemy. Where he has slowly tried to hijack it, remind him that you are there to be launched and that you refuse to be robbed, tormented, or discouraged a day longer. In Luke 4:14, it shows the end result of Jesus' wilderness experience, *"Jesus returned to Galilee in the power of the Spirit, and news about him spread through the whole countryside."*

The wilderness *empowers* you!

THE ONLY PATH TO PROMISE

If you are called to be a voice for God in some capacity, then the wilderness will always be part of your journey at some stage. I have seen plenty of emerging voices spring up without this phase of life, and the results are not good. I know that at some stage the wilderness will call them.

What qualified David to be anointed king by Samuel? He didn't have the qualities his brothers had. He wasn't the perfect package by man's standards but by God's he had everything. He was a man after God's own heart, and that was the result of David spending time in the wilderness. In the wilderness, you discover God's heart, you hear His voice, and soon you begin to sound like Him, too. This is a rite of passage, and we can't skip it. In fact, I encourage anyone who hasn't been through a season of being pulled away by God to give a season of their life to the Lord. No public speaking. Just Him. No public ministry. Just Him.

The wilderness is the best thing that can happen to you because it is where your purpose is birthed and you are launched. In the next chapter, I want to share our launch story with you to encourage you that the wilderness leads somewhere amazing.

The earth needs the wilderness voices because they are pure. They are no longer about themselves. They can't be sold, bought, or traded. They have been marked deeply for a purpose that Heaven will soon reveal. Years ago, the Lord said to me to look to the wilderness because a generation of all ages was going to emerge, and I haven't stopped watching for them to come and come in droves.

Just like David, their wilderness is coming to an end. Just like David, their time to emerge is *now*!

PROPHETIC SURVIVAL KEYS

See your season with different eyes. Empty is the setup for upgrade. You need spiritual eyes when you are either feeling the pull into a wilderness season or in the middle of such a season.

CAMPFIRE PRAYER

Lord, if it's You, I want it. Prepare me for what is ahead and protect me in the secret place of the most high (Ps. 91). I say yes to the come away season and the call of the wild You are leading me into, wherever it takes me, in Jesus' name!

CHAPTER 7

Off the Beaten Track

We abandon the most important journey of our lives
when we abandon desire. We leave our hearts by the
side of the road and head off in the direction of fitting in,
getting by, being productive, what have you. Whatever we
might gain—money, position, the approval of others, or
just absence of the discontent self—it's not worth it.
—John Eldridge

Have you ever done something that no one else was doing? Have you ever made a decision to move in a different direction than others or to go against the flow? Have you ever felt desperate, craving to stay in step with God, that you'd do anything, even let go of everything you have known and look foolish to everyone around you? Join the club.

Abraham knew that unless he left Haran and went to Canaan that all the promises God gave him for his life wouldn't come to pass.

> The Lord had said to Abram, "Go from your country,
> your people and your father's household to the land I
> will show you. I will make you into a great nation, and
> I will bless you; I will make your name great, and you
> will be a blessing" (Genesis 12:1–2).

If you know the story of Abraham, you know that God did make him into a great nation because of his faithfulness to go, but Abraham's journey wasn't easy. Interestingly, the name Haran where Abraham left means both "mountaineer" and "very dry road," which to me speaks of the difficult, unfruitful, and exhausting life he lived. The place that Abraham settled was in Canaan, which means "synchronized." Our obedience to go is what keeps us in sync with God and the Spirit. Often, when we don't listen and obey right away, we begin to feel dry and out of sync until we make the necessary adjustments to do what we were asked originally.

FORK IN THE ROAD

There are moments in our lives where, for us to stay true to the call of the wild upon our lives, we too will have to make a strong deviation from the road everyone else seems to be travelling. I have been there many times in my life, but there we one time that literally changed the course of my life in more ways than one. In the last chapter, I shared how the pull to our wilderness season began, but I didn't actually share when it happened or how we entered our wilderness. Let me tell that story.

It all started in my lounge room one day while I was practicing worship songs. I was about to lead at our church that Sunday when the Lord asked me two questions that offended me yet deeply convicted me. He said, "Why are you suppressing the full measure of the call I have placed inside of you?"

I didn't know what to say in response.

Then He said, "Are you okay with the dreams and desires I have placed upon your life to stay on the shelf?"

I quickly took stock of my life, all the projects I had done for people, the four church services a week I had been at since birth, the events I had run, the people I had poured into, and my life laid down at the altar. I felt as though I had neglected something I shouldn't have. In that moment, I realized I had been afraid of walking out what God had given me. As a result, I had found another Christian activity to do so I wouldn't have to face it. It was a good thing I was doing, but it just wasn't my core thing or my magnum opus.

WHO ARE YOU?

What was it? What was inside me? What was I called to do beyond serving others?

Then the Lord asked me something else that made me feel really insecure, naked, and fragile: "Who are you without your guitar? Who are you?" At the time we were part of a thriving church where God was truly moving, especially during the worship. It was normal for the worship team to just lie down on the stage during practice because the glory was still there from the last meeting. It was normal for people to be healed as they worshiped without anyone praying for them. It was normal for supernatural fragrances to fill the room, people getting set free, addictions breaking, and people going into throne room encounters as we worshiped. So, to ask me who I was without my guitar hit something deep. I had just been targeted for yet another ambush that would lead me and our family off the beaten path.

Not long after this encounter with the Lord, I felt that I needed to step down from my role as worship pastor for a season, so I met with my pastor about it. At the time the church was growing rapidly and moving into a new building. "Have a sabbatical? That's not God speaking," he said. So, I stayed. But every time I led worship, I felt like I needed to find out who I was without my guitar. Then our first one, Charlotte, was born, and she crashed into our world and seemed to reveal the longing of my heart even more. For the sake of my family and children, I needed to spend time digging my well and find what was at the bottom.

After six months of trying to be bold, I finally mustered up the courage and called my pastor, but this time I just said it straight, "I am stepping down," and I did. In that moment, our first official wilderness season began.

ROOM OF UNUSED TOYS

Instantly, we lost our community and tribe. We were still attending the church and did so for nine months after that, but it wasn't the same. It hurt, but God was beginning to do a deep work in me because I suddenly had no desire for anything I used to do. It was like God was stripping away the things I held onto for identity and value.

One night in a dream, I was sitting in the middle of a room that had objects hanging all over the walls all around me. They were all my favorite things, such as my guitar, a fishing rod, etc. I was unable to touch them, however. My first wilderness had begun, but it wasn't the one that shifted our lives completely.

FOLLOW ME!

Imagine being one of Jesus' disciples for a moment. The day you meet Jesus, He calls you to follow Him:

As he was walking by the shore of Lake Galilee, Jesus noticed two fishermen who were brothers. One was nicknamed Keefa (later called Peter), and the other was Andrew, his brother. Watching as they were casting their nets into the water, Jesus called out to them

*and said, "Come and follow me, and I will transform
you into men who catch people for God." Immediately
they dropped their nets and left everything behind to
follow Jesus. Leaving there, Jesus found three other
men sitting in a boat, mending their nets. Two were
brothers, Jacob and John, and they were with their
father, Zebedee. Jesus called Jacob and John to his
side and said to them, "Come and follow me." And at
once they left their boat and their father, and began
to follow Jesus* (Matthew 4:18–22 TPT).

In a matter of hours, these fisherman who had only known
how to catch fish their whole lives were leaving it all behind to
embark on a mission *outside* their comfort zone and area of
expertise. Have you ever wondered why they would leave everything behind like that in a moment? I know that answer, and I'm
guessing you do, too. When you have encountered Jesus, there
is no Plan B, no backup plan or other road. There is just Him,
and that's why you have been on the journey you have been
on. That's why you detoured off the beaten track, and it's cost
you everything—because compared to having Him, everything
is meaningless anyway. Riches, fame, fortune, acceptance with
others—they don't even compare.

SLAYING THE OXEN & BURNING BRIDGES

They say you shouldn't burn bridges with people, and while
I agree with that, unfortunately, it doesn't mean some seasons
with some people do end, especially those who aren't going
where you are going. It's common in relationships where someone is going after Jesus and the other is not or those who are
following the Spirit at all costs have to eventually leave behind
those who are happy to stay where they are. This has been my

experience many times. There are seasons God will ask you to end something—an assignment or relationship that is no longer necessary or is not going where you are going. In many ways, this feels like slaying the oxen.

In 1 Kings 19, God told Elijah to anoint and commission Elisha as prophet to succeed him.

> *So he departed from there, and found Elisha the son of Shaphat, who was plowing with twelve yoke of oxen before him, and he was with the twelfth. Then Elijah passed by him and threw his mantle on him. So Elisha turned back from him, and took a yoke of oxen and slaughtered them and boiled their flesh, using the oxen's equipment, and gave it to the people, and they ate. Then he arose and followed Elijah, and became his servant* (vv. 19–21 ESV).

What doesn't get explained in this story is that Elisha must have been a wealthy person of some level of social status in his region to have twelve oxen. When he left them behind, he was leaving behind a life that was set up for him with security and wealth. But when God throws his jacket over you, everything changes. You don't see things in the same way anymore, and the only thing in your sights is doing the will of God even if it means having to break away from the pack. Forging a new path feels so final.

As God mantles you, it initiates the ending of an old way of operation, an old road, and what you did and lived for before is now upgraded or completely changed altogether. Elisha slayed the oxen and burned the plow as a final ending to an old season and activity. When God throws His jacket suddenly, things that were part of the old assignment begin to end. Sometimes, relationships, doors, and even graces and functions change.

Reformers, pioneers, and forerunners all have something in common. They are all anointed to "break away" from the path and pave a new one for the sake of the Kingdom. What I wish I had understood early on was that, if I was going to really accept my calling, I also needed to accept the fact that many would misunderstand my mission, motives, and heart as I was faithful to walk it out.

THE STORY I WAS TOLD NEVER TO TELL

I never imagined I would tell this story, but for the sake of setting others free I know I need to. I honor the people in my life from all seasons, and I write this with not even an ounce of bitterness in my heart, knowing that, while seasons can be messy and there is collateral damage involved with following God, I know everything was all worked for the good. For that reason, I'm going to share this story I was told by well-known pastors and leaders never to speak about. Why? Because so far I have shared how embarking on a new path can be difficult and scary, and cost everything, but that is only part of the story. What if I shared how God can launch you regardless of where you are? What if I told you that you didn't need to be in leadership school, at every prayer meeting, running the ushers' team, singing every Sunday in worship team, greeting people at the door, or even going to church to be launched and used by God? Sounds heretical. Sounds rebellious. That's right. It does. But what if God uses the unbeaten path and the wilderness to be the very environment to birth you? How does it look to the rest of the religious institution? It looks like it's *not God*, but He is just as involved outside the church building as He is within the church walls, and right now He is launching people who are outside the system. He is doing that for a specific reason which I'll share more on shortly.

After our first wilderness came to an end, we felt God leading us to help a new local church plant in our city, so we did and enjoyed it. At the same time, I still felt that same uncomfortable stirring and pulling, but I was so busy serving in the worship team that I managed to ignore it for the most part until one day Christy and I both knew we had to leave and pursue what God was calling us to. We knew we needed to pay attention to what God had given us even though it may not be received or understood by our current church leadership. We had already been trying to survive as a family in a church culture that didn't value unique callings that didn't fit under the pastor's vision. We still honored them, but we were global Kingdom thinkers, not just local church-oriented leaders. We were pushing up against the system on all sides, and there was resistance. Breakdown starting to take place. We had to make a choice: Should we stay in this environment where the prophetic call on our lives is not valued, or should we step into the unknown with Jesus? The latter would possibly cost us everything, and it did.

YOU ARE ABORTING YOUR CALLING!

It was a Wednesday night, and I had arranged to meet my pastor at a local coffee shop to share my heart and let him know that my family was going to be ending our season at his church. We had been with the church since it had started up two years prior, and within those two years, attendance had grown to over a thousand people. When we first started attending this church, my family sensed we would not be everyone in the congregation's cup of tea. It wasn't out of hurt or bitterness we decided to go. As a family, we realized, to be free to be ourselves, we needed to leave and find open pastures.

As I sat down for coffee and shared my heart with the pastor, he asked me one question, "What church are you going to from here?" I told him there wasn't a church we felt to go to instead of his church. God hadn't put a new church on our hearts yet. We only knew it was time to go. Pastor seemed confused, and then told me this was not God calling us. His next statement was more painful to hear: "Well, I don't think there's anything I can do to get you to stay. So, I guess that's it, but I do want you to know that I think you are aborting your calling."

After this meeting, my family and I noticed our once close friends stopped calling. People from our former community would run a mile when they saw us at the mall. We were labeled "rebels" simply for chasing and pursuing God's calling for our lives. To these individuals, we went rogue. We chose the wild.

LEGACY BEGINS

After walking out the detaching process, which took a good year, something happened that we didn't anticipate. God handed us something new. It was like I finally had the capacity to open my heart and hands and say, "Okay, Lord, that thing inside us—that wild calling I have been ignoring—do what You want. I take my hands off, and I let go of all my man-made ideals and reputation, and I am all in for this road. I won't look back anymore, wondering what could have been, feeling shame or the words of disapproval from others. I won't fear this new road, and I won't dread the unknown anymore. Instead, I'll be a kid again, I'll live in wonder, and I'll do this because You are with me in this. You called me from my comforts and my apathy, and you didn't have to, but now I give my life to the call of the wild, in Jesus' name."

That day a legacy began that our children are now part of (and someday our grandchildren as well), and today your new path and legacy begins, too.

PROPHETIC SURVIVAL KEYS

You can't follow the unbeaten path and man's path at the same time. You will have to forfeit man's ways for God's perfect way. Your key is to listen to the voice and leading of Holy Spirit only.

CAMPFIRE PRAYER

Pray the same prayer I prayed, "Okay, Lord, that thing inside us—that wild calling I have been ignoring—do what You want. I take my hands off, and I let go of all my man-made ideals and reputation, and I am all in for this road. I won't look back anymore, wondering what could have been, feeling shame or the words of disapproval from others. I won't fear this new road, and I won't dread the unknown anymore. Instead, I'll be a kid again, I'll live in wonder, and I'll do this because You are with me in this. You called me from my comforts and my apathy, and you didn't have to, but now I give my life to the call of the wild, in Jesus' name."

PART 2

The Wilderness Discovery

CHAPTER 8

Agents of the Crossover

If we don't know who we are, we will never know our purpose, and if we never know our purpose, we will never even leave the front porch. We have to know why we have been created. —Nate Johnston

If you retrace your life and go back through every season, every year, every environment, and every situation you were ever in, you will see the thread you didn't see at the time. You'll see the signs of a life called to a different road and the unmistakable divine thumbprint of God. You just didn't know it at the time.

What can you remember? When was your awakening moment where things shifted or transitioned?

You'll realize that it is no recent stirring that you are experiencing, but that God has always marked you with this calling. With that comes two cries: the cry to know and the cry to be known. It's the craving to know Him and the craving to know yourself. It's the curiosity and wonder of finally beginning to unveil what has been hidden for so long and is now announcing itself with or without your consent. It's the journey commencing for a lifestyle that few know how to navigate. In this part of the guide, I want to address this journey and process and give language to you as you are trying to find yourself in this season and understand how you have been wired. Welcome to the discovery of the wild ones.

I WILL NEVER SEE THE SAME AGAIN

Whether you have had an encounter with God or just one day woke up on a different side of the bed and know that God has completely changed your projected path, you'll never be able to go back to seeing the way you once did before. This is the greatest struggle of this calling because you suddenly feel like you are speaking another language than others are.

Paul, or Saul before his name was changed, would have faced this beyond what we can read in the Bible text. A Jewish scholar who persecuted and executed Christians encountering God? Yeah, that created a stir. This is Saul's encounter:

> As he neared Damascus on his journey, suddenly a light from heaven flashed around him. He fell to the ground and heard a voice say to him, "Saul, Saul, why do you persecute me?" "Who are you, Lord?" Saul asked. "I am Jesus, whom you are persecuting," he replied. "Now get up and go into the city, and you will be told what you must do." . . . Saul got up from the ground, but when he opened his eyes he could see nothing. So they led him by the hand into Damascus. For three days he was blind, and did not eat or drink anything (Acts 9:3–6, 8–9).

Saul was then led to Damascus because he could not see, but God sent a man named Ananias to help him.

> Then Ananias went to the house and entered it. Placing his hands on Saul, he said, "Brother Saul, the Lord—Jesus, who appeared to you on the road as you were coming here—has sent me so that you may see again and be filled with the Holy Spirit." Immediately, something like scales fell from Saul's eyes, and he could see again. He got up and was baptized (Acts 9:17–18).

When God interrupts your life and calls you to this unique mandate, it feels like a conversion because you leave not being able to function the way you once did before. In Saul's case, he also got a name change to Paul as well just like Jacob did after he wrestled the angel of the Lord. What are the similarities with these two stories? Both men were in critical destiny crossover moments.

WHERE DO I GO FROM HERE?

2009 was my first Damascus road moment. I can see now how, while it was the week at Bethel that was the cherry on the cake, the whole year leading up until then God was removing blindfolds off my eyes. I remember one blindfold moment. Christy and I were at a church, and Nick Vujicic was speaking back-to-back services 45 minutes each, catchy intro, worship for 18 minutes exactly, segue, announcements, offering, message, and finish. Rinse and repeat. As I sat there in the third service, I felt the grief of the Holy Spirit that he was not given any or much space in the service outside of Nicks message. It was an uncomfortable thing to sense, and I didn't know what to do with it.

Have you ever experienced something like this? It's where suddenly your eyes are opened to see God's heart on something and nothing can make you see it any other way again. Once the blindfold is off, it is off.

The reformational call of the wild emerging voices means that we have been given specific access to see the way the Father sees because our commission is to make what we see a reality in the earth.

MY 11:11 DATE WITH DESTINY

This brings me to my date with destiny in 2011. After a year of being back in Australia since living in Los Angeles, I began working for my father-in-law who ran a church and a foodbank charity all in one. I was no longer a pastor there, but I helped him keep the charity running smoothly. While we were happy to be back home with family and about to have our first baby, we were most definitely in a wilderness season after being in ministry positions for so long. It felt like everything around us had died from the season we had just left, including friendships, goals, and even desires. We felt lost and even abandoned by God.

One Wednesday morning, I drove to work and felt very low. We had debt stacking up from the year before and were struggling to make ends meet. Then we were a one-wage family, and things were just difficult. "God, why are we in a rut?" I yelled. "What is going on?"

Later that morning, my father-in-law handed me the banking deposits to take down to the bank. As I turned the car off, I looked at the clock, and it caught my attention. Flashing back at me was 11:11. I shrugged it off and went about my day, but the strangest thing happened, for months every time I would go down to the bank, I would always look at the clock, and it would either be 11:11 or 1:11. *Am I going crazy?* I would wonder. Soon, it began to show up everywhere, from signs to car number plates, and even waking up at 1:11 many mornings in a row. I began to realize that somehow, even though completely off my grid, God must be trying to tell me something, but what? Then one morning, I received a text from a friend who simply wrote, "Was praying for you today, and God gave me this scripture for you, Deuteronomy 11:11, *"But the land you are crossing the Jordan to take possession of is a land of mountains and valleys that drinks rain from heaven."*

I can't even tell you how much this text lifted my spirit. Things began to connect that I had been perceiving but was unsure of how to reconcile. Then I found two other scriptures:

> In that day the Lord will reach out his hand a second time to reclaim the surviving remnant of his people (Isaiah 11:11).

> After he had said this, he went on to tell them, "Our friend Lazarus has fallen asleep; but I am going there to wake him up" (John 11:11).

As soon as I read these three scriptures together, it unlocked the message the Father was trying to get to me this whole time because He spoke, "Nate, I am leading you into a new path that you will have to see to believe. It's a road that many are called to but few follow. It's the road of the reformational call to awaken the Church to all she is meant to be. You don't need to fear not knowing this new path, but walk it with Me."

I was undone.

Here is a list of meanings of 11:11 that was put together by our revivalist friend Jodie Hughes: a

- awakening
- wake up call
- fresh spiritual awakening into more
- supernatural favor provision to take possession of promises
- transition and alignment
- revival

God is bringing life to the dead things and places. God is breathing encounters over you to *wake you up* into spiritual clarity, fresh connected relationship with Him, and an awakened sense of identity in God and your exciting eternal purpose.

THE EMPTYING OUT

Discovery seasons and wilderness seasons tend to go hand in hand, but why? Saul had to have his eyes recalibrated from how he once saw to the way God was wanting him to see. It wasn't an external process but an internal one. God was taking the eyes of Paul's heart through the wash so that he could then be able to see properly.

The wilderness is the emptying, but it's also the discovery. It's the removal of what no longer sustains and the giving of what carries life and breath upon it. In a season where God is leading you to discover who you are and what you are called to do, don't be surprised if you are also going through a very deep emptying and surrendering. It's the last few drops of the old wine falling to the ground and the new wine being poured into you all at the same time. Leviticus 26:10–13 says,

> You will still be eating last year's harvest when you will have to move it out to make room for the new. I will put my dwelling place among you, and I will not abhor you. I will walk among you and be your God, and you will be my people. I am the Lord your God, who brought you out of Egypt so that you would no longer be slaves to the Egyptians; I broke the bars of your yoke and enabled you to walk with heads held high.

God never changes, but His manna needs to be fresh, and because of that, we are meant to be filled daily with the Spirit and led daily by the Spirit. The wilderness always ensures that your operating system is updated, and you aren't falling prey to the bugs and glitches of religion's tacky maintenance program. It makes sure that you are current with Heaven, purged of the subtle and seductive apathy of the world and the lure of the culture. The wilderness is your fueling place, your setup, and your commissioning. The wilderness awakens what you didn't even know was hidden in you!

THE SLEEPY GIANT AWAKES

I strongly believe that without the wilderness David wouldn't have been prepared to defeat Goliath. His brothers weren't equipped to defeat David so that can only mean that the difference was the wilderness, and it was the wilderness that prepared him for his destiny. It brought who he really was to the surface so that he was ready in his crossover moment.

Can you see how your wilderness has only revealed what has been sleeping? It was your valley of decision where you had to choose to hold on to the old or embrace the new—and with the new came your awakening.

This generation of wild voices thought they were going onto the wilderness to die and to lay down their call, but it only graduated them in the realm of the spirit, armed them, and gave them a mighty voice. You are that generation. You are that sound. You are the awakened ones!

MENDING // CONNECTING THE SEASONS

The difficulties we face are trying to seamlessly connect the season we have been in to the season we are going into, and that can't always be done perfectly in the way we would want. Think of your seasons like the fabric and the wineskins:

And who would mend worn-out clothing with new fabric? When the new cloth shrinks it will rip, making the hole worse than before. And who would pour fresh, new wine into an old wineskin? Eventually the wine will ferment and make the wineskin burst, losing everything—the wine is spilled and the wineskin ruined. Instead, new wine is always poured into a new wineskin so that both are preserved (Matthew 9:16 TPT).

See how the fabrics can't be joined together and the new wine can't be poured into the old wineskin? Your seasons won't always connect seamlessly, and you won't have your ducks in a row, *but* you can take comfort in knowing that, while your crossover looks messy, you are going somewhere that God has promised will be better than you think!

THE MESS IS THE SIGN

If you are walking through this crossover phase of your calling right now where it feels like you are in limbo, everything is up in the air, and you are doing your best to navigate life as God leads you, you need some encouragement from God. Here's what He said to me, "Nate, don't fear the puzzle pieces scattered everywhere because the mess is actually the sign that I am upgrading you and taking you from glory to glory!" Proverbs 14:4 says, *"Without oxen a stable stays clean, but you need a strong ox for a large harvest"* (NLT). This means that, if we want increase in our lives, then from time to time we will experience a mess around us, but that is okay. It only means things are moving; we are moving!

Here are a few other signs of you being in a new wine, new path, crossover season:

- Doors close around you.
- Friendships change or end.

- Our old glasses/lenses must be thrown out.
- We see and hear God in a new way.
- Lies and religious beliefs are falling away.
- The new wineskin will confront and challenge what you know.
- The new wine will establish new infrastructure/belief system.
- You are continuing to feel the Holy Ghost pull.
- It feels like recession, but it's actually succession.
- You aren't in the driver's seat anymore.
- God gives you a new name (new identity).

SEEING PAST THE STORM

In the discovery process, there is purpose, not just for you, but for others. You see God is taking you this way because you are going to be a way finder for others. When other are freaking out and losing their footing and hope runs out the door, you are the one called to help lead people into their promise. I want to end this chapter with this amazing Jesus moment we have all heard before:

They all got into a boat and began to cross over to the other side of the lake. And Jesus, exhausted, fell asleep. Suddenly, a violent storm developed with waves so high the boat was about to be swamped. Yet Jesus continued to sleep soundly. The disciples woke him up, saying, "Save us, Lord! We're going to die!" But Jesus reprimanded them. "Why are you gripped with fear? Where is your faith?" Then he stood and rebuked the storm, saying, "Be still!" And instantly it became perfectly calm (Matthew 8:23–26 TPT).

What stands out to you? Authority? Yes. Faith? Yes, but what stands out to me the most is that Jesus wasn't unsettled by the storm or the possibility of it capsizing them. He saw beyond the storm. Also, interesting to note, they were between two places in the boat when this took place, which represents the transition we all go through.

We have been called to the breach, the chasm, and the wilderness so we can be the agents of Heaven to help people step out of the dead places, lead them through the storms, and march them into their promise.

PROPHETIC SURVIVAL KEYS

Keep your eyes fixed on where you are going. If you can't see far, attach yourself to the farthest that you can see and don't look back.

CAMPFIRE PRAYER

This is a prayer of activation to ask the Lord to open up our eyes, to open up our spiritual ears, to sharpen and activate our spiritual senses in this season:

Lord, anoint my eyes so I can see. I don't just want to see in the natural, so activate my spiritual eyes to see what is taking place in the realm of the spirit and where You are taking me.

Lord, help me discern, perceive, and understand this

season better.

Lord, I also ask you to open my ears so I can hear Your voice. I want to hear Your voice above everything else, in Jesus' name!

CHAPTER 9

New Wine Brokers

Jesus bring new wine out of me.
—Brooke Fraser

Ever heard the phrase "pulling a cart before the horse"? Growing up, I heard that phrase a lot, among other very Australian phrases that many wouldn't understand. "Nate, you can't pull the cart before the horse!" people would say to me. What they were saying was, "Don't do things backwards!" I always seemed to have a different approach to most things in life and responded a little differently than most would in similar situations. "That's not the way to do that!" people would say because my way was quite back to front from their way of thinking. I see now that it was the mantle of the pioneer upon my life. From a young age, God was already training me to pioneer in the Kingdom, but back in the day, it wasn't exactly doing me any favors.

My comfort is knowing Jesus was the same. Even before His ministry began, Jesus was messing up the system. I both love and cringe at the story of where Jesus went missing when visiting Jerusalem:

> *After the festival was over, while his parents were returning home, the boy Jesus stayed behind in Jerusalem, but they were unaware of it. Thinking he was in their company, they traveled on for a day. Then they began looking for him among their relatives*

and friends. When they did not find him, they went back to Jerusalem to look for him. After three days they found him in the temple courts, sitting among the teachers, listening to them and asking them questions. Everyone who heard him was amazed at his understanding and his answers. When his parents saw him, they were astonished. His mother said to him, "Son, why have you treated us like this? Your father and I have been anxiously searching for you." "Why were you searching for me?" he asked. "Didn't you know I had to be in my Father's house?" But they did not understand what he was saying to them (Luke 2:43–49).

The interesting things to point out here is that Jesus was twelve years of age—a number of completion and government. His parents lost him for three days—the same number of days from his death to resurrection. His parents' priority was different than his. And we learn from all this that Jesus saw things differently than His parents.

Often, when the Holy Spirit leads us in a way or direction or method that isn't like what has been done before, it looks rebellious or foolish, but it's quite the opposite.

RUNNING ON EMPTY

I was in worship and about to step up to speak a few years ago when I felt the tangible glory of God rest upon me heavily. I could barely stand. As I sat down on my chair to make sense of what God was doing, He spoke something loud and clear, "Will you come with me off the beaten path?"

"What Lord?" I asked needing clarification.

"Will you step out of the way tonight?"

Slightly offended but yielded, my response was, "Yes, Lord, of course!" As I got up to speak, I still felt the weight of His presence, and I had zero ability to take control. So, I just allowed the Holy Spirit to do what He was wanting to do.

Over the hour that followed, I felt like more like a fly on the wall than someone speaking as the Holy Spirit moved in an unusual way. I even laid down on the stage at one point! *What is happening?* I remember thinking.

That meeting was a marker for me, a point of no return. It wasn't setting a new trend or new pattern, but it marked a new level of surrender and flowing with the Holy Spirit to reap more fruit than could have come from simply doing what I had planned.

The next day, I opened up my Bible to John 2, where Jesus turned the water into wine, and a verse kept hitting my spirit:

> *He called the bridegroom over and said to him, "Every host serves his best wine first until everyone has had a cup or two, then he serves the wine of poor quality. But you, my friend, you've reserved the most exquisite wine until now!"* (John 2:10).

"What are you saying Lord?" I asked.

His response was simple, "It's time for the new wine!"

Ever since then, the Lord has been speaking to me about the significance of the new wine and the invitation to step into the new wine of the new era we are in. I believe Jesus' miracle of the turning of wine was a prophetic act and is a statement of the change of the era—from the water which in this context represents the ways of man and the wine, the things of the Spirit.

THE BEST SERVED LAST

Jesus was waiting, waiting for the perfect moment to officially begin His ministry and reveal what He was capable of. Of all the places He could have begun, it happened to be at a wedding. This speaks volumes to me of the Father's heart and intentions to woo back a church that was so far from Him and was separated from Him because of sin. He didn't send His Son so He could gain control again over His people and assert His position, but He sent His Son as a message of love that screamed, "I must be One with you!" But let's get back on track.

When Jesus was told that the old wine had run out and He went to perform the miracle, the interesting things to note from this part of the story are that:

- He used pots used for ceremonial cleaning as the place He wanted the new wine to appear. In this step, He was both prophesying and revealing the Father's heart that He was going to pour out His blood over that which was unclean and make it clean again. From the very first miracle, Jesus set this precedent.

- His wine tasted better than the first wine that was served, and so much so the master of the banquet said, *"Everyone brings out the choice wine first and then the cheaper wine after the guests have had too much to drink; but you have saved the best till now"* (Matt. 2:10). Jesus did this to prophesy what God was doing in the latter time was going to eclipse the former (fulfilling Haggai 2:9).

THE RUPTURED WINESKIN SYNDROME

A few years ago, Christy and I were approached by our good friend from Destiny Image, Larry Sparks, to contribute toward a prophetic word compilation book for 2019. Over the course of a few months, every time I pressed in for what God was saying for the coming year, I kept drawing a blank except these words kept coming to me: *new wine* and *birthing*. A week from the contribution due date, we were in Tasmania and just happened to be staying in a winery region when I had a powerful dream of that region being flooded by wine that was sinking deep into the earth. The flood began to expose what lay underneath. It looked destructive, but it was actually removing all the top layers of earth and hidden rocks and debris and realigning the destiny of the region. As I woke up, the Lord said something that sent shivers down my spine, "The old wineskin is about to burst."

When we talk about wineskins, we tend to think about it corporately rather than how it applies to us personally, but just as we have been in a change of wineskins season corporately, many of us have been dealing with what I believe is the ruptured wineskin syndrome personally. What does this mean? It's where suddenly the very methods and ways we lived don't work or have any grace or functional ease like they once did.

LOOK AROUND YOU

Look around you at the Church right now. We have seen the bursting of the old wineskin like a public exposé spread in a Hollywood magazine that read, "Church tries to run on old and outdated methods and systems. Breaks down and is facing extinction." That may be a little dramatic, but you get my point. We need the new wine *at all costs*! This will take laying down our reputations, what we have built, our pride and egos, and our faulty mindsets and beliefs. It's not a fun day when God has been warning us for a long time and suddenly the wineskin that was drying up bursts. Burst wineskins are messy and reveal the drive of man over the surrender to the Holy Spirit.

CHOOSE THE NEW WINE!

"Choose the new wine!" I hear the Holy Spirit saying over you. The old wine will not sustain you in this new season; in fact, it will only cause you to settle for the results and fruit of a past season. Often what carries new wine will also *defy* the current norms that are changing or transitioning, and you'll be faced with the decision to either bow and back down or push through the fear and embrace the fresh thing the Holy Spirit is doing.

As we crossed this threshold, there are two arms in the spirit. One arm is the might and strength of the Holy Spirit, and the other is the arm of man, the strength and ability of man that is rising right now. The temptation is even greater to operate in the strength of self and to push forward in the driven pursuit of man but choose the Spirit! We are going to see the sporadic fruits or contractions of labor of a move of God hit the nations, but it will take focus and discernment to bring it forth because the opposition is the competitive arm of man that wants to control, dominate, orchestrate, and order its own steps.

What looks like common sense in this season won't always be right either. The new wine is gushing forth, and it isn't necessarily flowing in the way most will expect. Only those who follow His voice will see it. The fear of man will always want you to trade in your chips for cheap wine, and religion will want you to police the flow. All the while, the Holy Spirit is saying, "Jump in! Jump in! Jump in!

Even right now you can feel the uncomfortable tension as God is calling you to venture beyond the expected, and you may even feel a great distaste for what you see others chasing who have settled for the old. Your womb is leaping, your passion is resurging, and you are longing to see the Lord move mightily upon your life at any cost! There is an even deeper defining taking place that will cause your lane to really be set for the years to come so you are not swayed, moved, or distracted as God brings increase to you. Allow him to refine your heart, realign your vision, and surround you with other carriers. It's time for the *new wine*!

It can look foreign carrying a new wine blueprint, even offensive, but never let the opinions of others make you forfeit it. You are creating the infrastructure for the future. It has felt like a fight to steward this new thing, but here comes a mighty *surge* of ease and fresh insight to carry it over the line. We are coming into a time where the plans will jump off the paper and *manifest*!

HOW DO I KNOW IF I AM A CARRIER OF NEW WINE?

A major marker of your discovery process is realizing that what you carry is a very different grape and vintage to what others carry—and that's okay! But how do you recognize it? Here are a few indicators:

- You have been through the process of crushing and pressing for more seasons than you can count.
- You live next to the spring, the well, the source of life. You don't like middlemen in your relationship.
- You live with your ear to the ground with a longing to hear what is hot off the print room of Heaven first.

- Your very presence and the revelations you speak seem to confront old methods and systems and get religious people unsettled.
- You speak of the new thing and never the old.
- You break new ground without any effort.
- You have a strong distaste for apathy and man-made systems.
- You see the old wine infrastructure a mile away.
- You bring a refreshing and life to those who will accept you and be poured into.
- You have a rejuvenation anointing that resurrects tired and worn-out people, and you put wind back into their sails.

PROPHETIC SURVIVAL KEYS

Being a carrier of new wine often rubs people the wrong way as they are still trying to save the last few drops of the ruptured wineskin. A key with stewarding the new wine is applying wisdom. Ask the Holy Spirit to give you wisdom to know how to walk out and speak out what you carry so that, instead of scaring people away, you can invite them into it.

CAMPFIRE PRAYER

In the words of Brooke Fraser's song, "New Wine," pray with me, "Lord make me a vessel, make me an offering, make me whatever you want me to be. I came here with nothing but all You have given me. Jesus, bring new wine out of me."

CHAPTER 10

Finding Your Voice

There is no journey like the journey of finding one's voice. It's the deep, soul-searching voyage to see what remains pure and untouched after the storm blows through and disappears, and when the lights go off and the music fades. —Nate Johnston

It wasn't the palace, the seminary, or the courts of the king that gave David a voice—it was the wilderness. The moments that aren't glorious unlock so much more than you realize. For David, his job of shepherding his father's sheep was the place where he learned to hear the voice of the Lord.

David discovered his own voice doing a humble, not-so-glamorous job. When David was alone worshipping the Lord, God gave David his voice. When David went against the lion and the bear, he began exercising it and it was as he faced more and more battles and obstacles in the wilderness where he soon realised the authority and potency of his God given voice arise. This prepared David for when it was time for him to stand against Goliath.

We don't always choose the environment where our voices emerge, but all voices are conceived in the wilderness. Voices that emerge from anywhere else will not carry the following:

- Anointing or unction
- God's power

- Weightiness and conviction

THE IDENTITY PROCESS

Discovering one's voice can be a difficult process. As I discussed above, David had to go against a lion, a bear, and a giant, and on top of this, David had to be alone in the wild. I have personally found the following portion of Scripture to be a great explanation for how we can receive and find our individual voices in God.

> The word of the Lord came to me, saying, "Before I formed you in the womb I knew you, before you were born I set you apart; I appointed you as a prophet to the nations." "Alas, Sovereign Lord," I said, "I do not know how to speak; I am too young." But the Lord said to me, "Do not say, 'I am too young.' You must go to everyone I send you to and say whatever I command you. Do not be afraid of them, for I am with you and will rescue you," declares the Lord. Then the Lord reached out his hand and touched my mouth and said to me, "I have put my words in your mouth. See, today I appoint you over nations and kingdoms to uproot and tear down, to destroy and overthrow, to build and to plant" (Jeremiah 1:4–10).

This passage reveals that Jeremiah was called to be a voice since his birth, but it wasn't until he reached adulthood that this voice was explained, revealed, and activated. Jeremiah's response to God reveals his lack of confidence. He says to God:

- "I do not know how to speak."
- "I am too young."

These statements sum up where Jeremiah was at mentally when God called him. He felt unready, unable, and disqualified, but God reminded Him of the only thing that matters: God is with us, and He will give us the words we need to speak. That sums up emerging voices who are responding to the call of the wild. Wild ones are called to be the mouthpiece that God uses, not the mouthpiece for a religious cause or man-made mission, but God's alone.

Moses struggled with this too when God called him to set his people free.

> But Moses said to the Lord, "Oh, my Lord, I am not eloquent, either in the past or since you have spoken to your servant, but I am slow of speech and of tongue." Then the Lord said to him, "Who has made man's mouth? Who makes him mute, or deaf, or seeing, or blind? Is it not I, the Lord? Now therefore go, and I will be with your mouth and teach you what you shall speak" (Exodus 4:10–12 ESV).

See how these two stories mirror the same insecurity and the same solution? I have seen far too many called and anointed voices give up in the discovery phase, even before they walk through the trial phase (that's coming up!), simply because they disqualify themselves. The most anointed people I have met in my life haven't been the most gifted and able. They simply have been the ones willing to let God fill their mouths with His words!

RECEIVER UP!

People ask me all time, "Have you always prophesied the way you do now?" and my answer is *no*. I have always had a natural prophetic "knowing," but most of it wasn't awakened or discovered until I was in my twenties. Initially, the prophetic call and gifting didn't come at some big moment. That "knowing" just seemed to slowly increase over the years until I begun to ask myself, "Why am I thinking this? This is not my thought!"

The first time I remember hearing God's voice in a way that I would say was clearly Him speaking was in 2005. Christy and I had just started running our church's youth group that January, and one day as I was driving to church for our Friday night meeting, I heard a voice on the inside begin to speak. It was as if thoughts and ideas were popping up that I had nothing to do with, and I recognized it as God speaking to me. I wrote down what He told me and what I heard. It was a prophetic word over that year, but at the time, I had no grid to understand what I was receiving. My receiver was up, though. Prior to that experience, my prophetic calling had been manifesting for years in my songwriting, but I had always just written off the random, "inspired" moments I would have as creativity even though they were more that, even surreal and other-worldly.

MESSING UP THE FLOW

Things began to change in a dramatic way during my 2006 "soaking season." I was so hungry for God that I wanted others to be just as hungry as I was. I was leading and being trained as a worship pastor at our church. Now, when I say "trained," I mean Holy Spirit trained, thrown in the deep end of the pool of trial and error. But I was all in. My encounters at home were spilling into every part of my life, and my worship leading began to be affected in way I didn't see coming. The first time in happened was awkward.

Our church was somewhat free, but we stuck to singing only the words of the songs for the full thirty minutes of praise and worship every service. Back then, there was no spontaneous worship, so we just sang one song to the next until we were through with our worship set. But this one day was different. I could feel my spirit burning to the point that I just wanted to put the guitar down and lay down and get drunk in the Spirit. I was not feeling like I was going to be able to keep my composure much longer, so as we finished the song we were singing, I directed the band to hold the key, and they did. I didn't know what I was doing, but I didn't want to move on from that place. I could feel words in my spirit begin to erupt out of me, but in moment of hesitancy, I stopped it and moved onto the next song with a confused congregation who didn't know what it was going on.

A few Sunday nights later, I was leading worship and didn't have the same feelings I had at the service weeks earlier, but my spirit was burning again like something needed to come out. We finished a song when I suddenly felt a strong surge of a word of the Lord bubbling up again; however, this time I let it erupt, and I prophesied over the church (but didn't know what it was). It felt amazing, but unfortunately, I had a few people tell me that it was nonsense, so I shut it down for many years thereafter.

LIKE A FIRE IN MY BONES

The problem with shutting down your voice is that eventually sooner or later it's going to come out again with a potency. Jeremiah learned this.

> But if I say, "I will not mention his word or speak anymore in his name," his word is in my heart like a fire, a fire shut up in my bones. I am weary of holding it in; indeed, I cannot (Jeremiah 20:9).

What a different tune Jeremiah has in this verse. He realizes that it's more exhausting to hold his tongue than free it. I learned this the hard way, too.

In my last worship pastor role, we were part of a church that loved Jesus but just didn't value prophecy, and as I had discovered, prophecy was my flow! I had been spiritually suffocated not being able to completely unleash the way I was supposed to. One day, I just decided that I wasn't going to shut it down the next time it happened and deal with the consequences. One Sunday morning shortly after that as I was in the bridge of a song, I suddenly felt the overwhelming bubbling forth of the Spirit inside me, and this time it felt involuntary as words from God gushed out. For about forty seconds, I prophesied to the horror of the pastors. That was the day I knew I had finally stepped into the wild prophetic calling God had always ordained for me. The rest is history.

FINDING YOUR HAMMER

Just like me, your discovery season normally is recognized by the moment you first find your hammer or you sense you are about to.

It's that moment that you suddenly feel an intense and overwhelming conviction about something or for something.

It's that moment that you feel "divinely disturbed" over something you didn't say before and you feel called to be a solution for it.

It's that moment that you wake up and out of nowhere have clarity that you must be a voice for that issue.

It's that moment that God pulls something out of your arsenal you didn't even know was there.

Sound familiar? If not, it will.

KEYS TO THE DISCOVERY PHASE

I know you are called to be a mighty voice, and I meet people every day who are similarly marked for this. Sadly, they don't step into it fully because they just don't know how. Here are a few keys to help you on your journey to being a mighty voice:

- It's less about trying to find your voice and more about finding God's. When you hear His voice, you'll know what you sound like.
- Stop doubting that God has called you. Stop making excuses and creating reasons why you can't be used by God.
- God calls you to this mandate and office not man. Don't live to appease people. Please God.
- Don't let the voice in you stagnate and lay dormant. If you hold it back, it will cause you to feel frustrated and unfulfilled.
- Shake off comparison and stop thinking up all the ways you don't qualify.
- Accept your calling today as an emerging voice in the earth.
- Pay attention to what unlocks your voice or causes the bubbling forth.

WAYS OF RECEIVING

What really helps the discovery phase is knowing different ways you receive from God. Here are a few ways you can receive from God:

- Through hearing His voice audibly

- Through worship
- Through dreams
- As you read the Word
- Through signs or numbers
- Through impressions and pictures
- Through visions

Do you hear God through any of these ways? These are how God speaks *to* us, but I believe the emphasis in the days to come needs to be on how He speaks *through* us because far too much of what God says stays on the shelf.

DIVINE MOMENTS

There are also what I like to call "divinely inspired moments" that God uses to speak through us. Here are a few examples:

- **Knowing**—it is like hearing God through osmosis. You didn't hear it or see it, but you just somehow know it in your entire being.
- **Bubbling**—it's where the Holy Spirit touches your belly and you begin to speak His words and not your own. It tends to flood or bubble out.
- **Lightning crack**—this is similar to bubbling, but there are moments of such intensity that the Holy Spirit will use His words in your mouth like the crack of lightning to scatter the enemy, break demonic activity, or shift an atmosphere.

WHAT KIND OF VOICE WILL YOU BE?

- We need clear voices for where we are going—voices that are so branded in the throne room that they effortlessly cut through earthly conflict and chaos and bring the focus back to Jesus.
- We need voices of truth, voices that set the standard and are the reminder to the Church of where true north lies.
- We need voices that keep the main thing the main thing and call out distraction and diversions sent to get us off track.
- We need pure voices that are atmosphere shifters and air clearers, exposing principalities and counterfeits and sending demons running when they are near.
- We need voices that don't just read the news but give us the roadmap and the blueprints and lead us forward in times of transition and many unknowns.
- We need voices that aren't owned by man, don't live for the praises of people, or never easily cave in and appease man. We need voices that live for the audience of One so that, when it matters, they hold to their post.
- We need voices that have felt the hot coals of Heaven touch their lips and they know what it's like to be a carrier of the unfiltered Word of the Lord.
- We need the undignified voices that aren't rebels but love-sick worshipers who will gladly speak and look stupid at the cost of seeing Jesus magnified.
- We need voices that aren't trying to rant, display their opinions, or have a soapbox moment, but voices whose sole prerogative is to share what God is saying.
- The church and even the world are waiting, longing, searching for the pure sound of the emerging ones that

speak a different language and are pioneering the NOW Word of the Lord.

- We need our warrior sound back where the enemy has tamed a generation and removed the fiery roar that the Church was meant to carry. It has made prophecy a psychic gift in the Church and rejected the office that shifts cities and nations.

- We need voices that are anchored in the Word of God and are rooted deeply in love so that they can last the distance.

- We need voices of reformation that unapologetically tear down idols and bring the Church back to her original design.

- We need the voices that are the builders and designers under the new wineskin that lead the Church out of outdated ways and systems and construct the new.

- We need voices of deliverance that are constantly addressing the heart and leading us into freedom, health, and wholeness.

- We need the voices of healing that are raised up to address and lead the way with social injustices, instead of allowing the humanism to lead the charge or deceptive counterfeit social justice reforms that do not result in real transformation.

- We need a new media system birthed through the Church because we are tired of truth being thwarted and muted and righteousness being censored and labeled offensive.

- We need voices driven by the testimony of Jesus so, when they speak, miracles, signs, and wonders manifest.

- We need voices that simply know how to be great listeners to Heaven's newsroom, the strategy room, and the Father's secrets so that, when they speak, it is *fresh*, carries *dunamis* power, and *births* what is released.

This is our mandate. Clear voices, arise!

PROPHETIC SURVIVAL KEYS

Don't shut down the gift you have been given. See your voice as a special gift from God, not a curse or burden. Then you will choose to steward it and not silence it. Give your voice room.

CAMPFIRE PRAYER

Lord, You have given me a voice for a reason, and I can look back and see the many times I let others and myself shut it down out of not knowing how to use it or out of fear. Today, help me begin to see the kind of voice You have called me to be. Help me own it and steward it well, in Jesus' name.

CHAPTER 11

Pioneers & Forerunners

Tomorrow, tomorrow, living inside of you.
—Kim Clement

This lyric from a prophetic song by Kim Clement captures the very heart and mandate of the voices God is raising up. One of the defining qualities and attributes of this new breed of voices is the call to pioneer and be voices that connect today with tomorrow. They are the ones who seem to speak a different language and different themes. They carry unique and unseen expressions and break open the way for others to walk through.

One very obvious characteristic of the emerging voices rising up right now is that they are all pioneers and forerunners, but what is a pioneer?

> pi·o·neer
>
> /ˌpīəˈnir/
>
> Noun: a person who is among the first to explore or settle a new country or area.
>
> Verb: develop or be the first to use or apply (a new method, area of knowledge, or activity. One who goes before, as into the wilderness, preparing the way for others to follow.
>
> A person or other entity who is first or among the earliest in any field of inquiry, enterprise, or progress.

Pioneer comes from a French word that means "foot-soldier" and was the role of a specific military unit that would be sent ahead of the main military unit tasked with making roads, digging intrenchments, and clearing the way in advance of the main body. A pioneer pushes boundaries to advance a cause or idea or break a record. A pioneer is the first to try something new and not yet seen before. I believe a generation of pioneers are mantled to advance the Kingdom of God in ways we haven't seen before.

FORERUNNERS

"Am I a pioneer or a forerunner?" you may have asked yourself before. The answer is both. They both mean someone who does something first.

As nouns, the difference between pioneer and forerunner is that pioneer is one who goes before, as into the wilderness, preparing the way for others to follow while a forerunner is a runner at the front or ahead of others.

fore·run·ner | \ ˈfȯr-ˌrə-nər
a runner at the front or ahead
Someone who leads out the competitors on to the circuit usually testing or checking the way.
a precursor or harbinger, a warning ahead.

A forerunner in essence is the fruit of being faithful to pioneer long-term, which is not an easy feat to accomplish. Pioneers are those who are faithful to go and endure the process of being misunderstood for a season, whereas a forerunner is one who has continued to stand and run when the odds were stacked against them.

Years ago, I saw a group of people in a vision, and they were running forward with fiery torches, even though there were many on the side lines yelling abusively and accusatively at them. This was their mission: to carry the torch into new and unknown lands and territories for the Kingdom. They were those who had continued to stay at the feet of Jesus throughout the process and had prevailed and were then running with fire, lighting the way for so many others.

A pioneer is called to open a new path, an untraveled path, whereas a forerunner will make it a three-lane freeway and direct traffic onto it. The last definition I want to give to distinguish these two is this: A pioneer is called to conceive and nurture a spiritual baby while a forerunner will carry it to full-term.

As God's reformational voices in the earth, your assignment is both. You will notice in some seasons you are carrying seeds that need propagating, which is the role of the pioneer, and in others you are leading the pack and driving the flag of victory into new territory. In some seasons, you will find yourself walking in the dark, clearing new paths, and in others you will be leading an army of renegades through the very paths you paved to spearhead mighty exploits.

YOU ARE THE NEW THING

Isaiah 43:19 says,

> I am doing something brand new, something unheard of. Even now it sprouts and grows and matures. Don't you perceive it? I will make a way in the wilderness and open up flowing streams in the desert (TPT).

Recently in worship, the Holy Spirit began to speak to me, and He said "I am doing a new thing, do you see it? I am doing something brand new, something unheard of. Even now it sprouts and grows and matures. Do you see it?" just as it says in Isaiah 43:19. Then He said it again "Nate I am doing a new thing; do you *see it*?"

I replied, "Yes, Lord, I see it!"

Then He said, "Nate, I am doing a new thing, do you see them?"

My spirit was quickened to the next chapter of Isaiah where it says:

> *"I will pour refreshing water on the thirsty and streams on the dry ground. I will pour out my Spirit on your children, my blessing upon your descendants. They will spring up like grass blanketing a meadow, like poplars growing by gushing streams"* (Isaiah 44:3 TPT).

I understood what He was saying. Not only are we in a *new era* where God is doing a *new thing*, but *we are* the new thing! Wow! Pioneers are the new thing!

IT'S IN YOUR DNA

Within the design of every pioneering voice is the DNA to long to increase, advance, multiply, and possess. It was within the original command that God gave Adam and Eve when they left the garden of Eden, and the same theme is woven throughout the history of humanity, where we have proven that this spiritual rule is deeply embedded into the way we have been constructed.

Of course, this revealed itself in negative ways too with the conquests of Rome, Britain, France, and Spain as the sole focus and measure of success was in how many other lands people could conquer and take into their possession. But that only reveals the longing in us to always be pushing the envelope and breaking new ground. It doesn't mean that we are some type of super-humans that don't experience fear. It simply means that, regardless of fear, we know we need to press forward into unsure places. There is a high cost of not moving forward that extends further than our lifetimes and is measured in generations to come. That's why it is important for us to put in the hard yards to do what we were called to do. Sometimes, I think of this when I feel like what God has called me to is too much to handle and know that my momentary discomfort will mean that my children get to build upon what I have pioneered and go even further.

You must advance forward no matter the cost. You feel it in your bones. The road for you and me seems a little different than the road for others, and there's a reason why. Let me make this clear. You are birthing something *new* and never before seen! That's why you wrestle with it. That's why hell hates it, and people judge it. That's why you question and doubt it, and yet heaven is screaming, "You got this. This is who you are!"

PIONEERS RECEIVE HEAVEN'S BLUEPRINTS & STEWARD THEM

In 2015, during our season of isolation, God began to speak, and Christy and I began to write. To our surprise, He gave us prophetic discipling content and curriculum that used words and concepts we had never heard before. Then in 2016, we officially kicked off our first online course in a time where few were doing them. Instantly and to our surprise, God blew it up, and we were seeing people's lives radically changed and transformed with many activated in their callings.

It shocked us, but then the persecution came from those who didn't understand what our hearts were and were unsure of our practices and concepts. I had many pastors I knew from previous seasons message me that they were very concerned we were not plugged into a church anywhere. These made derogatory remarks about our course content. They would see snippets of it online. They were troubled by the language of our social media updates. I had some of my closest friends call and tell us that online ministry was not legitimate ministry and that I needed to stop seeking online fame, which was not our hearts at all, but the hardest hit came closer to home.

One day, I received a call from a family member saying we were embarrassing the family. The individual warned us that going down this road would only lead to ruin. I was so grateful for Rick Pino's song, "Pioneer," back then. I would play it on repeat on especially hard days. It encouraged me to "keep pressing onwards beyond" my fear to the "uncharted wilderness" stretching before me and calling out to me.

Pioneers, you must keep going, even when what you speak isn't popular or seems out of step with the rest of the church. Please keep going. Be true to the call of the Spirit inside you. I truly believe history books being written hinge on your faithfulness.

LOOK TO JESUS, THE ULTIMATE PIONEER

But, pioneers, you aren't driven by the need to out-do or even innovate. That is not your motivation. It's *who* you are following that makes the difference. Being different and going a different path for the sake of standing out isn't pioneering; that's something else entirely.

I can imagine the disciples' journey for the three years they were with Jesus must have been an interesting one. Jesus showed up and said, "Follow me," and that was it, cold turkey. Their old way of life was over, and their lives were entrusted into the hands of someone who did things very differently than they knew or were taught. They were constantly unsure of which way He would be led or how He would respond to different scenarios. From the outset, Jesus was modeling a life surrendered to the Spirit and walking out the life of a pioneer. In fact, Jesus was the ultimate Pioneer, our Prototype. Just as in a car factory there is a prototype that a mold is taken from to construct the other cars, Jesus is the Prototype for us to know how to model the life we are meant to lead and reveal the path that we will follow. Hebrews 6:19–20 says,

> We have this certain hope like a strong, unbreakable anchor holding our souls to God himself. Our anchor of hope is fastened to the mercy seat which sits in the heavenly realm beyond the sacred threshold, and where Jesus, our forerunner, has gone in before us. He is now and forever our royal Priest like Melchizedek (TPT).

LED BY THE CLOUD

The Israelites would be led on their unknown path through the wilderness by the cloud in the day and the fire by night. Today, our standard hasn't changed. We follow the cloud of glory and the fire of His presence and nothing else.

The pioneering call is to worship; it's about intimacy not accomplishment. The venture itself isn't our goal; it's obedience and connection. Far too many get this wrong and end up disappointed. I don't want you disappointed. Follow the longing inside you. That's right. I know you have it. It's the longing inside you that says, "There must be more!"

In 2004, during the "Toronto blessing" revival, one of the marker songs of the outpouring was a song by Vineyard Music called "There Must Be More." The Spirit of God fell upon the people, and this song of hunger and travail would come upon those present, calling for the Holy Spirit to breathe on them.

This is the heart's cry of pioneers around the world. It's the cry of a people who want to see God touch them, anoint them, and use them mightily in the earth. Jesus actually said something interesting on this:

> I tell you this timeless truth: The person who follows me in faith, believing in me, will do the same mighty miracles that I do—even greater miracles than these because I go to be with my Father! (John 14:12 TPT).

The word *greater* here is the Greek word *mega*, which means exceeding, great, large, mighty, and epic. In other words, it's saying that we would continue on the pioneering legacy Jesus began and that we would increase it, multiply it, and raise up others with the same mandate!

There is so much more to discover, and this is one of the roles of the pioneer—to be revealers of God and His intentions to a world hungering for something more than we have known. That is now your mandate.

You see, we are created for intimacy with God and for the pursuit of His heart at all costs. When we don't feel that closeness, we know it. That's why pioneering and intimacy go hand in hand because, without intimate connection with God, we will never know what the "more" is. How can we hear the thoughts of God without laying our head on His chest? How can we see the unique path before us without seeing where He is walking? Your pioneering begins and ends with Jesus.

I pray that you also begin to deeply hunger for powerful encounters with the Lord that ignite the pioneer inside you.

HOW DO I KNOW I AM CALLED TO PIONEER?

- Do you carry unusual blueprints and never before seen concepts, ideas, and messages?
- Do you feel like you are living before your time or with the map of tomorrow in your spirit?
- Do you flow in ways, expressions, or methods that challenge the status quo?
- Do you see beyond the moment, beyond the storm, and beyond the temporal to a new day?
- Do you live with a longing for more than you can see?

Then you are a pioneer, and it's time to step into your unique path.

PROPHETIC SURVIVAL KEYS

Take stock of your life and see the areas God has given you insight into that are ahead of the curve. Your greatest key in pioneering is doing it for God as worship and not doing it for man. If you adjust that one thing, you'll step into another dimension of your destiny.

CAMPFIRE PRAYER

Lord, help me know how to pioneer well. So much is unknown, and I'm still trying to find my footing in it. I know that, if I keep my eyes on You, Jesus, I will run my race well and break through any hard ground before me. I'm following You, Lord, in Jesus' name.

CHAPTER 12

Unlikely Heroes & Unusual Tools

God is looking for Davids who know the difference between the armor of God and the armor of Saul. One looks foolish, but it wins the battle. That's the hero you were called to be. —Nate Johnston

Everyone loves a good underdog story. You know the kind where the unlikely woman or man faces an opponent or situation that looks like it would outdo them, but then to everyone's surprise they get the upper hand. Hollywood loves this script, but Hollywood didn't write it. God did. He wrote it into the life of David whose destiny was to defeat a giant and bring victory to his people, and he did it with His Son, Jesus, who came as the underdog from Nazareth. He would save the world by dying for humanity.

God loves to make the foolish things of this world confound the wise, and what you need to know in your discovery is that you are no exception. I'm not saying you are foolish, but I am saying that, if you think you need to have it all together before God will use you, then maybe you need to go read a few more Bible stories for inspiration.

Think of when Peter and John went about healing in a village:

When they saw the courage of Peter and John and realized that they were unschooled, ordinary men, they were astonished and they took note that these men had been with Jesus (Acts 4:13).

What's the only prerequisite to being used by God? To be with Jesus. Wow. I feel like you are going to feel some freedom come to you today and a fresh courage rise up in your spirit as you read this. I love how God used the foolish things of this world to confound the wise, and in this next move and next wave, we will see the most unlikely by man's standards rise to lead the charge forward.

MY DUCKS AREN'T LINED UP

Are you the kind of person who needs to have their ducks in a row before they move? You've put the fleece out so many times, hoping for a sign for you to leave your place of safety, but it's also cost you time and not really brought any more clarity? I want to give you some tools and encourage you today to step out or, at the very least, to begin to see that you have everything you need right now to begin.

I'm not trying to rush you or make you launch before your time, but I am wanting you to move. Whether it's your green light moment or not, a wild calling without movement is a sitting duck, and a sitting duck is a target for the enemy at which he can shoot discouragement, apathy, and complacency. So, get up for a minute, set the book down, do a crazy dance, shake your arms, yell if you need to, and then let's dive back in.

WHAT'S MY LANE?

We all have seasons that feel like the place of trial and error as we learn to navigate what God has placed inside us. I had always had people tell me what I was and who I should be, and the whole time I was missing out on the fun and adventure of cracking the kinder surprise open that was my calling.

Before I move on, I am suggesting that the church leadership's ability to discern and appropriate people and their giftings has often been secondary to its need to fill a role. I get it, but it hasn't been conducive to raising people effectively and is lousy recruiting at best. What if, instead of telling people what they should do, we give them an opportunity to serve while still helping them understand their own unique spiritual makeup?

In our isolation season, I was no longer serving in a church the way I had been for so long, and I had much time to spare but didn't know what I was meant to do with it. I was finally in a space where I was free to explore the burning inside me, but I didn't know where to begin, so I started putting raw worship videos up on YouTube. I hated it. I sounded horrible. I think I even sat in the bathroom next to the toilet in one video just to capture the echo sound, hoping that would help me out. Newsflash, it didn't. I was conflicted in myself. I did worship, but I also liked to prophesy. However, I was rusty at it and had never fit in church, so I didn't know how they both fit now I was out there on my own. Then an app called Periscope came out. It was a broadcasting app that I could go live with, and people around the world could drop in and listen and comment. I decided that I was going to face my fears and come on once daily until I broke through. With two people watching, I encouraged them with a word, then soon five were watching, then thirty, and then many more. I used to iron my pants for work and prophesy over people both saved and unsaved, and God was really moving! In this trial-and-error discovery phase of my calling, I really took note of when I flowed more effortlessly and when I didn't.

Your lives light up the world. For how can you hide a city that stands on a hilltop? And who would light a lamp and then hide it in an obscure place? Instead, it's placed where everyone in the house can benefit from its light. So don't hide your light! Let it shine brightly before others, so that your commendable works will shine as light upon them, and then they will give their praise to your Father in heaven (Matthew 5:14–16 TPT).

The most fruit seemed to come from two main areas for me: Father encounters, where people encounter the love of God as I shared my encounter stories, and then deliverance and inner healing. I couldn't keep up with the testimonies because there were so many. I began to see the strong and apparent facets to my calling emerge. The hard part was being vulnerable enough to release those giftings associated with my calling consistent enough to give them room to grow and develop.

KINGDOM SUPERPOWERS

One day while I was driving in the car with our two daughters, they started asking me about how God makes us all special. Sophie said, "Daddy, I have special powers Jesus gave me." Surprised by her statement, I asked what she meant, and she said, "I am a protector!" and this was true. Sophie has always had a justice mandate, and as an expression of that, she often sticks up for and looks out for those who are being bullied or hurt in some way. It's her expression of her mandate, a gift the Holy Spirit has given her to express her calling.

Charlotte then piped up, "My superpower is kindness and loving people!" and her statement was also true because of the way she naturally loves and cares for people. "Daddy, you speak Jesus' heart to people!" Charlotte said.

"So, what's mummy's superpower?" I asked curiously.

"Mummy prays!" Sophie said immediately.

Our unique giftings are a special gift from God, and even kids can recognize it!

UNIQUE TOOLS FOR A UNIQUE HOUR

Over the years, I have seen some unusual and amazing giftings, callings, and hybrid anointings that, because they didn't fit within the conventional church parking cones, they were rejected rather than embraced. I've seen some unique and powerful ways God has wired people to operate. Time and time again, I've seen God offend the religious, legalistic barriers to accomplish something. He has used interesting people to do it, too. What we must establish is that there are *no* bounds with God. Let me say that again. *There are no bounds with God.* If He can cause a donkey to speak, then who are we to say whom He can use and how He can use them?

If you discovered that God had given you a unique gift mix that went beyond the bounds of normal or acceptable, would you still be obedient to use it? What makes you you *is* that your message, gift, revelation, mandate, or expression won't always fit the mold. It won't necessary look like everyone else's!

David's mighty men were all "mighty," but did you know that God cleverly crafted each of them to wield unique skills in battle that made them stand head and shoulders above the mark of a normal soldier? These were skilled warriors who were created and crafted to serve a specific role. We as the Church are in an hour where the world is looking to us for answers ,and we need to look outside the box of confinement to see the blueprints to move forward into new ground. God really is releasing unique mantles and gift mixes in this hour. Are you ready to receive them?

UNUSUAL HEROES RISING

One morning last year the Spirit of God fell upon me heavily, and I began to prophesy:

> *Here they come! The unlikely ones, the misfits, the overlooked! Here they come! They will be like David, the unlikely king, the unlikely warrior, the unlikely victor, the ones who were overlooked and called useless and hopeless. Here they come! They are the carriers of the pure voice of the Lord leading the Church back to the feet of Jesus. They are the igniters and fire-starters of revival in the nations. They are the ones who have been silenced and constantly muzzled and sent back into the wilderness by the religious voices or the insecure. They are the ones who have been broken and shipwrecked, pushed to the side, and underestimated, but NOW HERE THEY COME! The wild ones are rising. The undignified ones like David who had nothing but a harp and a sling, but they will take down giants, smash through immoveable doors and walls, command mountains to move, and lead the Church forward into victory!*

God is raising up the unlikely ones right now who like David may be the last pick to be king, yet God is choosing them to impact the earth. Right now, there is a changing of the guard because God needs worshipers, kings, and priests to lead the Body of Christ forward. I say this respectfully, but the kingdom of Saul has had its day. The wineskin has burst, and we can't operate the same way we have. We must be a generation living at the feet of Jesus, not basking in the sun of ministry accolades. God is resetting the affections of the Body of Christ, and He is using these unlikely heroes to lead the Body of Christ out of dysfunction and back into alignment with the heart of the Father.

The ones God is using today are the wild horses who aren't in union with the culture of the world but are in sync and flow with the river of the Spirit of God that is building, rising, and flowing into the nations. They are the cool drink of water to a dry and thirsty land, and we are seeing them rise! No this is not an hour to stop your flow but to raise your voice and release into the earth what you have been carrying!

CRAZY ONES STORMING THE FRONTLINES

I remember reading about a crazy group of warriors called the "berserkers" who were probably demon-possessed madmen, but there was something about them that the Holy Spirit wanted to show me. They were so full of passion and rage that they would fight and not feel the blows while others were falling to their left and right. These "berserk" men were so loud and crazy that they would be positioned at the front of the battle to intimidate the opponents, and it would work!

What if God has called us to be so possessed by His Spirit that we were the ones who rush to the frontlines to intimidate the enemy with our worship and shouts of victory?

There is a modern Hebrew word for pioneer. It is *chalutz*, which also means "forward, pathfinder, striker, and one who goes first in a great venture." I found that in biblical Hebrew, this same word means "one equipped for war, one that is armed, warrior, rescuer, and deliverer."

In the original text of Numbers 32:20–22, this word is found twice and is translated as a *shockfighter*:

> Moses said to them, "If you do this, if you go to battle as shocktroops, at the instance of the Lord, and every shockfighter among you crosses the Jordan, at the instance of the Lord, until He has dispossessed His

enemies before Him, and the land has been subdued, at the instance of the Lord, and then you return you shall be clear before the Lord and before Israel; and this land shall be your holding under the Lord" (TJSB).

This is who we are! We are shockfighters who will "cross over" into new territory and dispossess the kingdoms of darkness in our wake!

BATTLE OF BEERSHEBA

In 2017, we took our family to Washington, DC, be part of the Awaken the Dawn and Rise Up events as we felt called to join the prayers of America on behalf of the nation of Australia. On the Sunday of the event, we happened to bump into Lou Engle, and upon hearing we were Australians, he began prophesying and sharing the significance of Australians being at the event and the synergy of our nations in this time in history. He then mentioned the Australian Light-horsemen at the battle of Beersheba.

That afternoon, I looked up what he briefly shared, and my spirit leapt. On October 31, 1917, eight hundred Australian and New Zealander mounted cavalry stormed the city of Beersheba as one against the Turks. Against all odds, they took back the city of Beersheba, freeing the Jews from exactly four hundred years of captivity, altering the course of the war! These were eight hundred soldiers who outsmarted the vast Turkish army just by being brave, courageous, and letting their wild out a little!

What I didn't know about this story was that the horses also had a large role to play in the story. Apparently, the horses were extremely thirsty from the hot sun. The horses did not enough water, but they could smell the water in Beersheba, which was a city that had many wells (Beersheba means "well of 7"), so as the infantry charged, the horses also charged with extra motivation. The rest was history.

This story has always spoken to me in more ways than one, but the part of the horses speaks to me the most because they were driven by their thirst. Does that speak to you about our motivation as God's wild horses?

GET OVER THESE HURDLES ONCE & FOR ALL

The recipe of your calling, giftings, anointings, and expressions will be *unusual* because God uniquely created you. He made you that way because you are the *missing ingredient*! Others may not recognize or appreciate your makeup, but don't let that deter you or stop you because your ingredient and mix will be sought after down the road. What you are stewarding now is for a day coming where the Church will be needing your mix of giftings to get her out of the rut.

To encourage you a little more about this, let's look at some examples of the "unusual" in the Bible:

- **Unusual weapons**—David used unusual tools for his conquest—not the normal weapons of his day for battle. He used a sling and stones, which were normally used to protect sheep and deter predators but not fight giants, yet these were the right tools for the task. David obeyed God in using them. The unlikely heroes of this hour will arise with unusual tools and methods to reveal the King of Glory. Will we recognize them when we see them?

- **Unusual sound**—When David hurled his sling in the air in that valley, it would have created a sound like rushing wind. He didn't use taunts or scream obscenities back at Goliath. He let the sound of his unusual tool of choice fill the air. The unlikely heroes of this hour carry a new sound, and in this season the soundtrack is changing. A new sound is going to fill the air and the airwaves as a sign of this new era, new day, and new outpouring.

- **Unusual armor**—When David rejected Saul's armor, it was not a dishonor but a realization of different wineskin. David wasn't called to do battle and rule the kingdom like Saul, so it wasn't that his armor didn't fit. It was that it was not the right armor for the new era he was announcing that very day. Don't be afraid to say no to the old methods and ways of the old era because, by doing so, you are not dishonoring those who have gone before you, but you are stepping into the new wineskin for this hour.

- **Unusual motive**—I heard the Lord say that the greatest distinction of the unlikely heroes is not methods or tools, but it is a distinction of the heart. God is raising up these unlikely heroes who are lovers of Him, not ministry or serving a role or purpose. Their motive is different. They live for the King and nothing else. In this mighty outpouring, you will see them and discern them because they won't be bought, and you won't find them looking for a platform. Because their motive is pure, God will take them before kings.

KEYS TO MOVING FROM STAGNANCY TO DISCOVERY

If you are reading this and are feeling stagnant and stuck and unsure how to begin, here are a few keys for you:

- Reject the lie that says you don't have what you need to begin. With that logic, you'll never be ready.
- What you have in your hands right now, today, is enough.
- Where you are at is enough. You are enough.

- Faith ignites movement. Find something to create movement with.
- Step out onto the waters and walk.
- Own your voice and know there is no one who sounds like you do.
- Practice your gifts daily.
- Explore your gifts.

PROPHETIC SURVIVAL KEYS

Pick up your stones and sling or your unusual tools or expressions and begin using them. In moments of feeling unqualified, remember that it's who lives in you that matters.

CAMPFIRE PRAYER

Lord, today I lean into You and Your ability to use me in ways beyond my capabilities. Help me discover how You have uniquely created me for this moment and activate everything that has been inside me that You want to use to take down giants and set captives free, in Jesus' name!

CHAPTER 13

Unexpected Birthing

"Do I bring to the moment of birth and not give delivery?"
says the Lord. "Do I close up the womb when I bring to
delivery?" says your God. —Isaiah 66:9

Though maybe you haven't seen any signs of spiritual activity and have believed you weren't carrying anything, wild one, this is your season of unexpected birthing. It's also the very moment God has chosen to reveal what He has kept a secret from others and even you. It's the moment when you haven't got the baby room ready because you are not anticipating that *suddenly* God will shift your life by bringing forth the promise you thought would never come to pass.

FOR THE RIGHT TIME

The greatest discovery you can make right now is this—"I didn't know how much I was carrying until this moment." There has been a long and slow pregnancy for a reason: God has been preparing what you carry for an *appointed time.* That's right. What you carry birthed in the wrong time would be catastrophic, and God is choosing this time in history to bring a baby boom of epic proportions in the wilderness. We are seeing those who have felt shut down and barren suddenly feeling the leaping of a baby in their womb and even the onset of contractions. Those who felt like they were past their birthing years are suddenly feeling the kicks of new life inside them.

I often wonder why Jesus didn't start His ministry earlier. Why didn't He start doing miracles, healing the sick, cleansing the lepers, and revealing the heart of the Father earlier? Because it wasn't His time, meaning that God had reserved Him for a specific hour, for a specific reason, and it is the same for the thousands upon thousands of hidden and seemingly barren voices around the world today who are beginning to feel the clock announce a new day.

> *For the revelation awaits an appointed time; it speaks of the end and will not prove false. Though it linger, wait for it; it will certainly come and will not delay* (Habakkuk 2:3).

THE WAITING & FALSE LABOR

Two of the most common things I hear wild ones saying are:

- "I feel like my waiting is longer than others'."
- "I have been stuck at forty-weeks pregnant for too long."

For this reason, the discovery process can often be full of frustration with feelings of constant false starts and false hope.

When Christy was pregnant with Sophie, we ended up at the hospital twice thinking she was going into labor when it was just Braxton-Hicks contractions, which was her body's way of saying the time for birth was getting closer. But these were false contractions. Both times we left the hospital feeling discouraged and tired. We all know this feeling, and it can be toxic to experience them long-term, but God's incubation period should never be confused with the enemy's assignment of delay. What's the difference?

The enemy wants to keep putting off your delivery date, luring you into false hope, so as to detach you emotionally from what you are carrying. He wants you to abort your mission, be lulled into apathy, be numb to the purpose inside you, and become so hope-sick that you never exhaust yourself by co-dreaming and co-laboring with God ever again.

Far too many have mistaken God's process as the enemy's, or mistaken the enemy as God, and it's been creating a cycle of barrenness that needs to be broken!

PERMISSION TO BIRTH

In 2017, as I was speaking at a prophetic conference, I began to sense that many prophetic people, especially intercessors in the room, had experienced warfare and opposition against their birthing. I felt the Holy Spirit begin to speak through me, and I prophesied, "Your delay and barrenness are over, and you have permission to birth!" As soon as I said that, screams erupted around the room. About ten people went onto all fours as if they were birthing in the natural and began to have spiritual contractions. Honestly, this was new to me, and I had never before seen Holy Spirit move this way.

WORD FOR THOSE IN DELAYED BIRTHING

Last year God gave me a word for those who have experienced this delayed birthing:

Then I saw a season of contractions and pushing that

ended in nothing and these pioneers were exhausted and wanting to stop pressing in for the promise.

I saw the books and manuscripts and songs that had been blocked and held back, the creative solutions that were NEEDED for the season we have been in, but they came under fire and were never birthed.

But then I heard it again in my spirit, "Soon the waters are going to break! The waters are about to break!"

There has been a global, demonic assignment of delay sent to stop the move of God in the earth and the movements that pioneers have been carrying from coming into fruition, but right now the waters are breaking!

Yes, this is the right time, the right moment in history, and the right environment to birth movements. Don't buy into what you see around you and the news headlines. What God has given you is *for this hour!*

What you are about to birth and build next is what the enemy is afraid of. He is afraid because it's been like the collecting of waters, the building of pressure through years of warfare, that has brought you to a moment where what you have been carrying has only increased in its potency and is going to do some serious damage to the plans of darkness!

All the attack that has come against you, the words, the assassination attempts, and the lies that told you that you were barren are going to be shown up as God reveals what has been incubating in secret, increasing through your worship. The delay has only increased the size of the harvest.

Where it has looked like a fruitless season of pressing forward without seeing any progress, you will soon see what you have been incubating and building in the dark!

Get ready to feel a surge of fresh creativity where it has been blocked and a fresh anointing to build and create, write, plant, and pioneer the new and unseen blueprints from the Lord's heart.

MULTIPLE BIRTHS

It was unexpected for us. We were always the cheering squads and the midwives to others' dreams but never our own until God led us out of the church we were in. Why? We didn't know why, but we knew He said it and we had to follow. We were suddenly in isolation with no signs of opportunities around us or any hope of seeing God use us in any way—until He did.

About sixteen months into this "no man's land" season, things began to shift. We started to see things super clearly as the fog of religious activity blocking our view and influencing our judgment finally lifted. I was speaking daily on Periscope, prophesying over people and regularly had thousands of people per week tuning in. There were testimonies of many healings, salvations, and miracles breaking out daily. Then, in March of 2016, I had my first word published on *Elijah List*, then *Charisma* magazine, and spirit fuel followed. In April of the same year, we launched our first online course. What was happening? It was our season of multiple births taking place right before our eyes.

Isaiah 54:1 speaks about this strange phenomenon:

> *"Rejoice with singing, you barren one! You who have never given birth, burst into a song of joy and shout, you who have never been in labor! For the deserted wife will have more children than the married one,"* says Yahweh (TPT).

People often say, "You get double for your trouble," but this passage says *more*, which in Hebrew means "abundant, abounding, numerous, many, exceeding." That looks like *multiplication* to me! This is what God does with all the delay and the long, drawn-out, preparation season when you felt like you were held back or forgotten. He uses it to bless you with more!

IT WON'T LOOK LIKE YOU THINK

Recently, the Lord said to me that it was time for "home-births," not hospital births, meaning that God was going to reveal Heaven's newest exports *outside* the four walls of the Church and through unlikely people. We have looked to the institution for so long for answers and for the lead forward, but God is raising you up to be the golden ticket carrier of this era. What you birth is going to turn heads and hearts and lead the Church in the way she should go.

When Mary and Joseph arrived in Bethlehem, they didn't expect they would have to birth Jesus in a stable. I mean that's the King of kings being born next to animals, but it was ordained that way by God because Jesus didn't come into a palace for the elite. He came humbly and for the lowly of heart. Remember this—regardless of where Jesus was born, He still drew kings. If you birth where God leads you, then He will always make sure He brings it before kings.

In this next season, we are going organic, natural, and raw. We are breaking away from the monotonous, carbon-copy, birthings of man-made, flesh-fueled religion, and we are only birthing what comes from the Spirit alone.

Michael Koulianos says, "If God didn't birth it, then he won't bless it, and if God didn't birth it, I don't want it!"

Many have tried to manufacture the anointing and the mighty thunderous voice of Heaven, but without the Spirit it *does nothing*! Imagine if the disciples launched out before Pentecost. What would have happened? Some fruit perhaps, but it would have looked like the ridiculous, man-driven, religious rubbish we see all the time that has lots of hot air words but no transformation.

What if you have been in the waiting to be preserved for this moment so that, when the Holy Spirit comes upon you, He makes what has looked dead alive? What if you have been in waiting so that, when the Holy Spirit activates your mouth, it comes with lasting fruit, power, and potency?

This isn't the birthing you imagined and hasn't looked like you thought it would, but what God is going to do through you is going to blow your mind! Well, done for holding on!

SIGNS OF A BIRTHING SEASON

- You feel the tension of natural barrenness (like nothing is happening) and the stirring of anticipation in your spirit.
- You strangely feel like you need to nest, to make room for what is coming.
- Everything around you feels messy and in disarray. There is so much up in the air, and dots haven't connected.
- You are experiencing extreme pressure and warfare on every side.
- You feel movement that you didn't feel before.
- God begins to awaken forgotten dreams and desires.
- You have a sudden longing to see the promise manifest.
- New blueprints and ideas are starting to come. New revelation is flowing.

So, whether you are in the birthing phase or not, know that God is working powerfully today in your life, and He will finish what He started!

PROPHETIC SURVIVAL KEYS

Cast off the lies that you are barren and will never produce anything of any use or purpose inside you. Your key is this: "Look for the kick!" Ask God to show you signs of life, small indicators that incubation is taking place. Ask Him to show you the signs mentioned in this chapter. Remind yourself of those often when you are feeling barren.

CAMPFIRE PRAYER

Lord, show me what I am carrying and about to birth. Show me what You have been weaving together behind the scenes that I cannot always see and bring it to fruition in my life, in Jesus' name!

CHAPTER 14

The Prophetic Toolbox

Knowing what is in your prophetic quiver will change how you navigate your destiny, how you overcome obstacles, and even determine the difference between whether you become successful or fall short. We need to know what we have been given! —Nate Johnston

Imagine having the ability to unlock people around you and reveal the treasure they have inside? One of the greatest gifts of being a wild one for the Lord is that He gives you this insatiable love for people of all walks of life and the anointing to unlock people everywhere you go, even opening their eyes to who they are and what they carry. It's like the Holy Spirit gives you a behind the scenes pass into their life and reveals their internal makeup . In this chapter I want to help You discover how you tick so you can begin to see others in this same way.

SPIRITUAL MECHANICS

Growing up, my stepdad was a mechanic and ran a garage under our house. I was always curious to know what the tools were called and what they did, but the mechanics I was always interested in were "spiritual mechanics." Spiritual mechanics involve looking into people and seeing how God has wired them.

As a kid, I didn't know that's what this was, but I was always curious of how people were wired, and I had a natural scientific aptitude lurking dangerously on the perceiving end of the spectrum. This carried over into ministry life without missing a beat, and no matter where I was, I wanted to know how to pull up or draw up the gold in others.

When I worked in local government, I wasn't allowed to preach to people, but I came up with a way to reach people anyway. Once a week, I used to send an encouraging email to our whole office that sounded motivational, but I had asked God what to write that would be specific enough to touch on things people were going through. After months of doing this, I started having colleagues come to my desk and thank me. They would share their hearts and struggles. My email somehow triggered them to do that. Soon, I was interpreting dreams regularly, praying for people, and seeing healings, but most of all, people got a papa hug from the Father and were reminded of how they were created.

I remember one colleague got really freaked out one day on the way to a site visit when I randomly brought up a toy she loved growing up, a dress pattern her late grandmother sewed for her, and then told her in great detail the business plan she had been dreaming about. This was not my doing but God's. He is in the details, and He has equipped you with *so much* more than you could ever know you possess.

TREASURE HIDDEN IN CLAY POTS

Jesus has this same heart and ability. He finds the least likely candidates for a baptism of love and then just opens up the windows of Heaven over them—despite their messy lives. One of my favorite stories of Jesus doing this was when He called Matthew the tax collector. After Matthew followed Him, He invited Matthew to dinner, but the Pharisees didn't like it at all:

> When the Pharisees saw this, they asked his disciples, "Why does your teacher eat with such scum? When Jesus heard this, he said, "Healthy people don't need a doctor—sick people do." Then he added, "Now go and learn the meaning of this Scripture: 'I want you to show mercy, not offer sacrifices.' For I have come to call not those who think they are righteous, but those who know they are sinners" (Matthew 9:11–13 NLT).

Jesus also had dinner with Zacchaeus who was also a tax collector. His invitation surprised the onlookers. Jesus talked to the promiscuous woman who was about to be stoned and saved her. He went out of His way to give a word to a Samaritan woman who had been with five men, and we can't forget the twelve disciples who had their own stuff going on. Yet Jesus only saw the treasure they carried, the potential and promise in each of them.

> He appointed his Twelve and gave Simon the nickname Peter the Rock. And he gave the brothers, Jacob and John, the sons of Zebedee, the nickname Benay-Regah, which means "passionate sons" (Mark 3:16–17 TPT).

I love the story Nathanael because it just shows just how much Jesus saw the hearts of people and would call them up into it.

> When Jesus saw Nathanael approaching, he said of him, "Here truly is an Israelite in whom there is no deceit" (John 1:47).

In your process and journey to discover who God has called you to be, don't forget that the Holy Spirit wants to help you discover the treasure that has been hidden in you for far too long.

Open your heart, release what God has deposited in there, and begin to let it impact the world around you.

> *We are like common clay jars that carry this glorious treasure within, so that this immeasurable power will be seen as God's, not ours* (2 Corinthians 4:7 TPT).

A few years ago, I had a dream where I saw a toolbox being opened and inside were a variety of different tools. Each of them had a specific purpose, and over the course of a few months, the Lord showed me what I believe are some very strategic expressions or tools in the Lord's hand in this hour for the powerful wave of the Spirit that is upon us.

Did you know that you are a potent and powerful tool in the hand of the Lord? You were born to display the splendor and majesty of your Creator to a world that is craving Him.

> *But the Lord said to him, "Go, for he is a chosen instrument of Mine to bear My name before Gentiles, kings, and the children of Israel"* (Acts 9:15 NKJV).

Let's look at some of the prophetic tools I believe the Lord is using in this hour. Before we do that, just know that these tools are not just for those who deem themselves as ones who hold the office of a prophet but for all of the Body of Christ. We all can operate in the prophetic gift or grace as per 1 Corinthians 12:8–10. Also, I believe God will use many in a mix of many expressions, so I pray that you would be encouraged as you discover and unearth some of the hidden gifts incubating inside you.

THE KEY

The first tool I saw was a key. The key represents the revelators, the equippers, the trainers, the disciplers, and the imparters that equip the Body for service (see Eph. 4:12) or reveal the secrets/ revelation of the Kingdom. These individuals help push out and extend the borders of the Kingdom.

> *I will place on his shoulder the key to the house of David; what he opens no one can shut, and what he shuts no one can open* (Isaiah 22:22).
>
> *I will give you the keys of the kingdom of heaven; whatever you bind on earth will be bound in heaven, and whatever you loose on earth will be loosed in heaven* (Matthew 16:19).

Key-givers, as I call them, will be integral in passing the baton and grooming those God is raising up, uncovering the unlimited resources of the Kingdom available at hand.

These key-givers will be those who unlock and unveil the road ahead for the Body of Christ. They will clear the debris of old religious mindsets, will champion truth, and will raise an army of powerful sons and daughters who will subdue the earth.

THE HAMMER

The hammer represents the integral role of those called to administer reformation in the Church, or as I have come to call them *refitters* because they are repairing and restoring areas of the Church from the inside out. They come across like hammers because they challenge and confront stagnant and stale forms that have no fruit.

Refitters don't belong to one denomination or stream, but they have been raised for the Body of Christ as a whole. Moving against the tide of cultural and religious norms, they have the language and scope to articulate Heaven's intention, remove the old and outdated ways, and clear the path to greater unity, connectivity, and effectivity.

Refitters carry a deeply embedded knowledge of Kingdom infrastructure and work alongside apostles to implement new wineskin strategies to build and grow.

The refitter's gifting is not to fault find but to open the door to the future. Instead of criticism, they see the gold each expression possesses and is given a blueprint of Heaven of how to break out of areas of stagnation and flow again.

THE PEN

The pen encompasses the scribes, songwriters, psalmists, authors, policy writers, and those who carry the Word of the Lord through their creative or administrative gift.

I saw a pen lighting up the sky with words of fire, and so it will be in this hour that those who carry the anointing of the scribe will light up the sky and draw the world to Jesus through their anointed words. Psalmists and songwriters will suddenly birth songs that the world will call a *revolution* because these songs will expose counterfeits and ignite a desire to encounter God.

> *My heart is stirred by a noble theme as I recite my verses for the king; my tongue is the pen of a skillful writer* (Psalm 45:1).

We are in a historical season for the Body of Christ, and more than ever God is raising these prophetic pens in His hand to be messengers and articulators of the Lord's heart.

THE BELL

Recently, we were speaking at a conference in another city of Australia when I had a powerful encounter with the Lord where He took me up in a vision as I was walking around the city at night. Suddenly, the bells from the inner-city Catholic church began to ring out its beautiful melody throughout the city.

The Lord began speaking to me about His bellringers in this hour. They are not just calling the Body to worship and prayer, but to announce a call to justice and a sound of liberty throughout the lands.

> Blow the trumpet in Zion; sound the alarm on my holy hill. Let all who live in the land tremble, for the day of the Lord is coming. It is close at hand (Joel 2:1).

So many have spoken about bells in this season because heaven is speaking loud and clear, "You are My instruments, My vessels of freedom and peace, to administer truth and justice throughout the lands!"

Justice carriers, arise and let your sound be heard!

THE TIMEPIECE

I had a vision about a timepiece much like the one I saw in the toolbox earlier in the year, but what I noticed was that this watch had hands that went forward and backward in an unpredictable way. The Lord reminded me of the sons of Issachar from 1 Chronicles 12:32 who understood the times. What made no sense to me as I looked at this watch could be interpreted by those God has gifted with knowing the times.

The gift of knowing the times and seasons is valuable because these prophetic timekeepers can sense the changes and shifts in specific epoch cycles and are able to predict when God is doing certain things. Timekeepers provide a roadmap and clarity to those walking through blind or unknown periods and connect the dots for those feeling lost and hopeless.

The name *Issachar* means "there is recompense," and just like the name suggests, God's timekeepers can see the promise arising from the ashes of the wilderness and speak restoration in the middle of calamity.

THE TELESCOPE

When I asked the Lord about the telescope, He didn't show me anything until months later. I was in worship one night when I had a vision where Jesus was handing me a long, old, wooden box. I opened it to find an old brass telescope laying in navy blue silk. I took the telescope out of the box and extended it, and as I brought it up to my eye, I was taken deeper into the vision and saw some specific events for a country that were years away from taking place.

I believe God was highlighting to me the gift of foresight and long vision—the ability to foretell for the sake of warning and guiding the Body of Christ. I instantly thought of the late prophet Kim Clement who operated in this gift with such accuracy and purity, and I believe it is a gift that is going to become more common than it has been in the past.

These prophetic eyes will be shown specific plots and plans ahead of time so they can be foiled and disarmed, prayed into, and broken. This gift can be seen in many places in the Bible. For instance, the prophet Isaiah foretold of Jesus many centuries before His birth (see Isa. 9:6).

This gifting is also able to perceive what is hidden.

> *"None of us, my lord the king," said one of his officers, "but Elisha, the prophet who is in Israel, tells the king of Israel the very words you speak in your bedroom"* (2 Kings 6:12).

Prophetic seers, arise!

THE LIGHTNING ROD

For a whole week, I had recurring dreams of lightning strikes. In one dream a scene played out that reminded me much of the scene from the movie *Back to the Future*, where the lightning struck the clock before sending Marty back to the future. The next morning, the Lord began to show me that He is raising up lightning rods around the world. These will be conductors of His power and glory, and as the lightning of heaven hit them, they will transport the Church out of the past and into the future.

I was also reminded how, when lightning hits, many times it shorts the power system, shutting down power to whole cities and regions. In that same way, these lightning rods will short the system and take back territory from the longstanding, oppressive principalities over regions and cities.

Lightning rods always stay at a high altitude and perceive and sense what many others don't. They are poised to strike and recover, and we will see many of these heavenly conductors transfer back the rights and ownership of many stolen and usurped regions and places around the world.

WHICH ARE YOU?

Did any of those register in your spirit? Did any give clarity about the expression God has been nurturing inside you? Maybe you knew God was doing something, but you weren't sure what or why.

Many prophetic people have felt lost or displaced and, in many cases, rejected and confused, but you need to know that your greatest hour is upon you! God has been preparing you for your assignment and shifting you into position for your most effective season of impact! Break out from the confusion of your past and allow God to move you into position as God's mighty warrior in the earth!

PROPHETIC SURVIVAL KEYS

Don't get too hung up over figuring out what you do or don't have or what you can or can't understand about your spiritual destiny makeup. Just begin to use what you have, and God will reveal the rest and define it. Your spiritual key is simply to open up the "toolbox" and see what's inside, even if don't recognize what it does yet. Understanding will come!

CAMPFIRE PRAYER

Father, I thank You that I have access to Your limitless King-dom and every tool and resource inside it that will enable me to fulfill my destiny. I ask that You show me what my gift mix is, what my tools are, and help me use them effec-tively, in Jesus' name!

PART 3

The Wilderness Trials

CHAPTER 15

Wounded Warriors

You will be wounded. Just because this battle is spiritual doesn't mean it's not real; it is, and the wounds a man can take are in some ways more ugly than those that come in a firefight. To lose a leg is nothing compared to losing heart; to be crippled by shrapnel need not destroy your soul, but to be crippled by shame and guilt may. You will be wounded by the Enemy. He knows the wounds of your past, and he will try to wound you again in the same place. —John Eldridge

As I sat down to write this part of the book, I suddenly felt the weight of God's glory rest upon me as well as the fear of the Lord, knowing that this is going to be a game changer for you. Earlier in the year, before writing this chapter, I dreamed I was having a coffee with my publisher, Larry Sparks, about this book, and he looked down at the manuscript and then back at me and said with conviction, "Nate, don't hold back on the chapters on warfare. It's going to be a game changer!" So as I sit here trembling under the weight of this glory, I know that God is going to unleash Heaven over you as you read it. I just wanted you to know that.

Ninety percent of the prophetic journey is indeed the journey or process, and with that comes a winding path of obstacles, mines, opposition, warfare, and tests to face and overcome. Like the *Hunger Games*, it is not God who has created the arena. That is the enemy trying to take you out and divert you, but equally God is wanting to make sure that you walk through this part of your walk learning the lessons that will set you up for a powerful and lasting odyssey in the Kingdom as His forerunner and reformer.

In this part of the guide, I introduce you to what I believe is probably the most significant quest of any heavyweight voice for the Kingdom: the wilderness trials. However, with the Holy Spirit, the odds are always in your favor.

A DIVINE MEETING

I looked at the man across the table at the coffee club in Mount Gravatt, Australia, and he looked back at me and said, "I know why you asked me to come here."

"You do?" I replied, a little shocked thinking that I would have to explain myself.

Chris Harvey is a true revivalist, and at the time, he was doing what no one else was. He was such an odd mix of prophet, psalmist, and reformer, but you wouldn't hear him say that about himself. "I just love Jesus," he always said, but every time I hung around him, I felt somehow normal or understood. It was 2007, and I hadn't figured out my calling yet. All I knew was that I was hungry for God and needed guidance desperately.

"You need someone like you to learn from, don't you?" I just nodded in reply and eased into my chair, realizing in that moment God had set this up! The very first meeting I was ever in where Chris ministered was the equivalent of taking a dive to the bottom of the ocean. I felt it revealed God's heart and nature to me in a way I had never known. It was as if Chris were inviting the whole room into his private worship session with Jesus, and it created such a longing in me for more. What also stood out to me was how "himself" Chris was. He didn't sugarcoat his words or speak to wow or appease people. He spoke exactly what God told him and nothing more, and he wasn't afraid to enjoy the Holy Spirit and get drunk in his own meeting. This guy was wild, I recognized it, and I needed it.

After talking back and forth for a while about Kingdom, worship, and his wild ministry stories, he looked at me with a serious stare and said, "This calling is all about the posture of your heart. Your gifts are just gifts. The anointing comes upon you then lifts, but who you are is who you are when you aren't ministering. Steward your heart well, and you'll last the distance."

These words have stayed with me all these years and have been an often humbling reminder to keep my heart right no matter how hard things get.

OUT OF THE HEART FLOWS

Remember what God said to Samuel when he was choosing the next king over Israel?

> *But the Lord said to Samuel, "Do not consider his appearance or his height, for I have rejected him. The Lord does not look at the things people look at. People look at the outward appearance, but the Lord looks at the heart"* (1 Samuel 16:7).

Time and time again, God reminds us that this journey is less about how amazing and interesting our callings and giftings are and more about our heart status. Proverbs 4:23 says this, *"Above all else, guard your heart, for everything you do flows from it."*

NOT A GAME OF CHINESE WHISPERS

Have you ever played Chinese whispers? It's the game where you gather in a circle and someone thinks of a word or phrase, then whispers it to the next person, then they whisper it to the next person, and so on. By the end of the game, the word or phrase is nothing like the one that was started with.

Like a game of Chinese whispers inside our own bodies, our spirits have to communicate with our hearts, and then our mouths speak. Imagine a pipe line that is meant to carry fresh water from the source (Heaven) to the place of impact (the world). As you are intimate with Holy Spirit, He pours in that fresh living water into you, then it travels down the pipe towards our mouths, but along the way there are two filters it travels through: our souls and our hearts. Now, for the message or whatever we receive to reach our mouths unedited, it takes quite a lot of heart and soul work and processing.

WHAT IS UNDER THE HOOD?

Religion has taught us that performance and service are more important than character until character flaws show, and then religion will bring out the cat o' nine tails. It's a system that keeps pastors and leaders working hard to please their congregations so the congregation keeps attending. These ministers feel the need to come up with fresh messages and content to keep people interested and keep tithes flowing in to pay off the huge building mortgages. As a result, the pastors and leaders don't have time to be the fathers and husbands they need to be, too. This is the perfect recipe for moral failure, affairs, addictions, mental health issues, and even suicide.

Religion keeps us running like a hamster on a wheel so fast and hard that we have no time to address the ticking time bombs that are heart issues we pick up along the way in life. These issues muddy the filter of our souls and hearts. But God is great at using situations in life to reveal the true state of our hearts. One of my favorite examples of this is when Jesus refused to go into a village:

> But as they approached the village, the people turned them away. They would not allow Jesus to enter, for he was on his way to worship in Jerusalem. When the disciples Jacob and John realized what was happening, they returned to Jesus and said, "Lord, if you wanted to, you could command fire to fall down from heaven, just as Elijah did and destroy all these wicked people!" Jesus rebuked them sharply, saying, "Don't you realize what spews from your hearts when you say that? The Son of Man did not come to destroy life, but to bring life to the earth" (Luke 9:53–56 TPT).

Now when I read this, I do cringe a little because I love James and John. I feel I relate to them a lot. The *sons of thunder* were the go-getters of the group, the fiery hot under the collar, let's take the world types. Yeah, that's me. I relate to them, so I read Luke 9 and gulp because I hear Jesus saying this to me. It's a massive heart checkup from Jesus, where He says, "I know you are passionate and you love Me, but *that* is not coming from the place you think it is. Check yourselves before you wreck yourselves, James, John, and Nate." Ouch.

It's scary that we can be living in such strong conviction yet be way off simply because there is a little mud on the windscreen blocking the view. I'll say it again. The state of our hearts matter in this.

THE DISABLED BRIDE

The wilderness season can be a worship if we let it be. It can be the preparation for major impact if we don't let it twist us and embitter us. But what happens if we do have wounds?

A few years ago, I had a dream where I was walking down this dark street in a city. I stopped at this alleyway where I saw all these people speaking and some singing, but something just felt off. I stopped to listen, and I instantly discerned that they were prophetic people I was hearing who had been hurt, rejected, wounded, bitter, and burned out. They were in pain, and they were prophesying *from* that pain.

The reason I say, "from," is because we can prophesy through pain, and it's like prophesying empathetically even though the wound is healed like David did in the Psalms, but prophesying *from* pain means it is muddying up the message. In the dream, these prophetic people were speaking all types of things that were just not from the heart of God. The calling and the mantle were real, but their souls were sick, their hearts were sick, and they were spewing out that same sickness onto people who passed by. I walked a little bit closer, and I saw something that startled me. They were missing limbs from their bodies. They were missing arms, legs, hands, and feet.

When I woke up from the dream, I said, "Lord, what have I just seen?"

He said, "What you have just seen is a sick bride, a limbless bride, and my Bride needs to be whole again!"

I broke down when He said this because only a year earlier God had said to me, "Who will go for them? Who will find them? Who will raise up the outcast, the rejected, and the bitter? Who will bring them home?"

Those in my dream represented both the outcast, wounded, bitter, and soul-sick, but they also represented the Church not being whole without her limbs. We are all different parts of the Body of Christ, all different and unique, yet we need each other. The Church has been missing the misfits, the reformers, and the ones who have been wounded, and God desires *us* to be whole; He desires the Bride to be whole!

Seasons of being under control, oppression, silencing, and muzzling can begin to cause your heart to get wounded and stay there without experiencing God's healing.

ICHABOD OR KABOD?

Last year, I dreamed I was with another prophetic voice, and we were both on pianos, playing the exact same tune. It sounded beautiful, but then the other person stopped playing. I started to play and sing a song, and the anointing of *reconciliation and restoration* began to flow out as I played. After I finished playing, the other person started playing the exact same tune but sang different words. The lyrics were of judgment against others, calling people out, vengeance, accusation, and slander. It came across as a song/message of purity, but it was a dagger to assassinate people and shut people down to protect territory. I instantly felt unsettled because I was expecting to feel the anointing, but there was none. There was no healing, only hurt, pain, and witchcraft masquerading as a prophetic ballad. So, I asked the prophet if we could play together again but sing my song, and as we did, this person began to cry as God set them free of bitterness, pain, and insecurity.

What was this dream saying?

- That we need to be singing the right tune right now. We need to be singing the same one that can be heard in Heaven—the tune of reconciliation and restoration. We can be saying the right scriptures, and our tune can sound right, but if our heart is wounded, there will be no anointing on our words, and the fruit will be bondage, not freedom.

- God is healing those who have been speaking from bitterness and hurt, and He is restoring those whose tune has changed.

- We cause damage when we aren't healed. Address your pain. Forgive often. Your heart matters as much as your message.

- Your voice matters in this season! Don't let the enemy change your message or divert your mission. Prophetic cop was never a thing. Loving people into their best looks better on His prophets.

WOUNDED DOWN TO THE ROOTS

Wounded means suffering from a wound, especially one acquired in battle, and suffering from an emotional injury. In Hebrew, the English word *wound* is used when translated from the Hebrew word *chalal*, which means "to bore, pierce, defile, break, stain, and create a wedge." From this word, we can see the effects that wounds have on us. They pierce deep, bore into our inner being, then cause damage, defile, stain, and create internal obstacles in us.

The Greek word for *wound* that you will be familiar with is *trauma*, which is made up of three Greek words. These are the words and their respective meanings:

- *thrauo*—crush, break, and shatter
- *tribos*—a worn path, a beaten path
- *trizo*—gnashing (torment) refers to the demoniac Jesus delivered

From this definition we can see the effects of woundedness also. Wounds crush, break, and shatter us internally. They wear us and beat us down, and they cause shame and torment.

BY HIS WOUNDS, YOU ARE FREE

As I wrote this section, I felt the intense pain someone reading this has carried and some may be still carrying inside. You need to know that the Father sees your pain and He sees the painful journey you have been through, but it doesn't have to continue this way. Jesus died so that you and I could live wound-free and live with our hearts clear and whole.

> But it was because of our rebellious deeds that he was pierced and because of our sins that he was crushed. He endured the punishment that made us completely whole, and in his wounding we found our healing (Isaiah 53:5 ESV).

The word for *healing* in this scripture is the word *rapha*, meaning to heal, to cure, to repair thoroughly, and make whole.

Jesus wasn't wounded for you so that you would stay wounded. He was wounded for you but so that the cage doors of bondage could be opened and you be set free! It's time to accept your full healing today!

WILD & WOUNDED

When I was working for government years ago, I was visited by our district manager who was always great to me. He hired me for a senior management position I had zero experience in, but I had shown him that I could do anything I put my hands to, and I was highly motivated and a forward thinker. I was thriving in the role and keeping up, but he said something profound to me that day.

We sat in the boardroom, and he asked me how I was liking the job and how different projects were going. We discussed the challenges I was facing, and then he made this statement: "Nate, there's no doubt about it. You are a wildcard, and we love it, but wildcards can also be liabilities."

That phrase echoed deep into my soul. A few years later, when we launched into ministry amid much opposition (more on that later), I remembered my manager's statement, reminding that a wild call can be what God designed it be, for the good, for the building up of others and the Church, or it can be twisted through woundedness into something that has the opposite effect.

INTERNAL WIRING

But why do we get so easily wounded? Why is this even a trial or a hurdle in our journey? I used to always feel like I was ultrasensitive to the world around me, which only made my calling even more difficult to navigate because it was sensing everything to a high-definition degree. Growing up, this felt like a curse because I would experience things deeper than most from triumphs to catastrophes.

One of the traits of a wild one is the heart of David, and what was that exactly? First Samuel 13:14 and 16:7 both say David had a heart after God's own heart, meaning he had the same heart as God. In both of these scriptures, the Hebrew word for *heart* is *lebab*, meaning inner man, mind, will, and tender heart. David's heart was soft—easily broken, cut, bruised, or damaged—and we can see that throughout David's life, he was like that. Saul's attack, for example, affected him deeply.

> *"After removing Saul, he made David their king. God testified concerning him: 'I have found David son of Jesse, a man after my own heart; he will do everything I want him to do'"* (Acts 13:22).

The Greek word for *heart* used here means the heart, mind, character, inner self, will, and thoughts and feelings. So, we can see the similar meanings in both passages. David's heart was, in fact, the recess of deep emotion, thought, feelings, and sensitivity. It was a blessing to him in the ways he heard and connected to God, but in other ways, it was hard to handle. In fact, I believe David really struggled to understand how he was wired as he matured, but at some point, he learned some valuable ways to manage himself. Think of the scripture when he prayed, *"Why, my soul, are you downcast? Why so disturbed within me? Put your hope in God, for I will yet praise him, my Savior and my God"* (Ps. 43:5).

The key here is that David, while being created as a tender heart for a purpose, had to learn how to manage it so it didn't manage him. I know I have often felt like my sensitivity managed me more than I used it as a helpful tool in my belt.

ARE YOU A FEELER?

God has created a unique and special group of people who are not only sensitive to His heart, but also are wired to be receptors of the reality of Heaven so that they can live, not in response to the chaos of the world, but out of the overflow of this higher reality and manifest it. The problem, however, is that for far too long the enemy has worked overtime to bombard these secret agents with warfare, insecurity, and noise to take them off course and wound them. I am of course referring to *feelers*, as I like to call us. Christy wrote this about feelers in her book *Releasing Prophetic Solutions*:

> A feeler is someone who I would describe as being the heart in the room where God's emotions, thoughts, and feelings for people and places are communicated to you in a overly heightened way. A feeler is always constantly tapping into the empathy of Jesus in every situation and sensing everything from the pain, grief, and sorrow He is feeling to joy, peace, and bliss. To be a feeler is a powerful gift of intercession—to be able to feel what God is feeling, to pray Heaven's solutions over it, empathy—to be Jesus on the earth and be able to be there in the moment with people understanding their pain, and for discernment—being able to see through the surface value to determine what is really going on. Feelers are God's special agents of His heart![1]

She continues to say:

> One of the greatest and hardest journeys I have seen in the body of Christ is people learning to steward being a feeler. There are many ineffective feelers and many effective feelers. The ineffective feeler gift is when we either take what we feel and make it about us. We internalize and personalize what we sense to the point it takes us out. Whether what we feel in a city we take on, or we keep taking on the burdens of others that God didn't ask us to. The effective feeler gift is being able to distinguish what WE are feeling personally and what we are sensing corporately. Without learning to know those we live a very messy and self-focused Christian life always thinking something

is wrong with us. Many of you have been ineffective in prayer because you keep coming under the atmospheres around you instead of ruling over it.[2]

Can you relate? So how do you learn to manage it better?

DEVELOPING EMOTIONAL INTELLIGENCE

Hebrews 5:14 says; *"But solid food is for the mature, who by constant use have trained their senses to distinguish good from evil."* This means that we can learn to develop our emotional intelligence in this area so that over time we learn the cues and discern better what we are sensing better, and this ultimately helps us not take on so much of the baggage we as feelers often do. So, if you have struggled with this here is something to remember: When you feel something strongly, instead of reacting, take a step back and access it. Ask yourself, "Is this coming from me, or am I sensing it around me? Then ask the Lord why you are sensing it and what He wants you to do with it. Pray this feeler prayer with me:

> *In the name of Jesus, I break partnership with the atmosphere. I ask that what belongs to the atmosphere go back to the atmosphere and what belongs to me be returned to me, completely cleansed by You. Jesus, I choose, no matter where I am, only to be aware of You in my atmosphere. Jesus, I also break off all soul ties with people I have been carrying burdens for that has been out of Your will, and I ask You to teach me how to feel and discern without it crushing me and sending me into heaviness, anxiety, and depression, in Jesus' name!*

You weren't created to live your life battling people or yourself. We don't battle flesh and blood, but we do battle the enemy. The enemy wants you to never leave the wilderness trials, so he tried to keep you in the never-ending boxing match of your inner world. Today, I pray and prophesy that changes in Jesus' name! Wild ones, wildcards, welcome to the wilderness trials. Your next moves will determine your destiny.

PROPHETIC SURVIVAL KEYS

Being wounded is inevitable, but it's not where we stay. Your key from the outset is that you aren't faulty or a failure for being wounded in your journey; it just means you are human, but Jesus took those wounds for you, and you can give them to Him and move on.

CAMPFIRE PRAYER

Jesus, I give You my wounds. I don't want to live disabled by the things that have happened to me, and I don't want operate in my calling with the potential to wound others or miss what You are saying. Today I shake off the wounded mentality that has caused me so much shame and begin step into my healing and hour of complete wholeness in Jesus' name!

NOTES

1. Christy Johnson, *Releasing Prophetic Solutions: Praying Heaven's Promises Over Your Home, Family, and Nation,* (Shippensburg, PA: Destiny Image Publishers, Inc., 2020).
2. Christy Johnson, *Releasing Prophetic Solutions.*

CHAPTER 16

Wilderness Syndrome, Lone Rangers, & Isolation

The longer the wilderness, the longer the isolation, the longer the waiting—the longer and deeper the road is beneath you. Soon, they will see what you and Jesus have been building when there was no spotlight, no hurrah or fanfare, just worship, brokenness, and a yes.
—Nate Johnston

One of the greatest trials you will ever experience as an emerging voice is the trial of being in the wilderness for an extended period. The wilderness either breaks you or makes you. It breaks you if you do it alone, and it makes you if you cling to Jesus through it, but it was designed for the latter and the glorious purpose, anointing, and voice that leaves the wilderness with you.

I want to be very direct in this part of the guide because I want to give language to what you have gone through or may go through, bring healing and closure to the wounds and pain sustained in your journey, and hopefully help you discern obstacles in the road and prevent you from having to be taken out by them. This part of the journey really is make it or break it. It's the trials that determine whether we end up moving into being commissioned or whether we stay in the perpetual cycle of going around the mountain without ever seeing any fruit.

The wilderness trials are not your average journey but a perilous one full of dangers, pitfalls, and many opportunities to turn around and find comfort. However, true destiny doesn't lay in the comforts of mediocrity, but in the risks of walking the unpopular path.

WILDERNESS SYNDROME

The Israelites wandered in the wilderness for forty years after leaving Egypt, and by their own complaints and disbelief, they signed themselves up for a multigenerational, scenic route when the journey to Canaan was only two weeks away. This mishap cost them more than just time, pain, and headaches. It further perpetuated an identity crisis that was already built into them through their years of slavery under Pharaoh.

Egypt taught them:

- They were worthless.
- They were the underdog.
- God didn't look after His own people.
- They would always be in captivity somewhere and to someone.

The wilderness taught them:

- They would always be in a fight.
- They were better off as slaves.
- God set them free from tyranny only to abandon them.
- God does miracles but only when it suits Him.

What happened over generations to the people of Israel is that this underdog mentality became ingrained in their identity, and so when the time came to cross over into Canaan (the Promised Land), they didn't feel equal to the task of taking the land.

But the men who had gone up with him said, "We can't attack those people; they are stronger than we are." And they spread among the Israelites a bad report about the land they had explored. They said, "The land we explored devours those living in it. All the people we saw there are of great size. We saw the Nephilim there (the descendants of Anak come from the Nephilim). We seemed like grasshoppers in our own eyes, and we looked the same to them" (Numbers 13:31–33).

Can you hear their confession? They said:

- "They are stronger than we are."
- "The land will devour us."
- "The enemies there are giants."
- "We are grasshoppers compared to them."

The real survey of the new land taken by Joshua and Caleb was this: Then Caleb silenced the people before Moses and said, *"We should go up and take possession of the land, for we can certainly do it"* (Num. 13:30).

What causes people who step out of the wilderness to still live like they are in it, and what causes people who see a brand-new day and opportunity to see the opposite? It's wilderness syndrome, and it's a spirit needs to be broken off the ones emerging; otherwise, they may come out with a fresh sound, a fresh message, and an anointing to break yokes, but they won't get far if they see themselves as inferior and as "grasshoppers."

THE TRANSITION BLUES

Pioneers who spend years in transition can also face similar internal conflict over the promise and the process. It's like living in the hallway between a door that is closing and a door that is about to open. Far too many who started off with fire in their bellies and big dreams for the new landscape end up giving up in transition and allow the same identity crisis and spirit of hopelessness cheat them out of the promise. The great mental hurdle of transition is that it looks like death all around—death to dreams, assignments, and people you once ran with—but it's actually the journey between where you were and the upgrade or the next floor where you are going. It's the emptying and the preparation for the new thing.

NOMADS & WANDERERS

Transition can also create an identity dysfunction that, if we aren't careful, can rewrite or override the call of God beyond the transition we are facing. I have said to God many times, "When will I be able to put my bags down? When will I feel settled and established?" I know what it's like to live as a nomad for Jesus, physically moving over and over to pursue the call of God. Over time, being a nomad or a wanderer isn't something you do, but it becomes who you are, and that's a hard mentality to crack.

> The Lord will establish you as his holy people, as he promised you on oath, if you keep the commands of the Lord your God and walk in obedience to him (Deuteronomy 28:9).

I'm afraid that we have created accepted identities and dysfunctions from our wilderness that are contrary to the heart of

God. The wilderness is there to strengthen you, refine you, add to you, and prepare you, but it is not designed to twist you into something you are not or take you out. That is the identity test.

MIGRATORY FAMILIES & THE PROMISED LAND

Migratory families are those who have packed up homes and belongings and followed God into the unknown for the pioneer call, and it has cost them everything. The challenge and trial of this call is holding the line when it feels like nothing has worked the way you imagined.

In migration, many get tired and feel grieved that the road has been so long and the battle to get there has been so drawn out and delayed. Then the endless and relentless warfare comes to take them out on every side. In migration, what we face is the enemy's attempt to prevent us entering our major promise because it's more than just us moving to a geographical location; this is about family legacy and revival. It's the setup for our children and the destiny upon them. It's the faith move that unties the knots that have been imposed upon family lines and activates purpose beyond what we can see.

Eventually, the carousel season of moving pieces, families, roles, and assignments stops, and rest comes, but in the process, it feels like treading water without any respite. This is so you see that God is faithful and see the signs of His goodness and favor, letting you know that He is still the Captain of this pioneering endeavor, the *Breaker* at the head of this migration!

If you have been shipwrecked by stepping out in faith, is that the end of your story? Did God steal, kill, and destroy, or did the enemy? Does God get the last say in your family's journey? Pick up your sword again and get on your face again and commit your future to the Lord, not to man, an institution, or ideal. Your future is the Lord's, and He who is faithful will deliver. If this speaks to you right now, remember this promise:

"Do I bring to the moment of birth and not give delivery?" says the Lord. "Do I close up the womb when I bring to delivery?" says your God (Isaiah 66:9).

He will do what He says He will do. Our job is to make it through with the help of the Spirit.

ISOLATION: EMANCIPATOR OR THIEF?

Isolation is the state of being secluded and alone, or separate, and many people ask me why they go through seasons of isolation. What does it accomplish? My answer is always the same. Just like there are two different wilderness seasons—the wilderness the enemy tries to send you to and the one God calls you to—there are two different types of isolation: one that corners you, traps you, and torments you, and the one that separates you, protects you, severs ties around you, and sets you up for a healthy season ahead. One is a Jezebelic tactic to bully you with no one around to help you, and the other is a God-ordained season of closure to many things that have been suffocating you. It just doesn't feel that way at the time. I have experienced both; in fact, I have experienced both types of isolation at the same time.

Many have been in a place of extended isolation, and for some it's been seasonal. Remember back to our four-year isolation? It was hard and confusing, but it was where God birthed in us what we are doing now. There are seasons that God intentionally hides us away like that to untangle us, encounter us, prepare us, and download to us what is to come, but there is also the isolation that seems to never end. It is a spiritual bondage and barrenness sent by the enemy to keep us from ever seeing what God has for us. This is also a tactic of the enemy to silence us and imprison us.

It was 2016, and my family and I were already in a God-ordained season of isolation. We were not in church, and no matter how hard we tried, we were just not able to find community or connection outside of being heavily immersed in a church.

After a year of fighting it, we recognized God's thumbprint all over it because we were experiencing freedom left and right. Our isolation was a blessing in disguise, and God was launching us. At the same time, I was working in senior management for the state government and loving it yet feeling the pull of ministry beginning. In February of that year, my boss who I got on so well with was mysteriously sent back to her prior role in another city, and a colleague of mine was promoted. This colleague was always against me, hated the God in me, and became the source of office gossip and strife. Within two days of her starting, she sent out an email listing her changes under her leadership. I would be called into private meetings each week to investigate my work, time on breaks, and logbook records. Then the worst part came.

One day, I was moved into a government office building with just one other colleague, another believer. I was moved without being given a reason. My manager would come weekly and watch us and scrutinize our work. It started to affect my health, and I knew I was on borrowed time in this job. This isolation was none other than a tactic of the Jezebel spirit to isolate me and then attack me. Sound familiar?

I have seen this in church settings quite often, too, where people are put aside or left out so they can be bullied. This is the enemy! There are also situations where you are being passed over as a protection of God! Which one have you experienced?

LONE RANGERS

"So you are a Lone Ranger, huh?" the pastor said to me. Newly starting our ministry, I had a friend wanting to connect me with other pastors in my city, so I met with a local guy just to get to know him. I was genuinely wanting to link arms with others and be part of what God was doing in our city, but my credibility was low. "Who is your accountability and covering?" Honestly, we had none by religious standards. We had many ministry friends who were involved in everything but no official covering at the time.

"No one, I guess," I replied, and you can imagine how short and awkward that meeting was. Yeah, exactly.

I understood. We were Lone Rangers, and I knew it had a bad connotation, especially involving prophetic ministers. Rogues, rebels, and heretics described how we were seen, but it wasn't of our doing at all. I won't lie. I started to believe maybe I was in error. I let it get to me a little too much, and I almost shut everything down until God visited me in a dream and rebuked me.

"Did man call Jeremiah and Isaiah to their post, or did I?" God's question still sends shivers down my spine.

HOLDING THE LINE WHEN THE SIGNS SAY DIFFERENTLY

The trial in being a Lone Ranger, isolated, in transition, migrating, and wilderness nomad is this:

- Will you trust that God knows what He is doing?
- Will you discern between the tactics of the enemy and the divinity of God's call?
- Will you cater to the religious pressure and feel foolish by its standards, or will you stand and stay the course?

- Will you build your life on the rock of who the Father says you are, or will you be tossed around by fractured identity?
- Will you find your worth in Jesus or in the religious standards and status quo?
- Will you keep moving in response to the sound of His voice or by the pressures to conform?
- And lastly, will you believe God that your Promised Land, your establishing, your settling, and your tribe are coming?

OUT FROM ISOLATION—YOUR TRIBE IS ON ITS WAY

Prophetic people need family. Pioneers can do seasons alone, but it's not a long-term situation. Reformers tend to move in small packs, and Elijah voices tend to roam around unpopular for seasons, but eventually they find their people. And so will you.

As I wrote this, I felt God's vindication over those who have been in this bondage because this will be the season you feel the cords of that break off your life. Where you have felt hidden and invisible, walking around the wilderness, alone and confused, the isolation breaks right now in Jesus' name!

There are also many Lone Ranger prophets, apostles, and evangelists whom God is calling out of isolation and into true connection. Years ago, God told me that my full potential would only be revealed in the context of community because isolation may help you learn to fight bears and lions like David did, but it's only when you have family around you who you really are is drawn out, leading you to impossible victories and exploits.

Remember all these seasons are temporary. The wilderness ends, isolation ends, and being a Lone Ranger ends. How you deal with this momentary reality is what matters. That is the trial at hand ,but with the Holy Spirit, you have got this, wild one!

PROPHETIC SURVIVAL KEYS

"God sets the lonely in families," and He doesn't leave us wandering and never settling (Ps. 68:6). Your survival keys are that there is a place with your name on it and a people to call family, so hold onto the hope of knowing that God is leading you to them.

CAMPFIRE PRAYER

Thank You, Lord that my family and tribe are coming and that there is a purpose in this crazy journey I have been on. Right now, I know You are connecting all the dots, and one day soon it will all make sense. I trust You that wherever I am going You are taking me from glory to glory and you will finish what You started, in Jesus' name.

CHAPTER 17

Tall Poppies, Competition, & the Fear of Man

For after years of living in a cage, a lion no longer even believes it is a lion . . . and a man no longer believes he is a man. —John Eldridge

If you are going to be an emerging voice for the Kingdom that has significant impact and influence, then you are must walk through the battlefield of people's opinions and misrepresentations of your character that you will never be able to change. You will have to learn how to steward big dreams and visions without selling them short, underselling your wins and successes, favor, and blessing, as well as being okay with soaring in high heights with Jesus and people calling you an opportunist or arrogant for it.

I felt like I grew up like this my whole life because I just knew I needed to break away from the norm and live passionately for Jesus, but this didn't go down well with family or friends who assumed I was arrogant, conceited, and full of myself. The reality for me was that I just loved God and wanted to serve Him with my whole being.

I remember the day I told my family that I wanted to preach and worship around the world—to see revival in dry and dead places—and their response shocked me: "Why don't you just choose a good, stable job that can provide for your family?"

I was shattered. How did I break out of this dreamless society and passionless culture?

STANDING A LITTLE TOO TALL

In Australia, we have a social stigma we call "the tall poppy syndrome," where if someone rises up, speaks up, seems to be overly confident, or stands taller than others, they are cut down and ostracized until they back down and accept defeat.

> Tall Poppy Syndrome
>
> a tendency to begrudge, resent, or mock people of great success, talent, or status.
>
> a tendency to downplay one's own achievements or talent in order to avoid the resentment and mockery of others.

I grew up in this culture, and it was very difficult to break out of because it creates a guilt and shame that seem to shroud every person who steps out or stands up. But whether you are Australian or not, or have encountered this spirit or not, this mentality has been rampant in the Western church where, as it celebrates people learning and growing within the church, the people who get a little too big are cut down by others.

JEALOUSY & ASSASSINATION

Joseph was a favored son who wore a coat of many colors that his dad made him. Joseph was a dreamer of superiority dreams, which is the perfect recipe for family conflict with ten other jealous and annoyed brothers.

> *Now Israel loved Joseph more than any of his other sons, because he had been born to him in his old age; and he made an ornate robe for him. When his brothers saw that their father loved him more than any of them, they hated him and could not speak a kind word to him* (Genesis 37:3–4).

What was it about Joseph that was so unbearable? The love and attention he received from his dad? His dreams of his family bowing before him? It was obvious: Joseph stood taller than the rest, and they didn't like it, so they faked his death and sold him into slavery. Pursuing your destiny will mean having to face this trial at some stage, the trial of Joseph's brothers whereby those who are jealous of you sell you out. If you have ever been the victim of people like Joseph's brothers, then you know how that feels.

SAUL'S JAVELIN & THE POISON OF BROTHERS

David was a tall poppy, a wild poppy, sent to Israel to stand tall for a purpose: to defeat giants in the land that were towering over them and intimidating them and to reveal to the people of the Kingdom that God was wanting them all to step up into this new standard and way. Saul, however, didn't see it that way and tried to have David killed time and time again.

> *As they danced, they sang: "Saul has slain his thousands, and David his tens of thousands"* (1 Samuel 18:7).

Jealousy, competition, and comparison were always warring against David the more he stepped into his calling. "Be less intense, David! Chill a little. Stop showing off!" people must have said. But David wasn't trying to show off or draw attention to himself but to God, and the people who once adored him and patted him on the back were now trying to get him to stand down.

I have experienced this in church leadership more than once. In one particular church, I struggled with this because it was the place God really developed me, and then suddenly I was being micromanaged and cut down. In that season, a well-known prophetic voice who was a guest speaker to our church said from the pulpit, "Just a word of warning for this house. There is an anointing here to raise up sons and daughters, but when they get too powerful, you kill them." This shocked the pastors who didn't expect this rebuke, but unfortunately, it was true.

The spirit of Saul like the tall poppy syndrome wants to cut you down when you surpass others in any way. I'll be sharing more on that at the end of this part of the book.

David's brother was similar. When David came to the army, this is what took place:

> When Eliab, David's oldest brother, heard him speaking with the men, he burned with anger at him and asked, "Why have you come down here? And with whom did you leave those few sheep in the wilderness? I know how conceited you are and how wicked your heart is; you came down only to watch the battle" (1 Samuel 17:28).

Have you faced Christians like this? People who are meant to be your brothers but because of insecurity hurl their fears at you in the form of character assassination? You just have to move past it and not let it take you out.

THERE IS ROOM AT THE TABLE

In a new church season years ago, the pastor took a liking to us and kept asking us to sit on the front row, which was so new to us after being in isolation for so long, but it ruffled some feathers with the other sons and daughters in the house who were being groomed. It took them years to warm up to us because they assumed we were going to take their place!

We as the Church need to expose and reject that plot and assignment against us that pits us against each other like schoolboys trying to protect our marbles. Why can't we share? Why can't we champion each other? There is enough room at the table!

QUEEN BEE SYNDROME

A strange phenomenon I haven't personally faced but have seen Christy and so many other mighty women of God face is the queen bee syndrome. Normally, this spirit tends to operate in women who have had to work hard to get where they are, but unfortunately, they have arrived there and spend more time guarding their throne than pulling others up with them.

I have seen far too many cut down by this spirit that says, "Watch your step, ladies. This is my territory and my hive, and there's only room for one queen!" Fortunately, the prophetic call is not a diva lifestyle, so their acting out ends up shooting them in the foot. Stay away from the prophetic divas who have traded their anointing oil for tanning lotion and have let flies spoil the honey.

GUILT, SHAME, & APPROVAL ADDICTION

I remember when we moved to LA in 2009 to travel on the road with our friend Nick Vujicic. I was shocked to receive at least five strange emails from present and former friends, making tall poppy remarks like, "Hey, remember where you came from" or "Don't get too big for your boots!" Or the worst one was "Just remember what goes up must come down!" It hurt me deeply because the last thing I wanted was to look like I was something big now or something that I wasn't. It plagued me for months because I was your Class A approval addict and wanted people not to misunderstand me. I tried everything to make people see that I was just following the call of God on my life, but nothing worked.

Every time I went to update what I was doing—a crazy testimony or photo of our travel—I would feel intense guilt and shame like I was a fake, a fraud, and phony. I felt as if I could dream more and genuinely have conversations with Americans on the amazing things God was doing, and they would be engaged in the conversation, celebrating wins with me. With our friends and family back home, however, it was a different story. I had a family member write to me and say, "Your photos are making your brother jealous, so you shouldn't post them." But then I came up with the best strategy: downplay everything to those back home.

The problem with my strategy was that I became used to downplaying God's goodness, downplaying miracles I saw, and downplaying everything that would cause anyone I knew to think I thought too highly of myself. By doing this, I was elevating myself and my reputation above God's. My approval addiction and concern for how people saw me needed to break.

THE CRITICAL CROSSROAD OF FEAR OF MAN & PROTECTING REPUTATION

But whether you are Australian or not, we all face this trial in a myriad of different ways during our process of emerging. At some point, we all come to the crossroad where we have to make a choice between pursuing and pleasing God or pursuing and pleasing man. Trust me, you can't do both.

> *For am I now seeking the approval of man, or of God? Or am I trying to please man? If I were still trying to please man, I would not be a servant of Christ* (Galatians 1:10 ESV).
>
> *But just as we have been approved by God to be entrusted with the gospel, so we speak, not to please man, but to please God who tests our hearts* (1 Thessalonians 2:4 ESV).

At its core, this mentality is a demonic ideology that puts the opinions and praises of man higher than obedience to God and pleasing Him. Some current examples of that would be cancel culture, virtue signaling, and political correctness. It's where we make an idol out of not rocking the boat and the cost. We accept and tolerate everything. We become slaves and put ourselves in bondage to thing we are afraid of offending. It's a lifestyle of fear.

UNAPOLOGETICALLY RADICAL

The isolation we went through was a blessing in disguise for me because we literally lost everything we once did life with. We lost our reputation and every other shred of our old life we once held dear. We were a blank slate, and being able to build from the ground up was a real gift. Imagine being able to design your dream home. You get to choose the colors, the bricks, the carpet, and the floor-plan. That's how we felt—like no matter what the outcome was, we were going to do it authentically with as much "us" as we could, so we did!

We decided to sit down and determine what we were about and what we weren't, what we wanted to achieve and what we didn't want to achieve. For the first time in our lives, we didn't feel pressured to be anything except who God had called us to be. I was reminded of one of Shakespeare's line, "To thine own self be true."

THE UNPOPULAR ROAD

Reformational voices stand out from the pack. We are often the ones who tend to do amazing exploits simply because we dare to dream and dare to step out into the unknown. We are seen as attention seekers, arrogant rule breakers, and the destroyers of peace when we are, in fact, the forerunners who choose to walk through the valley of constant criticism and opposition for the sake of the future.

We are the ones who stand firm with our faces set like flint when all around us people are choosing to replace obedience to the King of kings with the appeasement of another lesser king or settling to the level the world has set. We just don't live that way. But reformers have been bullied in their emerging, rising and shining process and have been slowly backing down over standing up and being counted for this hour. So, this is your test. Will you stand? Will you dream? Will you keep setting a higher standard when it is unpopular to do so?

PROPHETIC SURVIVAL KEYS

To pass this test, you need to be baptized in the approval of Heaven until the fear of man falls off you. You can only be governed by one and not both. When you are facing the fear of man, run into the secret place and get a second opinion!

CAMPFIRE PRAYER

Holy Ghost, baptize me in the love of God that burns away my incessant need to be liked and approved. Take away my fear of being looked down on and give me courage to rise up and be who I was called to be no matter what people do or say about me, in Jesus' name.

CHAPTER 18

Orphans, Outcasts, & Misfits

Without knowing what you mean to the Father you will live your life constantly trying to prove yourself worthy of something you were already qualified for.
—Nate Johnston

If the enemy can break your feet and make you lame before you even have a glimpse of your destiny, then he will try. I believe that the war on life, the war on women, the war on birth, the war on gender, the war on identity, the war on marriages, and the war on the family are all meant to prevent the emerging of a generation called to ring in the greatest harvest the earth has ever seen.

When Jesus was about to be born, the enemy used Herod to order the mass killing of babies in the kingdom of Israel. When Moses was a baby, Pharaoh had ordered the same thing, but both Jesus and Moses lived and fulfilled their purpose. This is why the enemy has tried to take you out since you birth—because you are a threat!

IN THE BARREN PLACE

We all know the story of Mephibosheth. He was the son of Jonathan who was lamed at around five years old when his nurse ran with him in fear at the news of his father and grandfather dying in battle. In her sheer haste and fear, she dropped him so severely it disabled him for the rest of his life. Fearing that the Philistines may take both her and the child as slaves, she ran to a town called Lo-Debar (means a barren place), where Mephibosheth spent the remainder of his childhood.

Mephibosheth lived in the house of Makir, which means bartered, an exchange, or compromise. Mephibosheth was living in a place that was desolate and without pasture, and it was far from the intimate inner sanctuary where he belonged. Lo-Debar was a wilderness, the complete opposite of his rightful inheritance.

Mephibosheth's life speaks into the outcast life on the sidelines of the Church that many prophetic voices walk through. Everywhere you go in this world, you can find people who are living outside the palace or a place God has given to occupy. It's an epidemic that causes identity confusion or rejection and can often lead people on a counterfeit path of it isn't corrected. This isn't to say that God doesn't call people outside of the walls of the church because my and so many others' stories show that He does, but I do believe it is the heart of God to restore the wild remnant back into the family of God, instead of be the estranged and strange distant family we have often been deemed.

The word *outcast* in Hebrew is *nadach*, which means "banished" and "violently thrust away." This word while similar to the English word *outcast* has more of a meaning of being separated from the main system or society. For too long, the Church has cast out reformers, and this is why we have seen a limbless church and a divided bride. But no longer!

OUTCAST NO LONGER

In early 2017, we left our season of isolation on the Gold Coast and joined Glory City Church in Brisbane led by Katherine

Ruonala. She called us into the family and just loved on us. She asked us that year if we would become part of the Australian Prophetic Council and had church members lay hands on us on the platform. As they did, the Lord spoke so loudly inside me that it shook me, "You are an outcast no longer," and I felt hidden weights and ties break off me that night. I'll never forget it.

> *"But I will restore you to health and heal your wounds," declares the Lord, "because you are called an outcast, Zion for whom no one cares"* (Jeremiah 30:17).

I know we use language like, "I'm a misfit for Jesus, or I'm a radical," and that's fine, but the test of the wilderness is will we continue to believe we are an outcast, or will we let it be a season we went through? Let me drive this home. Winter is a season, right? You went through winter, but that doesn't impart winter onto your identity or change your value because you lived through it. Winter was the season, and now springtime has come!

The Mephibosheth test that you and I face in our wilderness process is:

- Will we stay lame and de-feeted?
- Will be keep identifying by our dysfunction?
- Will we let our rejection and outcast season define us and rule us?
- Will we step into our rightful place in the Kingdom?

MISFITS & GENERATIONAL CURSES

I have called myself a misfit my whole life up until recently when the Lord said to me that He didn't like me using that confession because I was only ever a misfit to the institution and not to Him. I fit with God. I had a place and a home and a purpose, so it wasn't productive to keep seeing myself that way anymore.

The hardest hurdle misfits face is getting over being a victim because it can be so ingrained in them, and many times it passes on to future generations. We have grown up hearing our family members talk this way:

- "I'm a victim."
- "I'm overlooked."
- "I always miss out."
- "People always abuse me."
- "I am surrounded by abusers."

But there is good news. I grew up this way, then I got healed, and so can you. I want to be empathic in this but honest. Misfits are a secret weapon to the Church. Once the approval of the Father hits them, they go from being rebels without a cause to rebels with a chip on their shoulder for anything that opposes the Kingdom. Misfits, you are needed in this hour. We need your untamed voice. But we need you whole.

The crossroad and decision of every misfit when God calls them to the frontlines is will you stay feeling rejected, or will you get healed and say *yes*?

There is nothing more dangerous and volatile than an unhealed misfit, and equally there is nothing more potent against the kingdom of darkness than a healed misfit.

If this is you, I want to encourage you to take the negative identity label of being a misfit to Jesus and ask Him to heal you of rejection wounds. You can stay wild and untamed, but God wants you healed.

AN ORPHANED GENERATION

In chapter 17, we spoke about the tall poppy syndrome, and while it's a big subject on its own, it is not the root problem. The orphan spirit is.

My dad left when I was four, and my mum remarried my step-dad when I was seven. I always felt like an orphan, though, and struggled to know who Father God was because of it. In fact, I spent my whole life until my twenties looking for a father figure to approve and validate me, and I kept being disappointed over and over.

Outside of the acceptance and approval of the Father lurks a myriad of diversions to the prophetic reformational call, but there is none as destructive as the orphan spirit. The orphan spirit is what steps in when we are separated from Father God. After Adam and Eve left Eden and they had sons, Cain and Abel, what happened? Competition and jealousy turned into murder. It's the absence of the knowledge of the Father's love that opens a person up to a whole range of issues, causing a sense of abandonment, loneliness, alienation, and isolation. What comes out of that space are the greatest diversions to the prophetic call we see today. But let's look at the common signs or symptoms of an orphan spirit:

- Competition and comparison
- Jealousy and copycatting others
- Self-promotion and attention seeking
- Performance mentality and needing to prove worth
- Results driven over heart motivated
- Gossip, slander, and tearing down others
- Abandonment and self-isolation out of unworthiness
- Unhealthy independence and lack of trust
- Constant fear and feeling unsafe/unprotected

- Needing regular reassurance by others
- Lack of confidence in gifts and abilities
- Being territorial and protective in ministry/career
- Doesn't know how to champion or lift up others.
- Constantly scrambles for a place at the table
- Unshakable rejection and feeling dejected
- Battling others for position
- Operating out of insecurity
- Serving God and doing religious activities to earn His love

I can honestly say that I have experienced every single one of these in my life, and they had even become a part of my spiritual identity, and I had no idea! All I knew was that I was God's hireling and was going to live my life working hard to prove to Him that I was worthy even though I didn't think I would ever do an adequate job. My disconnection from the Father was creating a slight diversion from my calling in both my mindset and my assignment. From the outside, it looked like Kingdom, but in reality I was doing religious errands to make up for the massive void I lived with every day.

The most crucial and necessary road every prophetic voice must walk is the walk of healing the orphaned heart, reestablishing identity and original value, and stepping into a lifestyle of sonship. Otherwise, as we speak, we are just leading people back into slavery and bondage by the words we speak rather than true freedom and sonship.

What is sonship? Sonship is you in connection with God. It's recognizing God as Father, not just as Master or Lord. In that place, flows the purest expression you could ever imagine, and that is the very spring of life from which reformation is meant to flow. Today, I feel like the Father wants to encounter you and begin to shift you into a whole new realm of acceptance, healing, and wholeness as a reformational voice.

Because you are sons, God has sent forth the Spirit of His Son into our hearts, crying, "Abba! Father!" (Galatians 4:6 ESV).

See how great a love the Father has bestowed on us, that we would be called children of God; and such we are. For this reason the world does not know us, because it did not know Him (1 John 3:1 NASB1995).

Just sit in that for a moment. Read those scriptures again. Rinse and repeat.

PREVENTION TACTICS

These are some of the enemy's tactics to keep you in an orphaned state:

- He keeps you around dead religion that is void of the Father's love and freedom.
- He only lets you see father figures that don't represent the Father well.
- He keeps you out of the secret place and cuts you off from intimacy, acceptance, and identity.
- He makes you feel like it's normal to feel unsafe, alone, insecure, lacking peace, and having no real authority, power, anointing, or access to the Kingdom the Bible speaks about.
- He shuts you out from family and a real tribe who will accept you.
- He isolates and then assassinates you.

THE FATHERLESS TRANSITION & WILDERNESS

One night, I was praying for people at our church at the end of the service when a young man came up and asked for prayer. Instantly, without his saying anything more, I saw the pages of his book (his life) flicking before me, and I was able to see his journey that he had been through alone. He had been through some of the darkest nights I had ever seen without even knowing that the Father was wanting to be present with him in the mess of it. I told him what I had seen, and he was a mess. For the first time, someone touched on his deepest wound and spoke fatherly love and affection over him. He hugged me for twenty minutes straight, and the Father-heart of God did a major work as we held each other. It was amazing and unusual!

These are the symptoms of a fatherless wilderness:

- Feeling abandoned
- Feeling disconnected from God's voice
- Feeling let down and angry
- Feeling helpless and powerless
- Feeling like you have been teased into believing big things that haven't come true
- Feeling lost and alone
- Feeling like your hope is gone (your hope is in the outcome, not in the Person who is Hope)
- Feeling like everything you've been through is your fault
- Feeling unlovable and unworthy
- Looking for Plan B and second best
- Reliving old trauma
- Feeling unstable and like you are in sinking sand

THE FATHERED TRANSITION

These are some of the responses of those who know the Father as they go through transition:

- "I don't understand this, but I trust You."
- "That's not what I thought it would be, but I know You are good and You will work this toward my good in the end."
- "Your promises are *yes* and *amen*."
- "You have given me crazy hope that makes no sense."
- "I feel a fight and a worship in my spirit."
- "I still feel Your presence in the storm."
- "I can see beyond the mess."
- "I don't feel less loved, I just have more questions."
- "This is on You, Lord, and not on me."

CALL DIVERSIONS

A diversion means the act of deviating off course or operating in the wrong activity. It's the few degrees off course that takes a ship far away from its intended destination. Let's look at some prophetic diversions that happen because of operating out of the orphan spirit.

- Territorial/queen bee ministries that do not like to share the hive or work with anyone else unless it serves their purposes.
- Prophetic cop ministries whose purpose is to point out others who are wrong, failing, falling, or are in error.
- The "me, me, me" prophetic ministry that uses the prophetic gift to lead people back to themselves instead of Jesus due to their extreme lack of self-worth.

- Self-promotion and superstar ministries that exist to promote themselves and their achievements.
- The cheap swindler ministries that use the prophetic to sell prophetic words and prostitute the gifts of the Spirit.

ENTITLEMENT & PRIDE

On the other side of the spectrum of the "I am a dog" mentality of the Mephibosheth type is another fruit of the orphan spirit that few recognize, yet it has become increasingly prevalent today and the Church. It's entitlement. Entitlement actually means someone believing they deserve better treatment or conditions than others, and while this seems like something an orphan wouldn't do, the sense grows out of an orphan mentality.

Entitlement comes when someone tries to weigh up the balances of their lives like their own justice campaign and begins to believe that because of how they were treated they deserve to be compensated at everyone else's expense. It's revenge with an illusion of grandeur, and that's always a dead giveaway of the orphan spirit from the outset. It's someone who parades self-importance but inside is broken and craving affirmation. I have been so surprised over the years as I have met different successful people who aren't free of the orphan spirit at all. They have just morphed its shape from an under-the-table beggar to a pompous dignitary. Wild one, that is not who we are.

Just look at the word *entitlement* for a moment. What word within the word jumps out at you? That's right, the word *title*. In the secular entitlement culture, we can expect that the orphan spirit uses titles to cover over its gaping holes, voids, and deficits, but in the Kingdom, to operate in this same way is truly embarrassing. When titles become the gift wrap people wear to feel valuable, respected, and important, then sooner or later someone discerning is going to peak inside and see the reality of what's there staring back at them. How can we be sons and daughters yet idolize our titles, plastering them all over the internet like it changes one iota of who God said we were? I'm sorry, that's not honor. That's self-vanity with an orphan spirit.

SETTING A NEW TREND

So, this is where it leaves us—at a place of decision. Are we going to go through our wilderness holding onto the tattered rags of the orphanage, yelling out like Oliver Twist "Sir, can I have a bit more?" Or are we going to cry out, "Abba Father," and leave our fears and wounds in the dust?

It's time to set a new trend in the Church, and that's why your wholeness in this area matters because then you get to be the one who created healthy and safe environments that people can come to and be fathered and mothered and championed into who they were called to be. The Church needs to stop being extensions of the orphanages in the world and become launching pads again. Are you with me?

PROPHETIC SURVIVAL KEY

Long to encounter the Father. Speak to Him. Know you are a son or a daughter and walk out of the orphanage once and for all. Your key is the Father's perfect love, and it's time to encounter Him and use your key daily.

CAMPFIRE PRAYER

Father, heal me of the orphan spirit and reveal who You are to me. Show me who I am and break off every label and lie that I have accepted in my life, because I don't want to live looking through the lens of being an outcast anymore as I know You have called me into a role that requires I know who I really am in order to do it well. Show me who I am, Lord, in Jesus' name.

CHAPTER 19

The Muzzles of Silence, Narcissism, & Control

Jezebel wants to silence the church and send her underground but God is raising up a bride who will not be silenced! —Nate Johnston

"Let the prophets speak!" I heard booming in my spirit. "How dare you defy My mighty voices!"

I was invited to speak at a little church local to us and didn't know what to expect, but for a small church, I was surprised by the level of warfare I had encountered leading up to speaking there. As soon as I walked in the building, it was as if something zipped up my mouth. I couldn't sing, praise, or prophesy. I felt fear run up my spine, and for a moment, I wanted I run. Then I heard those words booming in my spirit.

What had happened there to stop the flow? The place was dead and dry in the absence of prophecy, and I needed to confront this spiritual stronghold. As I pressed in and rebuked it, I felt a sudden release and began praying for the church. I knew it wasn't going to be popular, but I needed to deal with this issue. As I addressed it from the stage, I could see the looks of shock on the pastors faces. *Wasn't he meant to bring an encouraging word?* they must have thought. But what's the point if there is a demonic agenda sent to steal the power of the prophetic words. As I prayed, people started falling over without me touching them. They were being delivered of the oppression that had been tolerated there. It was such a memorable meeting for me but maybe not for them.

A SILENCING AGENDA

There is no greater opposition and trial to the prophetic voice like that of the Jezebel spirit. It is one of the most formidable and frustrating trials in the path for the emerging voices. There is an overwhelming agenda to silence those who have already been in hiding long enough. The Jezebel spirit seeks to muzzle the prophets and assassinate them so their words have no effect or power.

Right now, more than ever before, the enemy is doing anything and everything he can to stop the voice of the Bride being heard. But nothing has changed in God's heart. You and I were born for this moment.

In 1 Kings 21, Jezebel wanted to turn Naboth's vineyard into a vegetable patch. Naboth means "words and prophecy," and the vineyard represents you and me grafted into the vine of Jesus. The enemy wants nothing more than a church of vegetables, not mighty branches grafted into the vine—branches that are carriers of the new wine! This spirit's intent is to silence God's prophets and remove the power from the Church, but I believe we are beginning to see prophets of purity and potency arising to take down this spirit once and for all.

The assignment of Jezebel in this season has been primarily to shut down the voices that God is raising up, those whom God is launching into new seasons of Kingdom exploits. For these, it has felt like a constant war of the mind battling fear, insecurity, and oppression. It has also felt like you have been muzzled, foggy headed, and unable to hear God like you used to. All of these tactics are to disconnect you from the heart of God so that you are diverted from your crossing over moment.

The enemy even uses people to squash you, trample you, usurp you, and delay you from your new doors and opportunities, but know this: God isn't going to let the enemy win.

THE TEMPTATION TO SHUT DOWN

In 1 Kings 19 after Elijah had called down fire upon the altar and killed the prophets of Baal, he heard the words of Jezebel seeking to take his life, and so he ran in fear. This was the same Elijah who just fearlessly defied the false gods in the land and saw God show up supernaturally! What happened? The Jezebel spirit caused Elijah to run in fear and even want to die.

> *Elijah was afraid and ran for his life. When he came to Beersheba in Judah, he left his servant there, while he himself went a day's journey into the wilderness. He came to a broom bush, sat down under it and prayed that he might die. "I have had enough, Lord,"* *he said. "Take my life; I am no better than my ancestors"* (1 Kings 19:3–4).

Have you been feeling that same assignment coming against you? The silencing muzzle that causes you to want to shut down your voice and hide in the wilderness again? That assignment that causes you to want to give up your calling, destiny, and call it quits? Have you experienced irrational fear, foreboding, or anxiety in mental warfare? This is nothing more than the adversary's assignment coming against your voice because you are coming into its *ripening*.

The bottom line is many have felt silenced so far in this new era. They have not felt empowered. They have felt under fire, attacked, and confused about how they can be a voice in this hour. Many didn't expect to leave the wilderness and be met with a world in crisis and chaos, but isn't that the perfect storm for the prophetic voice? Isn't that the perfect moment and opportunity to be a voice that cuts through all the noise?

NARCISSISM & CONTROL

I had an awakening moment one day when I was about twelve years old. I recognized something I hadn't seen before. It was as if I were on the *Hunger Games* and was suddenly able to see the invisible seams or forcefields of the game I was playing. A family member was taking me to go get some supplies for a hobby that I was really interested in. As we drove out of the driveway, they stopped the car and made this comment to me, "I will always gladly help you and get the things that make you happy if you listen to me and do what I say in your life, okay?" In a moment my spiritual discernment switched on, and I knew this was not right.

You see, there are insecure people who act out of insecurity to get their way, and then there are those who are influenced by the Jezebel spirit. We often like to say everyone is a Jezebel, but it's not helpful to demonize everyone. We need better discernment than that.

What I'm trying to get at is this: Narcissism is actually rooted in a Jezebel spirit. It has all the same characteristics and is birthed from the same scenario—hurting people who don't get healed and are driven by getting their needs met in whatever way possible. These are some of the traits of the narcissist:

- They gaslight, manipulate, and brainwash.

- They lie and exaggerate.
- They are aggressive when confronted.
- They love feeling powerful and making others feel disempowered.

This is Jezebel, people! Can you see her?

UNTANGLING URSULA'S TENTACLES

If you are a prophetically wired person, I guarantee there is someone the enemy has placed in your life to be the wet blanket to your raging wildfire. But look deeper, and you will see that they aren't just the naysayer to your destiny. They can be the greatest threat to your pure calling. How? Because they are close to you and they make subtle comments and suggestions about your giftings, abilities, and dreams. They even go out of their way to either control you so they control the gift, or they squash you so you are silenced.

I grew up around a few characters like this in my family. Other family members celebrated these characters as caring and thoughtful. But they were not because on the inside the characters were insidiously controlling and dominating. It was a poison to me that I didn't know I was ingesting because I didn't know any different until God turned the light on. After battling this spirit for years as it came against my marriage from family controlling and constantly disapproving our every step and causing strife between Christy and me, I was done because nothing I did worked. Boundaries didn't work. Trying to fix people didn't work. Reasoning with this spirit didn't work, so I asked God to show me what I was facing, and did He ever!

In a dream, I was in a spiritual realm that looked very much like a beach, but there was no color. It was just greys, black, white, and sepia. As I stood on the beach, I saw tentacles coming out of the water and snatching people up and wrapping around them before taking them under the water. Suddenly, a tentacle wrapped around me, but I held my ground, unraveled it, and began pulling this beast in one bit at a time until I was surprised to see an octopus with the head of a beautiful woman. She snarled at me and dragged me down a dark corridor full of prison cells with people suffering inside before I snatched my hand back and said, "No more!"

That season was a prison break season with instant results. I confronted the spirit in my life, and it unleashed my voice in a way I didn't know was possible. It was like the ceiling above me was no longer there.

Just like in the Disney movie *The Little Mermaid*, where the evil octopus Ursula stole the voice of Ariel (meaning lioness of God), so too does this spirit want to steal the voice of the lions rising up to roar in the earth, but there has been an awakening and a prison break! Many emerging voices who have been stuck in the grip of her tentacles or chained in her lair are beginning to break out of confinement and speak up for the first time.

UNEXPECTED TESTIMONIES

One night, I was ministering at our Friday night service at church when I felt to call people to the altar who felt muzzled and silenced. Surprisingly, at least half of the congregation came down. It was a long night! As I was praying for people what I expected would be a simple prayer time of freedom was more like a deliverance service of people coughing and sputtering as they got delivered. Another thing I didn't expect was the physical side of it. As I prayed for one lady, she started burping nonstop, and it was clear something vile was coming off her life and voice. Additionally, a guy I prayed for was healed in his throat, swollen vocal chords were healed, and people started prophesying, and even laughter broke out.

Ever since that night, I have continued to see much fruit from evicting this demonic assignment that so subtly and slyly enters into the Church, especially prophetic churches, and silences her. It must be confronted.

Over the years, I have heard these testimonies over and over. Last year, as an example, I heard a crazy testimony. In the middle of lockdown and restrictions, mask madness, and hysteria, I did a live video on living unmuzzled. Toward the end, I began speaking to the rising of the "wild ones" about whom God had spoken to me. A girl was watching me who had been so severely crippled by fear in her prophetic call that she had shut down for years and had felt as though the anointing and unction to prophesy had left her. In addition to that, she felt as if she had stopped hearing God altogether. When she would worship, a restriction would come over her throat and mouth, making it hard to concentrate. As I prayed, she began to lift her voice and declared, "I will not be muzzled another day longer! Get off me, demonic assignment that has been stealing my voice, in Jesus' name! I am a wild one for Jesus!" Instantly, something clicked and unlocked physically and spiritually. For the first time in years, she praised and prophesied. That night, she even began to dream and hear God's voice again.

We are living in an hour when the Church needs to be delivered from every assignment that has been muzzling her and keeping her silenced, unable to hear God's voice, and duped into counterfeit agendas. We need a good, old-fashioned deliverance session so that the Church can be shaken from her apathy and sickbed. We need new songs of revival to be written and sung in the halls and the streets, we need suppressed creativity to emerge, and we need all dormant prophetic expressions to erupt from their caves.

AN ENCOUNTER WITH THE LION

Many years ago, I was in a season where I was really struggling to navigate how to be a voice. It seemed that the more I shared what was on my heart, the more I was told that I shouldn't because I sounded anti-establishment and anti-Church. Furthermore, I was told I would only lead people away from God. My struggle was that this was not my heart at all, but God had placed a weighty message on my heart that I couldn't ignore; in fact, the more I fought it, the more frustrated I would become.

One Sunday, however, I was in worship, sitting at the back of the church feeling frustrated, misunderstood, and muzzled, and then I had a powerful encounter with the Lord. I suddenly felt the breath of God over my shoulders, as if the Lord was overshadowing me and releasing life and His very breath into my being. Then the sound came. It was the loudest roar I had ever heard, and it was coming from every direction. The sound was over me, overshadowing me, roaring over me and into my being. I know now that this was Jesus, the Lion of the Tribe of Judah, spoken about in Revelation 5:5,

> Then one of the elders said to me, "Stop weeping. Look! The mighty Lion of Judah's tribe, the root of David—he has conquered! He is the worthy one who can open the scroll and its seven seals" (TPT).

That experience was an awakening for me because I felt the fear of man lift off me where it had previously been choking the life out of me. I felt the fear of God in that moment so intensely that I was shaking. It was a good shaking as though the Lord was shaking all the fear and words off me that had been keeping me chained.

A few days later, I received a message by some people who had been leaders in my life at one time. They were ones who didn't approve of what I was doing. They had asked me to meet with them. I instantly knew that I couldn't meet with them because it would only be an ambush. The fear of man I normally would face didn't come over me. I said I wouldn't meet with them, I wiped the dust from my feet, and I moved on. The rest is history.

THE LIONS ROAR THROUGH YOU

I believe God is awakening your roar as well as the collective roar of a people called to speak into the darkness, into crisis and chaos, but without the roar, we will see *no real change*. The roar of the Lion of Judah is both the *breath* of God and the *sound* of God. The breath is the empowerment and anointing of the Spirit, and the sound is the weapon that heals, restores, breaks through, and destroys principalities and powers. That roar is wanting to come through you, but it isn't tame. No, like a lion this roar is wild, or like David said, "I will be so much more undignified than this!" (see 2 Sam. 6:22). He understood the wild nature of the Lion of Judah roaring through him. The roar wasn't a dutiful response but was a worshipful response, and because of this, it will never be clean and neat according to man's standards of religious customs/protocols. Rather, it will always carry an edge that stands out and "pierces through" the atmosphere you are in. That's what the sound of the roar through you does. It's not for show, and it's not for gain, but it is the natural response from your intimacy with God. You sound like the one with whom you have been. And right now, that's where God is calling us to be—with Him.

Imagine what it would like if the Church roared in crisis, adversity, trial, famine, and calamity instead of responding or reacting to appease the world and watering down the message of the gospel?

SYMPTOMS OF BEING MUZZLED IN A ROAR SEASON

I want to share a few of the symptoms that many have encountered this year:

- Excessive sensitivity to the fear of man/what people think
- Fear of offending or saying the wrong thing/political spirit
- Fear of being wrong or not pure enough/religious spirit
- Fear of your life, wanting to run and hide/Jezebel spirit
- Comparison and insecurity of feeling insignificant
- Feeling invisible and unheard
- Unrealistic fear and foreboding of the future/no vision or unclear future
- Wanting to give up/hard to get out of bed
- Demonic dreams and warfare/attack on sleep
- Demonic torment and heaviness against the mind
- Confusion, scattered mind, mental and creative block
- Unable or difficult to receive revelation like you used to
- Physical attack on your voice/throat

HOW YOU CAN BE A VOICE IN THIS SEASON

So, I want to give you some keys to help you be a voice in this season. I want to provide the following keys to encourage you to roar in a time when the enemy wants you on the sidelines:

- Spend time with Jesus, the Lion of the tribe of Judah.
- Make His voice louder than any other voice you hear and begin to let the sound of His voice and what He says become a greater reality than circumstances around you.

- Let Him pour into you more than you pour out. Keep your oil full and avoid running on empty.
- Learn to be more aware of how loved you are, and the fear will have less influence.
- Rebuke fear, foreboding, anxiety, and depression that try to come at you.
- Stop ingesting the lies of the media and being influenced by how culture wants you to think, act, and believe.
- Ask God for greater discernment and wisdom to be able to see past what you see in the natural, being able to discern the heart, motives, and intentions of things.
- Write down and journal what God shows you. Keep a record of it. Study it. Let it simmer. Ask for greater clarity and instruction on what you do hear.
- Decide that you are going to be a voice regardless of how you feel. Emotions and undeveloped senses can lie to you and cause you to move and live according to how you feel.
- Be responsible for your own destiny. No one can do it for you. No one can fight through the fog but you. You can do this!
- Take authority over your life and voice. The only permission the enemy has to you is what you give him by complacency, apathy, or agreement. Decide to stand up and not let him keep robbing you of your greatest commodity.
- Rebuke the enemy and be proactive with your spiritual armor according to Ephesians 6:10–19.
- Learn to be more aware of your atmosphere than simply emotionally reacting to it. Ask God questions daily like, "What am I sensing? Why do I feel this way?"
- Rebuke words, curses, judgment, and witchcraft chatter that comes at you. Isaiah 54:17 is a great defense.

- Shake off the disapproval of others or those who don't currently value or recognize your ministry or message. Bless them and keep your heart right.

- Do not be muzzled or suppressed. Don't tolerate Jezebel in any shape, way, or form. Don't partner with anything that shuts down the prophetic or is motivated by or uses fear, manipulation, or control to operate.

- Take stock of your alliances, allegiances, alignments, and partnerships. Are you in something that is shutting down your voice?

- Believe better things about yourself. Do you believe in your own voice?

- If you have been through previous rejection and any kind of church wound and have trauma, get healed. Find some people who can sit with you and walk you through healing.

- Be a son/daughter. You can't be a voice while thinking like an orphan or constantly feeling insignificant. Build yourself up in the Word and begin to see yourself as a mighty, powerful voice.

- Value people's opinions but don't live by them or make decisions based on anything other than what the Spirit of God speaks.

- Live tethered to the future you are speaking into, not the present that struggles to accept what you speak.

- Be a reformer if it's in you. Just make sure to increase in your love as equally as you swing your hammer.

- Live from eternity. Realize the afflictions and persecution you face are nothing compared to the glorious inheritance you have in Jesus (see 2 Cor. 4:17).

- Realize that, without your voice, the enemy will put something else in that vacuum. You have a role to fill!

- Wake up every day knowing that—regardless of position, platform, or followers—you have a voice that is powerful and known in the heavenlies. It's a new day to partner with Heaven and see your message impact the earth!

JEZEBEL IS LOSING INFLUENCE

One night the Lord woke me up and said, "Nate, the eunuchs are being freed. Voices that have been shut up are rising up!" I didn't know this at the time, but Jezebel had eunuchs. These were the ones who couldn't conceive or bring forth or produce. I know many have felt as if they have been kept from conceiving or reproducing. These have tried to speak but have felt silenced. If you have felt this way, the Lord says, "In this hour, I am healing and bringing restoration to those who have been silenced in the spirit, those who could not produce or bring forth." God says, "You will no longer be called eunuchs."

And He says, "I am raising up a new generation of prophets who will not live under the assignment of that Jezebel spirit. No, but," the Lord says, "I am calling those who will not operate from the fear of man but will simply raise up their voices. They will simply raise up their voices like a trumpet. As you raise up your new sound, there will be healing that will come because I am restoring a generation that knows My voice and sounds like Me, so know this, as you leave the wilderness, you're bringing out a generation of voices with you," says the Lord.

MUZZLES WILL BE THE STORY OF THE PAST— THE LIONS ARE RISING!

I need to prophesy to this generation. The controlling, manipulative, silencing, muting, stifling, oppressive, condescending, diminishing, purpose-stealing, roar-robbing, destiny-hijacking, gaslighting, narcissistic, and straight up demonic muzzle that you have grown up with and lived with *is being shattered*!

You will *not* take it with you into another season. You will not battle it constantly, having to fight for a moment's peace and for a second's freedom to lift your voice.

You will not be surrounded by Jezebel's assassins, queen-bee bullies, or Ahab's hired guns. You will not fall prey to the fear of man, political correctness, or cave into the seductive taming of culture and media that will steal your hot coals for the price of admittance. As Proverbs 28:1 says, *"The wicked flee when no one pursues, but the righteous are as bold as a lion."*

You will not carry over the trauma of your captivity any longer or live afraid to hear your voice ring louder than the pandemonium, but you will let your voice sound, and it will clear the air. This is your hour of getting back your greatest weapon—your creativity, potency, and prophetic decree—that will expose the darkness and release life into dead places.

This is the moment for this generation to be untangled from every tie and bond that keeps true prophecy at bay. It's time for every ceiling to be broken because the revolution of the wild, radical, *unmuzzled* voices is here!

Right now, that muzzle is coming off, and the irrational fear is leaving your life for good. You are not owned, and this spirit cannot claim what God has washed in His blood. You are His, and every cord attached to this kind of controlling and manipulative spirit is being severed. God is moving things and people out of your life that constantly keep you bound in a season you are meant to soar in. Even now, the chains are being broken in the name of Jesus.

Right now, cords are being cut daily. Ties are being severed. The tyrannical, spiritual muzzles and bondages that have held so many back from being a force to be reckoned with for the Kingdom are being dealt with, and God is using a time of extreme chaos and conflict to do it. Call it awakening, call it anything you like, but people who were once bullied and controlled are swinging their sword and beginning to encounter the *freedom* and the *permission* of Heaven to be a voice for the hour we live in.

I decree that we will no longer be a generation that tolerates the silencing, the cancelling, or the assassination of the Church's voice.

I decree that we will no longer edit/tame our voices in reaction to culture, the popular consensus, soulish opinions, or the worldly watchdogs.

We will boldly speak up for those who can't, we will be a light in the darkest places others aren't willing to be, and we will be part of the shifting of the tide of this hour and re-light the fires of this prophetic generation.

Fear, this is your eviction notice. You no longer rule us!

PROPHETIC SURVIVAL TIPS

Don't appease or tolerate any kind of muzzle. There are muzzles that are obvious and others that take more discernment, but the result is the same. If something or someone wants you quiet, *don't be!*

CAMPFIRE PRAYER

Lord, heal me of Jezebel bites and narcissism wounds that I have been carrying—wounds that have kept me silent in a time I know You are asking me to rise up. I give You my voice and ask that You would awaken and revive what I let muzzle me and put it in a tomb, in Jesus' name.

CHAPTER 20

Witchcraft, Warfare, & Character Refining

"But I promise you, no weapon meant to hurt you will succeed, and you will refute every accusing word spoken against you. This promise is the inheritance of Yahweh's servants, and their vindication is from me," says Yahweh.
—Isaiah 54:17 TPT

I could feel their words, but I didn't know what it was at the time. It was as if my mind was being bombarded by an invisible assault of demonic chatter and I didn't know how to stop it. I wanted to give up and never get out of bed. I said to God, "I'm done. I am never prophesying again!"

We had just delivered a warning word to our church leadership, and it didn't go down well at all. After a week of Zoom calls and being corrected and called judgmental prophets, we were exhausted. What was I experiencing? Christian witchcraft. But hang on, isn't that an oxymoron? Yes exactly. Even Christians can partner with the accuser if they are unaware. How do we do this? Anytime we engage in insecurity and out of fear toward people we can very easily start prophesying the enemy's lies over people and places. Proverbs 18:21 says that *"death and life are in the power of the tongue,"* so if we can speak and prophesy life, then we can also prophesy death, right? Unfortunately, yes, and as prophetic voices, we must understand this possibility.

I have had witches curse me and unbelievers say nasty things to me, but it has never been worse than the warfare that comes from Christians operating in witchcraft. Prophets can be the biggest offenders at this! I'll never forget a few years ago where I was feeling off, Christy and I were fighting endlessly for days, kids were waking up with nightmares, I was feeling sick, both of us were mentally under fire and discouraged, and our home was in chaos. We kept having doors suddenly shut in our faces out of nowhere, and sudden roadblocks appeared in our path. So, I was making coffee one morning when I saw a clear vision of two prophetic leaders I knew sitting at a cafe gossiping about us and judging our hearts in a very hurtful way. Then I saw them messaging other leaders in the Church and warning them about us simply out of that territorial and insecure spirit. After I had the vision, I prayed because I was thinking, *Was that real?* That very same day I happened to be on Instagram when a post appeared in my newsfeed of those two leaders. They were at a coffee shop three days earlier "catching up." Right away, I knew God was showing me the origin of the witchcraft so I could pray and break it in the spirit. Isaiah 22:22 says,

> *And I will place on his shoulder the key of the house of David. He shall open, and none shall shut; and he shall shut, and none shall open* (ESV).

WITCHCRAFT & HIRED GUNS

The other way the enemy has sought to shut down your voice in this season that God is increasing it is by assailing you with witchcraft and chatter. This is what I like to call "Jezebel's hired guns" because the main purpose is still to shut down your voice, but the Jezebel spirit will employ witchcraft prayers and chatter to come at you from all angles until you throw in the towel.

Anytime you are coming into something new, it's not unusual to suddenly sense that there are things swirling in the atmosphere around you. The enemy will find whomever he can to speak against you, judge you, and even prophesy things against you that didn't originate in God's heart. Often, the fruit of undealt with assignments of witchcraft are: wanting to give up, deep discouragement, complete defeat, a scattered mind (unable to get revelation the way you normally would), writer's or revelatory creative block, mental torment, and even physical symptoms, too.

In this season, discernment has been going through the roof as God is done with the immaturity of witchcraft in the Body of Christ. He is exposing sources of sabotage and hidden plots and slander that keep trying to take people down a few notches. Have your dreams been revealing this? Just remember your best defense is to break off and cancel their words, bless them, then move on. You don't need to hang out in this zone forever or make a full-time job out of knowing who is against you. *Break it and move on.*

COPYCAT PROPHETS & CASTING PEARLS

I received a call from a well-known prophetic friend, one day, who was going through a rough season. This person told me they were feeling dry and out of touch with God and hadn't been receiving words from Him like they used to, and so I prayed for them and encouraged them. Then they said, "What is God speaking to you about right now?"

Very excitedly I shared a word I was in the middle of writing.

"Oh, my goodness!" they exclaimed in reply. "That's amazing!"

Later that day I was on social media, and I saw a word from this individual with the topic and content I had just shared with them earlier. I couldn't believe what I was reading. I have been naive and trusted most people. I have always worn my heart on my sleeve, and so this was a good lesson in being careful what information I let people know and what pearls I was letting people trample on and steal.

Insecurity runs rampant in the prophetic movement when people aren't mature in their identity, and so they steal, lie, squash, and usurp to stay on top. They become copycat prophets when they run out of oil and think they can steal yours to keep up appearances, but sooner or later it catches up with them.

> At that time the kingdom of heaven will be like ten virgins who took their lamps and went out to meet the bridegroom. Five of them were foolish and five were wise. The foolish ones took their lamps but did not take any oil with them. The wise ones, however, took oil in jars along with their lamps (Matthew 25:1–4).

My advice to you is to stay genuine. Don't be like the foolish virgins. Stay full and stay authentic. Stay pure and stay true.

THE CHARACTER TEST

One of life's greatest tests in life is the test of character, but what is character, and why is it so important to the life of the believer? A.W. Tozer described character as "the excellence of moral beings."[1] As the excellence of gold is its purity and the excellence of art is its beauty, so the excellence of man is his character. Persons of character are noted for their honesty, ethics, and charity. A lack of character is to be without morals and biblical values, and persons lacking character tend to behave dishonestly and unethically. Our character comes from our overall maturity in thoughts, intentions, and desires.

I remember saying to the Lord that I never wanted to be more anointed than I had character and never more favored than my character, and I'd like to think God has answered me in that.

Basically, regarding our destiny, without character we won't be able to last the distance. Character enables us to *sustain* the gifts in us and the calling upon us. Character keeps your path straight so you have longevity and *end well*.

I once was given one of the *God's Generals* books, and as I read it, I was inspired, yet as I chewed through the chapters, I became grieved because, as anointed as these men and women were, some of them still didn't end well. I knew it wasn't the heart of God for them.

Solomon was the richest king in biblical history and possibly in world history. He had riches and wealth to spare as well as influence and, of course, wisdom. But he didn't end well:

> *As Solomon grew old, his wives turned his heart after other gods, and his heart was not fully devoted to the Lord his God, as the heart of David his father had been* (1 Kings 11:4).

His abundance in material wealth and his hundreds of wives blinded Solomon and led him astray so that he began worshipping other gods. This would have grieved the Lord, especially as Solomon was the son of David, the man had a heart after the Lord.

DON'T FIGHT THE FIRE

Romans 5:3–4 reads,

> *But that's not all! Even in times of trouble we have a joyful confidence, knowing that our pressures will*

develop in us patient endurance. And patient endurance will refine our character, and proven character leads us back to hope (TPT).

Character in this verse is the word *dokimé*, which means "a trial, proof; tried, approved character, proof of genuineness, a brand of what is tested and true, the process or test."

So often, we blame the enemy for the wilderness seasons, but God will lead us into isolation and obscurity to refine us. It's not to punish or hurt us but to *draw out* what is in us! Even as the Israelites were rescued from Egypt, God led them through the wilderness to *draw out* of them who they really were after being imprisoned for so long. He didn't intend for it to take forty years, but because of their complaining and grumbling, they extended the test! That should teach us that we can make our test longer than God intends for us.

> *You shall remember all the way which the Lord your God has led you in the wilderness these forty years, that He might humble you, testing you, to know what was in your heart, whether you would keep His commandments or not* (Deuteronomy 8:2 NASB1995).

Why do we fight the fire? Fire is the only route by which our character is formed.

> *And I will put this third into the fire, and refine them as one refines silver, and test them as gold is tested. They will call upon my name, and I will answer them. I will say, "They are my people"; and they will say, "The Lord is my God"* (Zechariah 13:9 ESV).

Your wilderness was never sent to harm you or inflict hopelessness upon you, but it was designed to be the perfect environment for destiny to be found and the character formed that will be the infrastructure for greatness to make its residence.

WILDERNESS WARFARE

I honestly didn't understand from a young age why I was always under attack. I felt like something was wrong with me. Let's set this straight. This is why you face warfare:

- Because you live in a world that the enemy and his demons also live in.
- Because you belong to a Kingdom the enemy doesn't and he is jealous and threatened everyday by your existence and what you carry.
- Because the enemy wants to rob, steal, and destroy you and prevent you from carrying out your purpose.
- Because he wants to stop your family from carrying out their purpose.
- Because you have authority over him and are here to embarrass his counterfeit rule.

   I have said these things to you, that in me you may have peace. In the world you will have tribulation. But take heart; I have overcome the world (John 16:33 ESV).

DETERMINE THE ASSIGNMENT/SPECIFIC SOURCE

Christy and I had to learn how to discern what we were facing. All warfare obviously comes from the enemy, but it's good to discern which of his henchman is behind it to know what the purpose of the warfare is and then apply different strategies to counteract each one. For instance:

- The assignment of witchcraft comes to bring confusion, delay, creative block, red tape, and abortion of your mission and what you are birthing. It also comes to attack your identity, worth, and what God says about you. It comes to close doors and opportunities.

- The assignment of Jezebel comes to stifle you, squash you, muzzle you, silence you, keep you in bondage to the fear of man, control, and manipulation through people (family, sometimes leaders, and wrong alignments). It's a destiny assassination assignment.

- The religious spirit comes to put the heavy on you, guilt you, slander you, condemn you, judge your motives, and make you want to run for the hills.

- The assignment of affliction comes to bring sickness to you and your home through accidents, mishaps, disease, etc.

- The assignment of barrenness is where it feels like nothing seems to manifest or move forward. It's like you are unable to *see* launched what you are carrying in the natural.

- Strife and division are fruit of witchcraft, so we treat them the same way.

When you learn the common symptoms of each assignment of the enemy, you discern it quicker each time and then apply the strategy you have learned.

> *Your hand-to-hand combat is not with human beings, but with the highest principalities and authorities operating in rebellion under the heavenly realms. For they are a powerful class of demon-gods and evil spirits that hold this dark world in bondage. Because of this, you must wear all the armor that God provides so you're protected as you confront the*

slanderer, for you are destined for all things and will rise victorious (Ephesians 6:12–13 TPT).

PRE-EMPT THE ATTACK & LIVE OFFENSIVELY

A few of the basic tactics/strategies we have learned over the years include:

- Worship is everything. The enemy hates you soaring in altitude. The snakes drop off the higher you go. (Ever feel like worship is hard to do when you are going through warfare? This is why.)
- Put on the armor of God.
- Pray in the Spirit.
- Read the Word like it's a weapon. Find loaded scriptures and fire them like bullets at the enemy.
- Be thankful. This makes the enemy mad when you take the focus off you and put it on God.
- Laugh and express your joy. Laugh at the enemy's attempts to distract you. Tell him his time is up.
- Rebuke the enemy and he must flee. Take authority over the situation.

Here are ways you can pre-empt and prevent warfare:

- Keep your heart right with the Lord.
- Don't create landing pads/open doors for the enemy by engaging in silly things. Don't have anything in common with the enemy.
- Stay away from bitterness and unforgiveness.
- Forgive often and keep your heart healthy.

- Create an atmosphere of worship in your home. Worship as a family.
- Take communion often, especially at the beginning of funky days.
- Take stock of what you are letting feed you, what you are letting in and listening to.
- Be wary of those who have access to your heart and information about your inner workings of your life.

Disarm attacks and living offensively:

- When you discern witchcraft, attack right away by not engaging in talking bad against people. Bless them and release them. But rebuke the words. Take communion and guard your home. Flood it out with worship and get your head in a good place. Sometimes, you must fight/ press in for peace.
- When you discern Jezebel/control and narcissism at work, take communion and take care of that in the spirit realm. Look at who has access to you and ask God for insight into the source of it. Often, you will have to confront sources/ people and define boundaries. Then worship in the secret place and break off the muzzle and demonic silence placed over you. This can also be a process of unlearning as it's a common way many are raised.
- When you discern the assignment against what you are birthing, stand and take authority. Rebuke the barrenness and declare that all doors are not shut for you, that you will birth and it will not be delayed. Pay attention to who is in the delivery room with you. Are they the right people?

THE BOTTOM LINE

Always remember:

- We have won. We worship up and warfare down. We aren't trying to battle to get victory. We are applying the victory we already have to our situation.
- We aren't victims; we are overcomers. We shift the narrative.
- There is nothing wrong with us if we go through warfare. We shake off that misconception.
- We know that God is fighting with us and for us!
- We are more than conquerors through Christ Jesus.
- We are seated in heavenly places.
- We overcome by the blood of the Lamb and the word of our testimony!
- We are going from glory to glory, and what we are doing by learning how to warfare is we are *pioneering* our family into greater health and legacy. We must keep going!

PROPHETIC SURVIVAL TIP

Don't curse others because they curse you. Your words are powerful, and the way you deal with those who speak against you matters. Bless them with your words!

CAMPFIRE PRAYER

Lord, I rebuke the words that have come at me and the chatter sent to keep me in bed. Lord, I cancel and command them to be null and void and disarmed. Lord, give me discernment in this journey and help me not to fight people but the principalities and powers I face. Arm me and equip me for this in Jesus' name.

NOTE

1. A.W. Tozer, "God's Character Is Infinitely Holy," *The Alliance Tozer Devotional*, Sunday, June 6, 2021, https://www.cmalliance.org/devotions/tozer?id=730.

CHAPTER 21

Father Wounds, Betrayal, Dishonor, & Forgiveness

How we deal with the deepest wounds matters, and there are wounds that do seem to go deeper than others. They go deeper than words of accusation, being rejected, or being passed over. These are the wounds that far too many who experience them never seem to move on from them, but that statistic is changing. I am talking about father wounds, dishonor, and betrayal.

I have already spoken about Saul from the perspective of competition, jealousy, and assassination, but let's talk about Saul as someone who was a father in David's life. You see, we forget Saul was David's father-in-law. David was married to Saul's daughter Michal, and while Saul started off admiring David, he became extremely jealous of the favor and presence on his life, and Saul sought to kill him.

> *The next day an evil spirit from God came forcefully on Saul. He was prophesying in his house, while David was playing the lyre, as he usually did. Saul had a spear in his hand and he hurled it, saying to himself, "I'll pin David to the wall." But David eluded him twice. Saul was afraid of David, because the*

Lord was with David but had departed from Saul (1 Samuel 18:10–12).

Saul represents the fathers, leaders, and figures we all know in life who are meant to champion us, raise us, empower us, and cover/protect us, but because of insecurity, they fall prey to being a Saul in our lives. It's quite ironic that a parental, spiritual figure that is meant to nurture and enhance the call of God on us can be the greatest threat to it. Many gifted and anointed people I know haven't survived the Sauls in their lives. They are derailed and assassinated and alienated from their destinies.

People ask me this question all the time: Then if Sauls can be so destructive, why does God allow them? Firstly, you must remember that what is a "Saul test" to the Davids, is a "David test" to the Sauls. When we deal with a leader who acts as a Saul out of insecurity, the test we face is equally for them. Will they lift us up and propel us further than they have been? I'll talk more about fathering in the chapters to come, but for now, I want to focus on the wilderness trial of dealing with Sauls, and then walking out the pain of being at the scary end of a Saul's insecure rampage.

As I shared earlier, it's one thing to raise people from orphans, but the real test is what fathers and mothers do when they mature and become powerful. In our years of raising up world changers in our school, we have seen time and time again people surpass us, and it blesses us, but if we got insecure, we could potentially be the greatest threat to their calling.

PINOCCHIO'S CONUNDRUM

The story of *Pinocchio* has always spoken to me in an unusual way because I felt like a puppet on strings in the institutional church setting, but especially to the spiritual fathers I submitted, knowing they wanted something from me. In the story of *Pinocchio*, these are the characters and whom they represent in this context:

- Pinocchio—orphan (not real son) who desperately wants to prove himself. Nose grows when he lies, which shows how Pinocchio sees his personal shame as external.
- Geppetto—Father God who desires family at any cost and loves even when we stray from Him.
- Jiminy Cricket—the voice of the Holy Spirit who tells us right from wrong.
- Stromboli—the counterfeit father who controls, extorts, and uses Pinocchio for money and gain.

There is a strange dynamic and almost a synergy between the orphan and the counterfeit father in that they are both looking to each other. The orphan desires validation while the insecure father wants people he can control and manipulate for his devices to use as stepping stones for his goals and dreams. I know this because I was Pinocchio, desperately wanting a father figure's approval. I would have done anything for it, even if I was oppressed in it.

Many years ago, when I was beginning to realize this unhealthy dynamic, I had a call from a friend of mine who said, "I have a word for you."

"Okay, great what is it?" I said.

He replied in a comedic way, "The Lord says, 'You're a real boy!'"

This strange word really blessed me and made me sever a tie I had a with a Stromboli in my life. I didn't need strings. I didn't need flattery and false validation at the cost of my destiny. That day, I stopped trying to find fathers and began to pursue *the* Father.

HEIRARCHY & ELITISM

My first experience with a Saul leader or a spiritual father like Stromboli was in a church environment that was known for championing the sonship message. This leader constantly made distinctions, separating orphans from the sons and the ones who flattered him the most, served his vision the most, or was the most loyal subject who treated him with honor. It was a hierarchy or tier system that you could climb based on how much you allowed him to control you like a marionette. I was blinded to it because I wanted to belong and be accepted.

> elitism ĭ-lē'tĭz"əm,
> The belief that certain persons or members of certain groups deserve favored treatment by virtue of their superiority, as in intelligence, social standing, or wealth

I didn't know it, but this was elitism at its finest. Because I was in the "in club" for a short season, I was blinded to seeing the way others who weren't in it were being treated. It took a hard hit for me to wake up and realize this, and when I did, I could see how much of a counterfeit of the Father's heart this was, leaving so many damaged and hurt people in its wake.

TOUCH NOT GOD'S ANOINTED

So how do you pass the test when dealing with a Saul? I have asked God that for years as I've walked through some of the most painful woundings by people I trusted and gave my all to serve. The answer is actually found in 1 Samuel 24, where David finds Saul sleeping in a cave and instead of killing him cuts off a piece of his robe and then walks away.

Then David went out of the cave and called out to Saul, "My lord the king!" When Saul looked behind him, David bowed down and prostrated himself with his face to the ground. He said to Saul, "Why do you listen when men say, 'David is bent on harming you'? This day you have seen with your own eyes how the Lord delivered you into my hands in the cave. Some urged me to kill you, but I spared you; I said, 'I will not lay my hand on my lord, because he is the Lord's anointed'" (1 Samuel 24:8–10).

What David did was more than just fueled by the fear of the Lord not to touch God's anointed. It was fueled by his love and honor for someone who betrayed and dishonored him. The fruit? Saul was repentant, for a while at least.

BETRAYAL'S POISON

Only three years ago, I faced a deep betrayal from a close brother. I didn't see it coming at all. It hurt so deeply that I felt lost in the pain and dishonor of it and wanted to give up ministry altogether. I felt done because the road of trials had finally hit its peak. In the middle of that, we happened to be in the States and were invited to lunch with good friends of ours who had no idea of the situation. Halfway through catching up, one of our friends said, "I need to give you something," and he took off his jacket and gave it to me. As soon as I put it on, I began to cry. It was the presence and anointing! I felt the covering of a brother over me where I had been exposed. Then he handed me his recently acquired black belt in martial arts and said, "This kind of warfare will not take you out ever again!"

In 1 Samuel 18:4, Jonathan took off the robe he was wearing—along with his tunic, sword, bow, and belt—and gave them all to

David. It was a sign of friendship, covenant, and honor while Jonathan's own father was operating in fear, jealousy, and insecurity.

It was the seed of honor David needed to continue acting in honor toward someone who wasn't acting honorably toward him. Think about the story of where Saul was chasing David and David found him sleeping in a cave. Instead of killing Saul, he cut off a corner of his tunic to show that he would act honorably even when Saul didn't. Honor is an art I don't feel like we have fully tapped into yet, but it is a key component for reformers because we will meet many Sauls in our journey, but how we deal with them will be the test.

Have you encountered a Saul in your life? Someone who should have been a leader, mentor, father, or mother but because of insecurity actually warred against you? Have you experienced witchcraft like I spoke about but didn't understand the symptoms? Pray Isaiah 54:17 today over yourself and rebuke every word curse, forgive the Sauls, and ask Holy Spirit to help you move on.

Dishonor comes in many ways and forms. Here are three examples from the Bible:

- Joseph's brothers were so jealous of him that they threw him in a pit and then sold him into slavery.
- David's brother Eliab was so jealous of David being anointed king that he spoke nasty hateful words when he was thinking of taking down Goliath.
- Absalom was so power hungry and jealous of his dad that he raised an army against his own father and sought to kill him!

HONOR IS CURRENCY IN A TRIAL

David used honor to see Saul in the way God saw Saul, even when Saul didn't see it himself. That's what honor is at its core, seeing and treating someone according to what God says about them and not according to their shortcomings or actions. I am so grateful for starting to learn this in the middle of my greatest seasons of attack and wilderness. I'm glad I'm learning how to honor those who don't honor me back.

I remember the first time I applied this in a moment of dishonor, and to be honest, it didn't feel satisfying at all. My innate sense of justice roaring in me was wanting to let this person know how wrongly they had treated me, but God's Band-Aids and healing balms often look different to ours. The Saul test we all go through is will we throw a javelin back when one is thrown at us? Will we touch God's anointed when they abuse or hurt us? Will we throw them under a bus when they have placed us in oncoming traffic?

If you are going through this trial, here are some practical actions of honor.

- Don't speak badly about those who have spoken badly about you.
- Speak to who they are. It doesn't excuse what they did, but it keeps your heart right.
- Bless them. Send them flowers or a gift.
- Break off the words and betrayal. That's honoring yourself.
- Break the soul tie. This detaches you spiritually from them, their ownership of you and their judgment, and it removes the ceiling they placed over you.

It's only when you are dishonored that you truly learn how to honor. It's in a moment of potential bitterness that you choose to not prescribe the same poison to others they inflicted upon you.

Can you be a reformational voice who speaks truth in boldness but also honors? Right now, the Father is releasing double honor upon you where you have been dishonored.

MY LIFE'S GREATEST HURDLE & GREATEST BREAKTHROUGH

I have never written my testimony before anywhere, and I'll be sharing it later in the book, but for now you need to know the nutshell version because there is one part of my story that has by far surpassed every trial I have faced as my life's greatest hurdle.

My dad left when I was four. Then my mum remarried again when I was almost seven. She married a pastor who was a great guy who my younger brother and I really liked, but he ended up being physically, emotionally, and verbally abusive. As a result, our home seemed spiritually healthy on the outside while the inside was quite cancerous, unstable, and bipolar.

From a young age, I became quite bitter toward God, especially Father God who I thought hated me and wanted to punish me endlessly. I became so bound by unforgiveness that I was demonized until I found God again after a failed assassination attempt of the enemy to take my life. I didn't know how to deal with the unforgiveness I carried around. It was there, and I knew it.

In 2004, Christy and I started running our church's youth group, and God was working on my heart. One morning, I heard Him speak so loudly inside me that there was no doubt He was talking. "Nate," He said, "it's time to forgive your stepdad." I remember feeling stunned because I just used to suppress my anger and bitterness and busied myself so I didn't have to deal with my feelings. But I couldn't hide from it anymore. "Nate, I have too much ahead for you to be held back by the wounds and bitterness you are carrying, so it's time to forgive him."

"How?" I asked, as if it was as hard to do as climbing Mount Everest.

"In a few months, your family will invite you to a gathering at your aunty's house. If you forgive him that night, then the whole bitter root will be plucked out and the wounding closed."

As God has said, I was invited to a family gathering, and I reluctantly went because I wasn't seeing my family very often at them time. I felt so much anger when I saw my stepdad walk in the door, but I noticed something had changed about him from the last time I had seen him. He had a calmness, a peace. Toward the end of the night, we were all sitting outside when people left, and we two were left alone. It was awkward. He started telling me stories of his dad and the painful things that happened to him as a child. It was horrific, and it far worse than what he had done to me, so I started to feel a little compassion for him.

"I forgive you," I suddenly blurted out as I couldn't hold it in any longer.

He looked stunned, emotional, unsure of what to say next, but he told me he had been having inner healing. God had begun to heal him of his father wounds and wanted to know if he could pray with me to heal mine.

I agreed.

UNDER THE DONALD DUCK BEDSHEETS

My stepdad asked me what I had been carrying and feeling for years. I told him I was angry all the time. I felt like a victim and felt cast aside, and that I mattered to no one because from a young age I had to figure life out completely alone. I was an orphan, and I felt like God orphaned me. He told me that Holy Spirit wanted to go back and heal the roots and entry point of those lies and then remove them once and for all. What took place next, I didn't expect.

As I prayed, "Holy Spirit show me," I went into a very real vision. My feet were on the ground in Bribie Island, Australia, when suddenly I was transported in the spirit to my home in Redcliffe in 1987. I was in the exact moment my dad was leaving, and in the vision, I was my four-year-old self. I could see everything so clearly—the decor, the pattern on the couches. I could even smell the place. I ran outside onto the porch where I saw my dad leaving, and he was crying and upset to leave me, but then he just drove away. Inside, I could hear my mum crying, so I walked inside to find her screaming into a cushion on the couch. Instantly, as a four-year-old, I felt a wave of new emotions I hadn't felt before: abandonment, fear, guilt that this was my fault. In the violent clashes of tense emotions, I ran down the hallway to my bedroom and hid under my bed that was made with the Donald Duck bedsheets.

As I was crying under my bed, I heard someone next to me and looked up to see Jesus kneeling with His head in His hands. He was crying with me. Suddenly, something that had been bottled up in me for almost twenty years broke. In an instant, the root wound that I was abandoned by God and left alone was plucked out and so were the abandonment of my biological father and the wounds inflicted upon me by my stepdad. I was free! I came out of the vision and gave my stepdad a big hug and said again, "I forgive you!"

If you have been through this trial or are still walking through it, you need to know that God has not abandoned you. That lie will keep you in obscurity for the rest of your life if you let it. Today, ask the Father to encounter you in a new way, release your wounds, let them stay behind you so you can finally move on into what God has called you to without being tethered another day to the past.

PROPHETIC SURVIVAL TIP

Camp your life around the Father's feet as Mary did at the feet of Jesus. This is the place upon which you can build your life and not be shipwrecked. Honor is your greatest currency. Use it well!

CAMPFIRE PRAYER

Father, baptize me in Your love and heal me of every father wound I have encountered in my journey. Today, I choose to forgive those who manipulated and controlled me, used me, and squashed me and my calling. Lord, I want to walk in honor, so please give me your eyes to see people how You have created them to be, in Jesus' name!

PART 4

The Wilderness Commissioning

CHAPTER 22

Look Here They Come!

*The entire universe is standing on tiptoe, yearning to see
the unveiling of God's glorious sons and daughters!*
—Romans 8:19 ESV

Have you ever arrived too early at the cinema to see a movie and had to wait through twenty advertisements and information videos, not to mention the trailers of six other movies, even before the movie you paid for began?

I have felt that way my whole life in the Church. I have felt like I was personally waiting for a green light moment where certain elements lined up and it was time to really *go!* Does that make sense? Globally, I have felt that waiting. It always felt like my Christian experience was a one of suspense for this unknown hour that I couldn't describe or explain but I just knew was coming. Romans 8:19 says it well. Believe it or not the world has felt it. It's a limbo, an eleventh hour gasp before the tick of midnight. But what are we waiting for? Jesus' return? No, I don't believe so yet. I believe it's the waiting for the Church to arise in her era of "greater glory."

"'The glory of this present house will be greater than the glory of the former house, says the Lord Almighty. And in this place I will grant peace, declares the Lord Almighty'" (Haggai 2:9).

It's the era of the Church coming out of the dark ages of religion and ineffective, weak Christianity and into being the glory-carrying, Jesus-revealers we were called to be!

Isaiah 60 paints an amazing picture of this revealing of God's sons and daughters;

> Rise up in splendor and be radiant, for your light has dawned, and Yahweh's glory now streams from you. Look carefully! Darkness blankets the earth, and thick gloom covers the nations, but Yahweh arises upon you and the brightness of his glory appears over you! Nations will be attracted to your radiant light and kings to the sunrise-glory of your new day (vv. 1–3).

I don't think God could be any clearer and more obvious about this one. The Church is being readied for a new moment, a new era, an age of commissioning. But who will lead the pack and be the catalysts of this re-formation, re-grouping, and awakening of God's people? You guessed it—the Wild ones.

In this chapter, I want to share something very personal. It's a word the Lord spoke to me one morning a few years ago.

LOOK TO THE WILDERNESS

"Nate, the wild ones are coming! Look to the wilderness, can you see them emerging? Can you see them springing up out of isolation and obscurity?"

Of all the words I have heard the Lord speak to me, this was one of the weightiest I have ever received and was my green light for writing this guidebook. I knew it needed to be done.

For if you remain completely silent at this time, relief and deliverance will arise for the Jews from another place, but you and your father's house will perish. Yet who knows whether you have come to the kingdom for such a time as this? (Esther 4:14 NKJV).

"Here they come, Nate. Here are my wild ones!" I heard the Lord say. These words rattled me to my core and pulled on a thread that went deep into my own life and journey. As I sat stunned by the weightiness of this simple sentence, I took out my phone and wrote down what the Spirit of God was wanting to say.

"I have opened the gates, and I have decreed that the time is over for those who have been in waiting for this moment. The moment I have prepared them for is here, and now the earth is in for a rude awakening because my front-liners are stepping into the light. They are my movers and shakers and demonic stronghold breakers, and here they are to usher in a season of the revealing of My glory through My Bride.

"Right now, I am bringing them out of exile. I am gathering them from all over the earth where they have been hidden and in waiting for a long season. They have wondered if I had abandoned them or if they would ever be used in the Kingdom because they were never fully accepted as a part of it, but right now they are emerging in the world's greatest moment of pain and the Church's hour of desperation.

"They are my undignified Davids who care more for My presence and My will and My plans than the wise plans of man. They aren't politically correct or motivated by reputation, but they have only one thing in their sights, and that is worshiping Me and giving Me glory. Can you see them coming? Will you have eyes to see them? Will My Church accept them? Will she keep turning them away?

"They haven't been given a red-carpet welcome, but they will be clothed in so much glory it will be hard to deny them anymore. The fire of My presence is all around them, and they aren't here to play games but to carry the torch of revival and establish My Kingdom on the earth."

THEY AREN'T REBELS; THEY ARE THE RESCUE TEAM!

"Remove the barricades and the gate-checks, for they aren't the rebels they have been seen as, but they are in fact the rescue team! They didn't quite fit the mold, and they didn't measure up to the standards of the institution, but they are sons and daughters who know My heart and know My house well. They have been in hiddenness for this very moment to bring *hope* to where many are prophesying hopelessness. They are the ones who have My eyes and see how I see. They know what is to come next. They aren't swayed by temporary storms, but they are the ones who will point the way to where I am moving and what I am doing.

"Look now. They are peeling back the veil and lifting up the curtain. They are speaking into what is to come, and they live from that reality. If you want hope again, watch where they are going! They are setting the stage for the new production and unraveling the new blueprints and plans I have given them.

"I am using them to raise a new standard for My people. Where there have been foxes that have stolen from my people and their faith for generations, I am restoring faith. Where foxes have come and stolen the revelation of My abiding glory, My signs and wonders, and My healing virtue, they will restore It. They will point the Church back to true north and clear the overheads. They will come with their hammers and chip off the pieces of rock that have been stumbling blocks and not building blocks, hindrances and not steppingstones. They are coming as a sign of the new wine and the beginning of a new era of My Church. I am not shutting down church as we have known it, but at the same time, the Church will never be the same way it was ever again. What had to be shaken was shaken. What had to fall and die fell and died, and what didn't have My Spirit upon it is right now breathing its last. For I am jealous for My Bride to be the *pure* Bride!

"What they thought was rejection from the mainstream culture was in fact My protection for an upcoming season. And that season is here now. They have been set apart so they could usher in a move of My holiness and power—a holiness so mighty that it will reveal the thoughts and intentions of men and reveal who is for Me and who is about building their own kingdom. This is a move of purity that is exposing the double-mindedness, duality, and mixture that has subtly crept into the hearts of believers and disconnected them from My heart."

THEY WILL BE THE BRIDGE BUILDERS & RESTORERS

"Their hammers will be mighty, and they will seem ferocious, but it isn't out of rage. It's out of righteous conviction to set the record straight and *rescue and lead* the Church forward. In fact, I am right now baptizing them afresh with a love for the Church in all of her expressions and parts so that they won't be the demolition team but the bridge-builders. Like Nehemiah, they will grieve that parts of the city are in rubble, and they will build and restore what has been broken down.

"They will raise up other builders and teach them to build the new while still honoring what has been built before them. They will seamlessly connect the seasons and the moves of My Spirit and reveal the pathway forward for My pioneers to run in. For many have said, "They are against what I have built!" but I have not raised them to tear down what I have given you to build, but to tear down the enemy's work and add and increase what you have been building. I have given them an anointing to see the cracks in the foundations and to fix and address them.

"And as they build, they will breathe life into the dry bones of dead and burnt-out movements that religion tired out and caused to expire before their time. They will be revivers of revival fire, and they will cause fresh fire to enter those who have been barely flickering, and they will get a second wind to finish the purposes I gave them to accomplish. Broken systems will be reinvented and reinvigorated, and My Spirit is going to cause wheels to turn where there has been no oil.

"They will especially revive the dead movements and dreams of those who were shipwrecked. They will cause hearts to start beating again in tune with Mine and begin to burn with love-sick desire where they have grown cold and deeply discouraged. In moments, they will take the weariest, oppressed, and wounded of soul and cause their furnace to be ignited again.

"They will find the hurting and derailed fathers and mothers of previous movements and restore honor to them, purpose to them, and give them a reason to believe in the impossible again. They will unearth the gold in people. But to get to gold you need the hammer, not just water. The hammer and the shaking, but soon the gold emerges.

"I have asked the Church, 'Will you stand up and be a voice? Will you confront the opposition and advance the Kingdom, or will you cave in and either maintain or retreat?' The intimidation and assaults have been relentless, but I have raised up a remnant who will not stand aside when evil is at their doorstep. This remnant will confront the giants that no one else will. They will be the Davids who will choose to fearlessly face the principalities in the land and call them for what they are. They will not water down the gospel or sell out to win the favor or man, but they will bravely move in offense against the assignments of the enemy that have defied the Church.

"Innocent blood has been shed for far too long in the nations, and there has been but a few who have stood in the face of true evil and given their lives to see it overturned. But My wild ones will not be those who back down. No, they will be like Esther who chose to give her life to see every injustice overturned."

THEY WILL BE A VOICE WHERE OTHERS CAVED INTO FEAR & SPEARHEAD CAMPAIGNS OF MY JUSTICE

"As they march into battle in places that none have dared to tread before, they will break open the way for the Church to gain back ground and advance where she has been slowly shrinking back. These wild ones will be like battering rams that break open the way and will be the spearheads of justice that enter into new territory that the Church has not had influence in before. If you think you have seen the positioning of My people in high places, you wait to see where I take them next. I am sending My reformers into the lion's den and the leopard's lair for the sake of the outpouring that is going to take place on the enemy's own campground.

"These wild ones will speak when I tell them to speak, and they will not have a religious filter that edits or politically corrects or adjusts what I ask them to say. They have not been tainted by the fear of man, and they will simply *speak*, and the word will go forth. As they speak, it will set in motion a domino effect of courage in those who have been afraid to speak.

"They will leave all behind this season to launch wildfire movements that have less concern for the tangible structure or program, but they will be focused on the people. They will have an apostolic anointing to build quickly and easily gain momentum, and I have given them favor to do it. It will look messy and foolish at the beginning, but soon fire will spread effortlessly.

"And I will move upon those who man would not choose. I will choose who I choose, and I will move on whom I move upon, and I am going to pour out My Spirit upon the most unlikely people in the most unlikely ways. So, get ready to see undeniable fruit from places that would offend the pious and self-righteous because I have come for all, not for a few, and I will pour out My Spirit upon *all*.

"I have given them an anointing that will be like a clear clarion call to the Bride to come back to her first love, and it will clear the air from all noise pollution and chasing vain desires and bring the hearts of My people back to Me again. Above all, My wild ones will offend the Church out of her idolatry to her own brands and reputation and cause her heart to return to Me. My wild ones will usher in a move of repentance that will cause those who have veered off course to correct their path, the lukewarm to run to Me, and those who have been chasing buildings and empires will forfeit them like crowns at My feet. They live for one thing, and this is to point and lead people to Me, to reveal Me in the earth.

"Their keys were stolen, and it's time they got them back! And I am using this remnant to remind the Church of what she has settled for in this season. Religion has caused My Church to forget how loved and accepted she is and the permission I've given her to do what she has inside of her. But they will usher in a new season of permission to those who were squashed and crushed under religious red tape and protocol.

"The gates of my affection will suddenly fling wide open for them, and they will see Me, not as a hard taskmaster, CEO, or head bishop, but as Father and Friend, and suddenly, every seed and idea inside them that has been lying dormant will begin to germinate. Suddenly, innovation and creativity will spring forth, and hope-deferred will lift.

"When was the last time my people boldly came to the throne? Religion has created a minefield of impossible hurdles to get to Me, but I am not like that. It has created a mindset of unworthiness that has stopped people from encountering Me and even longing for Me to make them feel known. To replace encounters, religion has instead made an intellectual idol out of Me, and I am removing it from the Church in this season, and My wild ones will overturn the tables and restore My presence again!

"They will be the brokers of Heaven's storehouse for this hour. They will be the ones who lead the Church back into My domain and open up the forgotten storehouses of access and authority they have forgotten existed. They will take the empty-handed and hopeless into My house and put back hammers in the hands of reformers who had theirs stolen, songs back into the mouths of worshipers who were shut down, books and pens into the hands of the scribes, and restore the voice of the Church where she has been silenced and voiceless. At first, it is going to feel foreign as they hear the sound of their voices rising again and seeing the powerful impact of their mantles upon darkness and injustice, but this is the awakening of My Church in the revelation of who they are in me!"

THE CONVERGENCE SEASON & THE LEGACY OF LAID DOWN LOVERS

"They need to know that I am so proud of them. I know it hasn't been an easy road to walk, and at times, it has felt like I have abandoned them or dealt them an unfair hand, but *now* it will all make sense why I made them the way they are. *This* is the moment that every season converges together, and they finally see the purpose in the pain and the pressing that has turned into power and anointing to break yokes of bondage and set captives free.

"Watch them now, running out of the wilderness, out of the hiding, out behind the facade of other roles that were limiting them and keeping them at bay. Watch now as My wild ones begin to emerge from all walks of life and all streams. I can see the look in their eyes as they are right now standing to their feet. This is worship to them, not a task. This is the life of laid down lovers, not the objectives of a servant. These are My friends and My Spirit is in them, upon them for this magnificent hour of the unveiling of the Bride, the great *turning* of hearts, the harvest at hand."

THE WAITING IS OVER

This word was like a key in my hand to turn on the ignition of the commissioning movement of exiles and pioneers who have been in hiding and bring them to the frontlines. The waiting is truly over, and God is now revealing a hidden remnant that are called for such a time as this. Are you ready?

> *And to present her to himself as a radiant church, without stain or wrinkle or any other blemish, but holy and blameless* (Ephesians 5:27).
>
> *"'But I will restore you to health and heal your wounds,' declares the Lord, 'because you are called an outcast, Zion for whom no one cares'"* (Jeremiah 30:17).
>
> *Who is this coming up from the wilderness leaning on her beloved?* (Song of Songs 8:5).
>
> *You will be known as Repairers of the Cities and Restorers of Communities* (Isaiah 58:12 TPT).

PROPHETIC SURVIVAL TIP

Please own this word. Recognize yourself somewhere in it and let it be your cry in this season that your waiting time is over. Begin to shake off the dust from your mantle and shine up your hammer because the sidelines can no longer have you.

CAMPFIRE PRAYER

Lord, here I am. Here is my heart and my life. Use me. Have all of me. This is the moment my whole life has been leading to, and I don't want it to pass me by. So, here I am. Do what you want, in Jesus' name.

CHAPTER 23

The Wave of Reformation

The yearning to know what cannot be known, to comprehend the incomprehensible, to touch and taste the unapproachable, arises from the image of God in the nature of man. Deep calleth unto deep, and though polluted and landlocked by the mighty disaster theologians call the Fall, the soul senses its origin and longs to return to its source. —A.W. Tozer

In December 2009, I had an encounter where I was shown a coming reformation to the Church that would change everything for the Body of Christ. It was clear that God was bringing a dramatic shift that would awaken and revive those in slumber and remove the stale and stagnant form we had placed like concrete around a God who can't be defined by our finite understanding. This reformation was poised like a tsunami wave of love and power that was about to send ripples warning the Church of its impending impact. I was undone witnessing it, and my life has never been the same since.

But seven years to the week of this encounter, I had another encounter. In it, God revealed to me that there was another kind of wave coming. It was a surge and influx, an emerging of sorts of the agents of reformation that would be positioned, not just to administer the new regime of Heaven, but to be models of the gates and doors to let the King of Glory in!

But who are these agents of reformation? I believe there is a unique remnant God is commissioning in this hour. The remnant are the exiles, the outcasts and marginalized, the displaced and forgotten! They are the ones who march to a different drum and will be given a blueprint for a season of the Church to come. These are the ones who tried desperately to fit in the mold when God had already busted them out!

During the transitioning years of reformation, many of these pioneers fell into disillusionment and disappointment, not understanding how and why they didn't fit anymore, not realizing God had placed upon them a powerful mantle for a season to come. But now, I believe is the kairos moment we have been waiting for, where the key turns in the lock and the door opens.

THE SPECIALISTS HAVE ARRIVED ON THE SCENE

I remember the moment I had an epiphany that changed my whole world, well at least how I saw my whole world. It was the moment I realized that I wasn't the problem or part of a problem, but I was the solution. God wasn't punishing me in making me the way He had, nor were all the rejections meant to make me hurt and bitter, but they were meant to preserve me for something unique and incredible. He had been keeping me and training me for a coming season, where I would need to be untangled from the institution enough that I was free to follow His leading without any stops or gate checks.

He wanted me pure and separated from the allure of religion's appetites and untethered from a systemic way of living that disabled me from embarking on the journey of true Kingdom living. You, too, have come a long way to find yourself here at this point. Maybe you're still detaching, maybe still unlearning and still being prepared, but you are beginning to realize the same thing I did. You are not the problem. You have been created as an agent of change. You are the answer to something the earth is crying out for. You are not only part of the mightiest move of the Spirit the earth has seen, but you *are* the move! This is your quest. This is your moment.

DEEP IS CALLING

Waves remind me of my days surfing with my friends on the Sunshine Coast and Gold Coast in Australia. We would go on these extreme surf and camping trips, where we left with barely any money or idea of where we were going. We would just drive, find a location, surf, talk about Jesus, and talk to Jesus. They were some of my most treasured memories. It was a wild adventure, and Jesus was in the middle of it. That's the adventure I feel like Jesus wants to take you on, where He and you journey into the unknown together, where pressures and weights from the world just fall away, and existence simply becomes about Him and you and nothing else. Now that we have established that premise, let's begin.

I can't even tell you how many dreams and visions of waves I have had over the years. Too many to count, and if you are prophetic, I'm sure you also have had one before. It seems to be part of our language, but have you ever wondered why? Is it the wildness? The rawness? Maybe, but waves also represent the move or moves of God, the flow of His Spirit, and yet I believe there has been an element we have missed. I saw the wave as God's power and might crashing against the shores of the earth. It was Heaven invading earth. But I didn't imagine that I was the wave, not until about five years ago.

One day, I had a vision where I saw a massive tsunami approaching the shorelines of nations, and it looked violent and daunting, as if it would cause damage if it collided with the approaching land. As I looked closer, though, I saw figures in the outlines of the waves. It was wild horses or *wild brumbies* as we call them in Australia. They were running like a stampede and with a fierceness in their eyes. That stampede was you and me. The wild ones were not rebelling against God but in formation *for* God. We are the new wave of the Spirit, and we look scary to religion. We are fierce and unstoppable, powerful and potent.

Throughout Bible history, God has continually used wild reformers as the front-liners, the first line of defense, the crazy and radical and unstoppable ones to storm the gates in times of great resistance, and as we do, we ignite others to the same call. Then the wave grows. When John the Baptist came on the scene, he didn't just prepare hearts for the Messiah's coming, he ignited a fire and a hunger in people that they didn't know before.

> *From the moment John stepped onto the scene until now, the realm of heaven's kingdom is bursting forth, and passionate people have taken hold of its power* (Matthew 11:12 TPT).

Reformers are contagious. They oppose the boxes and every man-made system that dares to defy God's freedom and power. When you get around them, they cause you to tap into a hunger and authority you didn't have before that moment, and they make you think, "Am I living in my full potential?" That's what *you* do to others!

But this is the key here. This is the wave you were always meant to catch because you are this wave. This is your moment. It's time to be part of this exciting move of wild brumbies, powerful voices, and mighty messengers for Jesus in your nation. Crash upon the shores of culture and be an inconvenience just like John was. In your wake won't be destruction, but a sea of awakened ones ready to ride and *be* the move of God with you back into the heart and intention of God and shaking the nations for Jesus!

RIDING THE WAVE

To catch a wave when surfing, you need to be intentionally paddling and positioning yourself perfectly to catch it. Timing it wrong will either cause you to miss it or get you dumped over with it. So it is with the move of the Holy Spirit. It's an art that many are right now learning to step into the *flow* of this current move and not operate or live independent of Him.

Ask Holy Spirit to help you ride the wave in this season and not miss what He is doing. In the wave is the rest you need to be able to keep going and the reset from the religion that has tried to wear you out.

Are you tired? Worn out? Burned out on religion? Come to me. Get away with me and you'll recover your life. I'll show you how to take a real rest. Walk with me and work with me—watch how I do it. Learn the unforced rhythms of grace. I won't lay anything heavy or ill-fitting on you. Keep company with me and you'll learn to live freely and lightly. (Matthew 11:28–30 MSG).

BREAKING LIFELESS PROTOCOLS

In one of my favorite movies, *The Lord of the Rings: The return of the King*, there is a scene where Gandalf and Pippin travel to a city of men called "Minas Tirith" to warn them that war is coming and they need to prepare to fight and gather armies to join them.[1] Upon their arrival, the steward of the city rejects them (sound familiar yet?) and their claims and refuses to do anything. In response to this, and knowing this was a life and death situation, Gandalf and Pippin come up with the plan to go against the steward's wishes, access the war beacon of the city, and light it, which in turn causes all those guarding the other beacons all over the country to light theirs as well so that reinforcements are gathered. This was a bold move but under the circumstances was the needed move to save a city.

Now I'm not endorsing overriding authority figures, but I am endorsing following the leading of the Spirit to oppose stale and religious protocols and methods that defeat our main purpose in the first place. On that note, let me introduce you to the ultimate reformer and the best role model to learn from in this season. That's right, it's Jesus! "But whoa! Hang on, Nate, wasn't Jesus God, not some crazy reformer?"

Actually, the Bible says that Jesus was a forerunner and pioneer, which are both major components of the reformational life. Read Hebrews 6:20 and Hebrews 2:10. But before we go any further we better define what reformation actually is:

- Is it breaking down religious systems?
- Is it offending people who are stuck in a rut?
- Is it being loud and opinionated?
- Is it telling people off who are blind?

THE CHIROPRACTIC CALL

The word for *reformation* is the Greek word *diorthosis* and is only found in the New Testament twice. The first time it is used is in Acts 24:2 when Paul was brought before Felix the governor of Judea and Samaria to answer to his crimes. Turtullus the law-yer praised Felix by saying, *"Your Excellency, through your wise leadership we have lasting peace and reforms that benefit the people."*

In this context, we are viewing reformation in a worldly stan-dard as Felix was not reforming on behalf of God but according to man's standards. Felix was reforming Judea to look like Rome essentially, but it does raise a clear point regarding reforma-tion. Reformation is the re-forming of a place, people, or society according to another standard. In the Kingdom, what does that look like? Making Earth look like Heaven.

The second time reformation is mentioned is in Hebrews 9:10–11, which talks about the old way of worship and ceremonies that applied under the law but was made obsolete when the *diortho-sis* had come to remove the man-made from their belief system. Wow! This is exact opposite of the first mention.

The word *diorthosis* also means "straightening" literally and metaphorically as an orthopedic straightening, a making straight, or restoring to its natural and normal condition. For instance, something which in some way protrudes or has got out of line is shaped back into its *original design*.

So, the very foundational concept of reformation is to bring the Church back to her original design, and that's what Jesus did. Jesus was the greatest reformer because He settled a debt that the sin in the garden had accumulated. He was restoring us back to the garden while simultaneously leading us forward as a pioneer or forerunner does. That's the life of the reformer!

Jesus has this unstoppable knack that you may relate to in that, everywhere He went, He constantly "reformed" whether by His action or by speech. He constantly offended the Pharisees, not because He was there to upset people, but He was there to upset expired and outdated systems. When He read the scroll in the synagogue in Luke 4, He couldn't help but to say, *"This was fulfilled before you today,"* and made Himself a heretic in their eyes. He told them He would destroy the temple (their most beloved symbol of connection to God) and rebuild it in three days, which was His way of speaking of His death and resurrection. He said to His own followers that they would have to eat His body and drink His blood (speaking of His death on the cross).

Jesus was on a mission to usher in a new way and a new Kingdom covenant, and in that mission, it meant that tradition had to be broken, and He was the perfect vessel for the job, and so are you.

SEEING WHAT OTHERS DON'T SEE

I can see a reformer a million miles away. While reformers come in all sizes and packages, they tend to wear a different set of glasses than others wear, and these glasses require training to use them well. It reminds me of the *Spider-Man 2* movie (have you figured out I like sci-fi yet?), where Peter Parker is given the late Tony Starks's special artificial intelligence glasses that control his whole database, military system, and arsenal called *EDITH*.[2] In the beginning, Peter is excited to use them because they give him special abilities, but he soon realizes after he almost blew up a bus that he has to learn to use them first.

Reformers see the gaps. They see what others don't see, and while this is a gift and special anointing, to the untrained it can be less than a gift and more frustrating and destructive to those around them.

After my 2009 encounter, my eyes were opened to both the *potential* (what something was meant to or could be) and the *deficit* (what it wasn't). I could see the systems and programs that were expired, the tired practices, and the gaps in the spiritual infrastructure of churches and ministries. One person who always dealt well with me was Katherine Ruonala. She knew I was a wildcard and could see the gaps, but she didn't judge me for it. Instead, she still gave me opportunity to speak into the church as a whole, including the congregation, leaders, and also her personally. I'll forever be grateful for that season of learning to use my glasses correctly while not despising what God was doing in the house.

PUT ON YOUR GLASSES

Has religion made you put your glasses away? Has it made you ashamed to see the way you do or convinced you that you operating in a critical spirit? Here's the test:

- Do you despise religion but love the Church?
- Do you see the shortcomings and issues but also see the beauty?

Then you are a reformer.

PROPHETIC SURVIVAL TIP

Own the way you see that's different. Be proud of those peculiar glasses because they see what others don't. You are a specialist for a problem that only a specialist can see, diagnose, and fix.

CAMPFIRE PRAYER

Father, thank You for making me this way. I see now how You haven't given me this call to alienate me but to use me powerfully to see the Church come back to what matters. I give my life to be part of this wave of reformers arriving on the scene, in Jesus' name.

NOTES

1. Peter Jackson, *The Lord of the Rings: The Return of the King,* New Line Cinema, 2003.
2. Laura Ziskin, *Spider-Man 2,* Columbia Pictures, 2004.

CHAPTER 24

The Ark Has Moved

I will become even more undignified than this!
—2 Samuel 6:22

At the beginning of last year, God told me that the ark was moving and asked me if I would move with it. This was before Covid was even a thing, so I didn't know quite what He meant at the time, but I said *yes* regardless. I had this overwhelming sense that things were about to get bumpy, and He wanted me to hang on to Him for the ride.

When God spoke to me about the ark, we were in the process of packing up our house in Australia to prepare to move, but we also had some major things to organize in the USA. We hadn't finalized everything and wondered if we were to delay the trip and just get everything settled. Then Christy had a dream one night of a March calendar showing all dates crossed out except March 10. We knew God was saying to go on that date and no later. On March 10, we flew into San Francisco, and only a few days later flights were being turned away and the borders closed. We instantly felt a massive shift. It was as if the old wineskin burst and the new began.

Churches were forced to close their doors, and suddenly social media was inundated with live videos in the absence of face-to-face church. I felt as though I was living out my visions from back in 2009, where God showed me what reformation would look like. The four walls were emptying. Home churches were springing up like fires around the nations, and fields and parks were becoming gathering places. Two things became clear:

- The ark definitely moved.
- It was *go time* for the reformers.

You see, anytime God shifts the program, you will be guaranteed that He sends His reformers in to manage the transition. Over the last few decades, the goal posts have pretty much stayed the same in the Church. Not many of us can remember a time where the Church was in such a unique place as right now, which means that reformers have never been more needed than right now.

The ark has moved, and the Church hasn't known what to do. But God is commissioning His specialists today who have been in the sidelines. They are pregnant with strategies and ideas that carry the fresh wind of God upon them. They have new eyes, fresh perspectives, and creativity and scope beyond the growing pains of moving into a new era and the new wineskin and beyond the storms of transition. This is what you have been created for, after all the years of wandering in obscurity, trying to figure out what your purpose was, suddenly you are here with your tools in hand, ready to join the taskforce of the hour.

Reformers are the transition specialists because transition has been their wilderness experience. They can write the book on it and give you tips on tourist hotspots. They are anointed to be the cleanup team because they aren't afraid of mess and they are the damage response unit that has been gifted to know how to move forward in very precarious situations. What's their secret? They move with the ark. The ark is where the blessing is. The ark abides in God's presence.

David knew that, above his call to be king, he must steward what mattered to God. While Saul was driven by resources, assets, and land, David was led by the Presence and had his sights set on the gaze of the Father and his interests in establishing the tabernacle, worship, and advancing spiritually as a nation.

DANCING THE ARK BACK TO ITS RIGHTFUL PLACE

Let's look at the story of David's dancing before the ark of the covenant in 2 Samuel 6:14–22.

Wearing a linen ephod, David was dancing before the Lord with all his might, while he and all Israel were bringing up the ark of the Lord with shouts and the sound of trumpets. As the ark of the Lord was entering the City of David, Michal daughter of Saul watched from a window. And when she saw King David leaping and dancing before the Lord, she despised him in her heart. They brought the ark of the Lord and set it in its place inside the tent that David had pitched for it, and David sacrificed burnt offerings and fellowship offerings before the Lord. After he had finished sacrificing the burnt offerings and fellowship offerings, he blessed the people in the name of the Lord Almighty. Then he gave a loaf of bread, a cake of dates and a cake of raisins to each person in the whole crowd of Israelites, both men and women. And all the people went to their homes. When David returned home to bless his household, Michal daughter of Saul came out to meet him and said, "How the king of Israel has distinguished him-self today, going around half-naked in full view of the slave girls of his servants as any vulgar fellow would!" David said to Michal, "It was before the Lord, who chose me rather than your father or anyone from his house when he appointed me ruler over the Lord's people Israel—I will celebrate before the Lord. I will become even more undignified than this.

This story to me wasn't just about bringing the ark back to its rightful place, but it demonstrated a reformational move to recover and restore what was *out of place*, and David knew this was his primary mission.

What we can learn about reformation from this story:

- Reformation isn't an activity or religious profession but an act of worship.
- When ministry and service become about obedience and worship, it removes the desire to worry about reputation.
- Reformation is warfare.
- Reformation is full abandonment to God above the ways and thoughts and fear of man.

I love how David said "I can be so much more undignified than this." It's like saying, "Do you think that was the highest mark of my praise and adoration for God? I can look even more foolish for Him!" This passage has forever marked my life. It's all about Him. Nothing else. Reformers only have Jesus in their sights.

I have had those moments in my life more times than I can count, where you can feel judgment and people gasping at what to you is an act of worship. But it shouldn't ever stop you. This is your life's call.

THE MARK OF THE LAID DOWN LOVERS

Many have been in this same space feeling the pull of the wild, David-worshiper path light up through the unknown and facing the opposition of those who don't see the worship. They see the broken protocols and the defiance of religious norms, but this is as honest as it gets. This is raw-hearted devotion to Jesus and nothing else. I see worshipers and laid down lovers throughout my travels, and then I see the territorial leaders trying desperately to "police" them and shut them down like a game of "whack a mole." And my heart is always so grieved by it. I feel like saying, "Do you see who they are? Yes, they have rough edges, but so did you. Yes, they are the unlikely, but so were you!"

Many choose to stay with the tried-and-true or camp around the past move of the Spirit, the old wave, but few choose to abandon everything for the new wave. Reformers go for the new wave. They aren't in this for a desk or title, a front row seat or a VIP car park. They are pursuers of Jesus, so that's their motivation. They are the ones who can't be shackled anymore. They won't be bought for a price, and these unlikely ones are right now erupting seemingly out of nowhere with an undignified composure and a fire in their eyes.

RESTORING ALL THINGS

There are two words that are often interchangeable with "reform" in most Bible transitions: *restore* and *repent*.

> *"If my people, who are called by my name, will humble themselves and pray and seek my face and turn from their wicked ways, then I will hear from heaven, and I will forgive their sin and will heal their land"* (2 Chronicle 7:14).
>
> *From that time on Jesus began to preach, "Repent, for the kingdom of heaven has come near"* (Matthew 4:17).
>
> *Jesus replied, "To be sure, Elijah comes and will restore all things"* (Matthew 17:11).

Read those two verses with the word *reform* in them. Can you see the pattern? This is God's heart—to reform *all* things and bring *all* things back to where they were before they were defiled or taken off course. We must reform to see the Kingdom of Heaven. The world is always wanting us to have baggage and be taken this way and that, but the reformational heart of God is for us to come back to our roots. Reformation brings us:

- Back to our first love, rekindling intimacy.
- Back to what matters and removes what doesn't.
- Back to the beginning where things were new and fresh.
- Back to the place of purity and removed from other influences.

WE ARE THE GUARD RAILS NOT THE POLICE

I remember getting lost when I was five at a local fair. For a while, I ran around asking people to help me find my mum. I was scared and worried I would never find her, until I remembered what she said to do if I ever got lost: go back to the seating area where people ate their lunch. As soon as I ran back, my mum was there waiting for me to find her. In the same way, reformers bring us back when we are lost. They are the standard, the plumbline, and the guard rails in case we ever venture too far to the left or right.

Reformers are the bellringers of a new day and constantly point the Church back to the news headlines of Heaven. They confront the distractions and expose the diversions and demonic paths of derailment that the Church often takes when she moves away from the heart of God. Reformers bring us back there.

It's time you stood up and led the Church back. This is your mission if you choose to accept it.

PROPHETIC SURVIVAL TIP

Make sure your motivation is worship and wanting to please God, not trying to be a rebel for shock value. That never changes anything, but a people who live passionately with their faces to Heaven will shift the course of history.

CAMPFIRE PRAYER

Father, I am following You wherever You go. This is worship to me. It's my life of abandon to seek You and do what pleases Your heart. Lead me and I will go. Show me where You are going and what You are moving upon, and I will leave everything behind for it, for Your glory, in Jesus' name.

CHAPTER 25

Hammer & Oil

You have been fashioned like a war-hammer for the greatest days of reformation the earth has seen.
—Nate Johnston

The Word of the Lord came to me strong one morning, "I am releasing My war-hammers into the earth! I have been forging them in secret, fashioning them through the fires of opposition and hardship, and now they are going to be a weapon of reformation in My hand for the hour!"

Then I saw a vision of the Lord taking all the conflict, chaos, warfare, accusation, slander, betrayal, pressure, crushing, and demonic assignments that had come against God's people and using it all to forge weapons of warfare—mighty hammers that would be used for the Kingdom.

I saw the intense opposition that drove many to their breaking point, but now they were rising up with a new strength and authority, commissioned as God's *breakers* in the earth.

> *Every warrior's boot used in battle and every garment rolled in blood will be destined for burning, will be fuel for the fire* (Isaiah 9:5).

I saw them rise with a strange and unusual instinct to oppose the things that had been robbing them, others, and the Church from their inheritance.

These reformers were standing up and finally accepting that they were not weak and powerless but a weapon of war that God was going to move through in the years to come.

You are my hammer and weapon of war: with you, I break nations in pieces; with you, I destroy kingdoms (Jeremiah 51:20 ESV).

THE ROLE OF THE WAR-HAMMERS

The war-hammers are coming to hammer out the kinks and the bumps in the Church. They will take the old, worn-out, bent, scratched, and dull blades in the Body of Christ and hammer these into shape. They will tear down religious idols and structures and throw them into the pit. They will take down the giants and the spiritual opposition that has been threatening the Church but has not been dealt with.

They will be unafraid to speak and expose the lies of the enemy who is trying to cast a veil over the earth and silence the Church.

They will break up the ground, smashing weak foundations and establishing new and strong foundations to stand on.

They will expire and retire the old system, wineskin, language, and infrastructure of the old move and introduce new infrastructure, building tools, and supplies for the new thing God is building.

They will bring new plans and blueprints to build God's new era projects, and they will have the wisdom and know-how to do it.

RISE UP WAR-HAMMERS

If you have been feeling the intense pressure in the last few years, the crushing, the refining, the purifying, and the heart test, mark my words—like the pulling back of an arrow, God is about to release the trigger and fire you into places of *influence and impact*. Those who have stood their ground are about to see the fruit of going low (buying low) when others didn't and when the opposition was at its highest and when the enemy took them to their breaking point.

You are about to see what happens to those who set their face like flint in the storm! "Watch them crumble!" the enemy said, but you *did not* crumble. You may have felt the heaviest blows of your life and are needing refreshing, but look! You have been fashioned like a war-hammer for the greatest days of reformation the earth has seen. What you thought was your breaking was not the end of the story. It was only the beginning!

ALL HAMMER & NO LOVE—THE MISSING PIECE

So, as we have been learning, the heart condition or posture greatly affects what the fruit of all your reforming looks like. I wish I knew this years ago when I was all hammer, hammer, hammer. I would swing that thing as often as I could in the name of being a reformer, but I kept wondering why my fruit wasn't always what I was hoping it would be.

When I first started swinging my reformational hammer, I was a little careless. I loved the Church, but I suddenly saw the weak areas and expired practices and protocols that were keeping her stuck in the past. I could see where she was ineffective, powerless, and redundant. I took religious license to swing my hammer and say Jesus Christ endorsed it. This is the same mentality that has started so many religious wars over the centuries. People who used Scripture but with the wrong heart. It's a tragedy that there are many amazing and gifted prophetic people out there who are using their reformational call to accuse and assassinate other Christians and tear them down in the name of God. From the outside now, I can see how it was perceived. I was young and passionate and often spoke from a place of brash, fiery passion instead of wisdom. I felt the Lord's heart that He detested these things, but I did it know how to use my hammer well. I was creating damage and carnage for the sake of being obedient.

Then one day, God revealed a missing piece that I didn't know I needed. He said to me, "Nate, I need you to love just as much as you swing your hammer," and I was convicted deeply.

"But how do I love while I tear down?" I asked myself.

Jesus hit the nail on the head when He said He didn't come to destroy life but to bring it. How does that apply to you and me? What if we need to expose something bad?

LEARNING TO BE THE REFORMER WITH THE LORD'S HEART

Ecclesiastes 3:3 says there's *"a time to kill and a time to heal, a time to tear down and a time to build."* Safe to say, I was on a learning journey to discover the beautiful marriage between the tearing down and the rebuilding, and maybe you are as well.

Reformers are the guard rails of the Church in her journey. They are the guides on the trail that help the Church not to fall or slip off the side of the cliff or be led down the wrong path. This role has great weight and responsibility, so for that to happen, we need to be on the right path and track ourselves.

I've heard it said that a false prophet is just a loveless prophet, and I believe that's true—not because they are wrong in what they say but because it's not just their words that matter but the spirit in which they are speaking them.

> And though I have the gift of prophecy, and understand all mysteries and all knowledge, and though I have all faith, so that I could remove mountains, but have not love, I am nothing (1 Corinthians 13:2 NKJV).

I have seen some of the most gifted, prophetic people lose their love and become robots who speak accurately through a gift but are no longer dispensing the oil. They flash their PayPal up on the screen and promote their next book, but they haven't been at the threshing floor in a long time.

Jesus said He only did what He saw His Father doing, and we should do the same. If we prophesy without the love of the Father, then what do we expect the fruit to be? Information? Isn't that what psychics do?

When I was working for local government, many of my colleagues were wiccans, witches, and those in the New Age. God gave me such a love for them, and because I loved them, relating to them wasn't weird because I loved them. That was one of the best seasons of my life because I got to learn how to love purely and honestly without the religious pressure to make a sale, so to speak. It gave God a place to work in amazing ways.

It was common for me to see my colleagues talking to people and trying their psychic abilities on them. I would hear it in phone calls and out and about. Then when I had the opportunity and they agreed to it, I would share what God was speaking to them and His presence would show up, and people would start tearing up. It constantly messed up the enemy's system.

One day after a long drive with a colleague, we arrived back at work, and she stopped me and said, "Can I ask you something?"

"Sure!" I said.

She continued, "How come when you speak what your God is saying to people it feels clean and pure and when I do my readings it feels muddy or dirty?"

My answer was simpler than she expected. "It's love," I replied.

THE WRONG KIND OF REFORMATION

What are some wrong kinds of reformation, some counterfeits or diversions?

In the last chapter, I spoke of the Roman reformation that was man-made, full of man's ideas of what should change, and not God's. It was the reformation to establish the Roman kingdom in the place of what was there before. It was the tearing down of the old to construct something man-made.

Reformation man's way can often look and smell like true Kingdom reformation, but you may have to look closer to see its true origins and spirit.

"Lord, do you want us to call fire down from heaven to destroy them?" was the famous phrase spoken by the disciples James and John who Jesus called *the sons of thunder*. He loved their wildness and *their* ferocity for the Kingdom and how they were go-getters. They were like the bouncers of the Dozen, and Jesus probably loved their raw passion and devotion, their rough edges, and their wit. They were His top students in His reformer school, but what they didn't know in this moment was that they were about to get a memorable schooling moment.

> *Jesus rebuked them sharply, saying, "Don't you realize what comes from your hearts when you say that? For the Son of Man did not come to destroy life, but to bring life to the earth"* (Luke 9:55 TPT).

They were using their hammer, but they were missing a key element.

The wrong kind of reformation looks like it is solving real problems, but because it is off its axis, it does not result in transformation or change, just more mess and division. In fact, the wrong kind of reformation fans the flames of dysfunction in the name of God.

Examples of the wrong kind of reformation are:

- Using man's intellect, culture, and ideas to solve problems by criticizing something to get there.
- Dealing with social issues, injustices the wrong way, without the redeeming blood of Jesus.
- Fighting fire with fire, hurling insults back to settle a case.

In essence, the wrong kind of reformation is the one that doesn't need Jesus at the center, and it comes with accusation against people and people groups instead of against demonic systems.

Real reformation begins when you stop trying to battle personalities and people and start battling principalities.

RIGHT KIND OF REFORMATION NEEDED RIGHT NOW

True reformation, while quite confronting, is still honors what God has done. It bridges the old to the new and removes impurities in between in the process. Right now, we need the bridge builders.

If you think I've come to set aside the law of Moses or the writings of the prophets, you're mistaken. I have come to bring to perfection all that has been written. Indeed, I assure you, as long as heaven and earth endure, not even the smallest detail of the Law will be done away with until its purpose is complete (Matthew 5:17–18).

True reformation realizes it needs the old to build upon and establish the new. It's reinforcing what Jesus came to restore, not creating something that isn't biblical. True reformation is not dishonoring, but it is confronting!

True reformation is bringing the Church back to true north again. It is simply *re*-forming what was already formed by God.

Reformation means to bring something back to its original condition. It's seeing the pure state of someone or something and contending to bring it back to that place.

When Paul confronted the Galatians, he said, *"Oh you foolish Galatians!"* He was seeing who they truly were and bringing them back to the purity of the message and call, and he did it all in love.

True reformation sounds like the Father correcting and guiding his sons and daughters, not the nasty shouts and screams of a master disapproving of his hired workers. Can you see the difference? This should change everything about the way we speak and reform. This should be our cornerstone and our source of swinging our hammer. It must be from the heart of the Father who wants to see His Bride uncluttered and moving forward, unstuck from all that binds and free from all bondages.

Emerging voices, we are voice of the Lion, but we are also the sound of the Lamb. Can we be both? Absolutely!

We can love those who walk in sin while hating the sin. We can love what God is doing in others while not endorsing their double standards. Let me say this loud and clear: Love is *not* tolerating and excusing dysfunction in the name of loving like Jesus. Real love is pulling people out of it. The tension or the reformational call is loving well while destroying the chains around their feet.

It's weeping with those who are mourning while untangling the ropes of death around their feet.

WE CAN ONLY CHANGE WHAT WE LOVE

We only can change what we are willing to love, whether a city, a people, or the Church. We need to shift out of fighting personalities and start evicting principalities. That's our role.

Earlier last year, I was being schooled in another level of this. God spoke to me and said, "Nate, its the hammer and the oil, and you use them together."

What did He mean by the oil? The oil represents many things, but I knew He meant healing and restoring.

> *"Is not my word like fire," declares the Lord, "and like a hammer that breaks a rock in pieces?"* (Jeremiah 23:29).
>
> *And they were casting out many demons and were anointing with oil many sick people and healing them* (Mark 6:13 NASB1995).

Reformers are commissioned to a unique task that creates a tension. Reformers break down religious and demonic strongholds and bring healing and restoring. They aren't destroyers of people but of ideas, strongholds, principalities, and counterfeit moves. When it comes to the Body of Christ, reformers are the bridge builders who lead us from one level of glory to another.

Remember my vision of the wave? The wave is both *destructive* and *healing*. It's a shock to the system, yes. It's going to come in and tear down everything that isn't rooted, but it's also going to unleash healing and freedom if you decide to yield to the Holy Spirit in this season. That's your commission, mighty one.

Have you found it difficult to operate in both heavy conviction and love? Which one do you naturally swing toward? There are three possible results. depending on your inclination:

- More hammer, little love = People hear truth but may disconnect because they feel attacked.
- Less hammer, great love = People feel loved, but truth wasn't represented well enough to convict their hearts.
- Equal hammer and love = People feel loved, built, and supported while lies are being exposed and error is being removed.

Are you ready to walk in both power and love? Truth and deep heart-embracing impact? Then let's go!

PROPHETIC SURVIVAL TIP

Put on your love before you swing your hammer! Create a pathway of demonic destruction in your wake as you tear down, but know it's in your ability to love that you build! Remember that you aren't called to be "Wreck It Ralph," known for what you destroy. You want to be known for what you correct and build.

CAMPFIRE PRAYER

Lord, give me a love for people and even systems and institutions that often frustrate me. Give me such a heart for the areas I am called to reform so that I do it with Your heart and not out of a heart of disgust or judgment. Help me flow with Your healing oil in Jesus' name.

CHAPTER 26

The Changing of the Guard

Gideon and the hundred men with him reached the edge of the camp at the beginning of the middle watch, just after they had changed the guard. They blew their trumpets and broke the jars that were in their hands.
—Judges 7:19

"Here they come! The unlikely ones, the misfits, the overlooked! Here they come! They will be like David, the unlikely king, the unlikely warrior, the unlikely victor, the ones who were overlooked and called useless and hopeless. Here they come! They are the carriers of the pure voice of the Lord leading the Church back to the feet of Jesus. They are the igniters and fire-starters of revival in the nations. They are the ones who have been silenced and constantly muzzled and sent back into the wilderness by the religious voices or the insecure. They are the ones who have been broken and shipwrecked, pushed to the side, and underestimated, but *now here they come*! The wild ones are rising. The undignified ones like David who had nothing but a harp and a sling, but they will take down giants, smash through immoveable doors and walls, command mountains to move, and lead the Church forward into victory!

God is resetting the affections of the Body of Christ, and He is using these unlikely heroes to lead the Body of Christ out of dysfunction and back into focus with the heart of the Father. They are the river of wild horses who aren't in union with the culture of the world but are in-sync and flow with the river of the Spirit of God that is building, rising, and flowing into the nations. They are the cool drink of water to a dry and thirsty land, and we are seeing them rise! No, this is not an hour to stop your flow, no this is not an hour to cater to the half-truths of the silencing agenda of the insecure, but it's an hour to raise your voice and release what you have been carrying into the earth!

LEANING ON THE BELOVED

I see the generation rising right now out of the wilderness for such a time as this.

> *Who is this one? Look at her now! She arises out of her desert, clinging to her beloved. When I awakened you under the apple tree, as you were feasting upon me, I awakened your innermost being with the travail of birth as you longed for more of me* (Song of Songs 8:5 TPT).

I see the ones who have been in hiding and in waiting, the ones who have been taken out and decommissioned, the ones who have been through painful seasons of trauma and woundedness, the ones who have lost all hope. They have been outcasts, abused, or just didn't fit the box, but God has been awakening them and *commissioning* them! And now all of Heaven is singing this song, cheering them on, and the Father is speaking this over you!

Song of Songs 8:5 is so pregnant with an activating message for so many right now. Let's break it down:

- *"Who is this one?"* They will be the *unheard*, never-before-seen ones stepping onto the scene.

- *"Look at her now!"* The Father Himself is cheering her on and sending wave after wave of love and approval over her.
- *"She arises out of her desert, clinging to her beloved."* These ones are coming out of their wildernesses, not tangled up with the world or with the past but clinging to Him!
- *"When I awakened you under the apple tree, as you were feasting upon me."* They have been in a season of intimacy and feasting on God's presence.
- *"I awakened your innermost being with the travail of birth as you longed for more of me."* They are in a season of birthing!

Recently the Lord began to speak into the process that many had been through and the moment they were about to enter into.

THE RE-IDENTITIFICATION

He said:

- "I am giving them a new ring and a robe. The old clothes, armor, and old glory needs to be removed."
- "I am removing past labels, words, titles, and witchcraft that were spoken over them."
- "I am giving them a new name like Abraham and Sarah. I am putting the *Ruach* in them again. It's the wind of My Spirit."
- "They are in a season of a fresh infilling, of fresh rivers of living water flowing, which is purifying stagnant waters/ still and barren wombs."

- "They will hear My voice louder than the world's. I am making them untouchable and unreachable by the noise of the world."
- "They will not be professional ministry career people but simply full-time lovers of God who desire Me more than anything the world or man could offer them."

THE HEALING & SEALING

- "They have been through the final shaking off of the past season and healed of trauma, woundedness, religious abuse, witchcraft, betrayal, and bondage from the Jezebel spirit that sent many into the wilderness."
- "They will be unshackled from people's words and opinions, the fear of man, the political spirit, the politically correct mindset, the religious spirit, and culture."
- "They will not come under the Jezebel spirit in any way, shape, or form or tolerate anything that silences them or others."
- "They will be free from defilement/mixture or what the world calls *balance*. I call that double-minded, and they will not be on a fence."
- "They will carry My heart and be healers and restorers where others have tried and failed to bring restoration and healing."
- "I am going to use them to deconstruct all idols that the Church has constructed in My image."
- "They will be people of honor even though they have received double dishonor."

THE RE-ACTIVATION & RE-COMMISSIONING

- "They will be like Samuels who live for My voice alone and restore My voice to the land" (see 1 Sam. 3:1).
- "They will be water dispensers in a dry and thirsty land" (see Ps. 63:1).
- "They will be the fathers and mothers to a rising generation and join the family of God and the army of God together."
- "They will bring healing to orphans and be healers of the land" (see Malachi 4:5–6).
- "They will usher in the spirit of adoption."
- "They will know the *voice* of the Lord, not the voice of at the accuser so they will be used to *unite* not divide."
- "I am making them like sharp arrows" (see Isa. 49:2).
- "They will point the Church back to her original purpose— to intimacy, to the garden."
- "They will give back permission to a generation of those who have been controlled and stifled."
- "They will reveal Jesus in an *apocalyptic* time" (the Greek word that means to reveal and uncover).
- "They were born as specialists for such a time as this!"

He gives me words that pierce and penetrate. He hid me and protected me in the shadow of his hand. He prepared me like a polished arrow and concealed me in his quiver (Isaiah 49:2 TPT).

THIS IS THEIR MOMENT

In 2019. the Holy Spirit spoke to me in my sleep and warned me, "There's a changing of the guard coming, and those who pass the test will be those who drink." I was confused at first but oddly knew exactly what He meant.

We are witnessing that changing of the guard in the Body of Christ today. There have been role shuffles, demotions, promotions, and vacancies filled in epic proportions. There have been a refining and a redefinition of roles and the refueling of those who have come to the end of an old role in an old era.

> changing of the guard (noun)
>
> a ceremony during which the soldiers or other officials guarding a major government building or state residence, especially Buckingham Place in England, are replaced by a new shift.
>
> changing of the guard (noun)
>
> any situation in which an individual or group charged with a task or responsibilities in an organization is replaced by another individual or group.

The wild ones are the new guard that God is bringing on shift, not to usurp or override but to serve and usher in the new. But they are coming to bring the power of Heaven to roles in regions that topple the principalities that had been allowed to remain under the previous occupier of that role. This goes globally. God is placing reformational heavyweights in roles of influence and power to evict evil and bring restitution to the land. This is one of the core mandates of reformation. It's for redeeming the land and nations and bringing them back to their original design and purpose. Our love for America began this way. We began to have the Lord show us what He was doing and how He was restoring the land back its original roots, shutting down abortion, bringing the Bible back into schools, and removing all censoring so that the voce of the Church could rise to counteract the darkness.

GIDEON'S ARMY

One of the characteristics of this change of the guard is that God is refining His remnant. In Judges 7, Gideon was about to go into battle when God told him that he had too many men and that it would only cause them to boast after the battle. He wanted Gideon to defeat the enemy with the least men possible so they knew it could only be God who won the battle. This is how God reduced the number of men:

> So Gideon took the men down to the water. There the Lord told him, "Separate those who lap the water with their tongues as a dog laps from those who kneel down to drink." Three hundred of them drank from cupped hands, lapping like dogs. All the rest got down on their knees to drink. The Lord said to Gideon, "With the three hundred men that lapped I will save you and give the Midianites into your hands. Let all the others go home" (Judges 7:4–7).

In the change of the guard season, God separates those who drink and those who don't. He doesn't need 10,000 men, just His 300 who are His faithful lovers. The change of the guard in this season is sending the dry and burnt-out on religion to the rest zone for recuperation and detoxification. The former guard are the ones who have tried on their giftings, popularity, and titles but in that pursuit and pride have left their first love and dropped their authority and responsibility to impact their cities effectively. In their place, God's wild reformers are being sent to their new posts.

TARES & WHEAT

Jesus told them a parable about weeds that were planted alongside wheat;

*"He answered, 'This has to be the work of an enemy!'
"They replied, 'Do you want us to go and gather up all the weeds?' 'No,' he said. 'If you pull out the weeds you might uproot the wheat at the same time. Let them both grow together until the harvest. At that time, I'll tell my harvesters to gather the weeds first and tie them all in bundles to be burned. Then they will harvest the wheat and put it into my barn'"* (Matthew 13:28–29 TPT).

What I found out about these weeds called *tares* is that they look exactly like wheat until it's harvest time, for then they are easily distinguished because the wheat plants have heavy wheat kernels attached that weigh them down into a bowing position, whereas the weeds stay the same.

In this change of the guard, God is decommissioning those who have not been seeking His face (bowing) and those who no longer operate in the glory (weightiness), and He is setting His reformers in to new seats and roles for Kingdom impact.

ELIJAH'S MANTLE

One of the greatest change of the guard moments was when Elijah was taken up into the heavens. Elisha was bold and asked for double of the anointing that Elijah carried. Elijah said to him, *"If you see me when I am taken from you, it will be yours,"* and sure enough he did.

"You have asked a difficult thing," Elijah said, "yet if you see me when I am taken from you, it will be yours—otherwise, it will not." As they were walking along and talking together, suddenly a chariot of fire and horses of fire appeared and separated the two of them, and Elijah went up to heaven in a whirlwind. Elisha saw this and cried out, "My father! My father! The chariots and horsemen of Israel!" And Elisha saw him no more. Then he took hold of his garment and tore it in two. Elisha then picked up Elijah's cloak that had fallen from him and went back and stood on the bank of the Jordan. He took the cloak that had fallen from Elijah and struck the water with it. "Where now is the Lord, the God of Elijah?" he asked. When he struck the water, it divided to the right and to the left, and he crossed over (2 Kings 2:10–14).

The interesting thing to note here is that Elisha tore his own garment and tore it in two. Was it out of grief of seeing his spiritual father go? Possibly, but there was more to it than that. He was tearing the mantle he carried to make room for the new one—the double portion mantle he was promised. The changing of the guard can feel like a tearing away and a receiving all at the same time.

Signs you are being commissioned into new roles and mantles:

- You are suddenly pulled in a new direction and focus.
- You feel the tearing away of the old thing and mantle you used to wear.
- You don't seem to have the grace you used to have for a certain role or activity.
- You feel temporarily displaced or lost.
- God is expanding your influence and authority.
- You are receiving new revelation you aren't sure what to do with.

- You are beginning to notice a new anointing or grace in an area you didn't have before.
- You feel a fresh conviction/burning call for the new area and the pull to a new spiritual office.
- You feel like overnight you have shifted, and you aren't sure how to move forward.
- Doors are opening in areas you didn't ask for or expect.
- You feel your voice rising up to speak into things you didn't in the last season, and words feel like they carry weight they didn't in the last season.

Reformers this is your changing of the guard, commissioning moment where God is sending you into your new roles and capacities you didn't see coming. Are you ready to grab your new mantle and strike the water with it?

PROPHETIC SURVIVAL TIP

Be flexible and willing to go where God sends you and to take whatever post He gives you. And know this—when He calls you, He anoints you for it. Wear your jacket and use it!

CAMPFIRE PRAYER

Lord, mantle me for this purpose. Commission me for a life of being sent into the places that need me most, in Jesus' name.

CHAPTER 27

Reformational Messages, Roles, & Unusual Blueprints

Great moves of God are usually preceded by simple acts of obedience. —Steven Furtick

The life of a reformer is like a never-ending treasure hunt of clues, signs, strange experiences, divine moments, and encounters that all paint the picture God is wanting the reformer to broadcast. The challenge of this unique commission is that it can take a while to bring all the pieces together, connect the dots, and make sense of the elements, tools, and fragments of mission plans in your hand. It can often feel like the story of *Hansel and Gretel,* just following the next breadcrumb until you make it to your destination.

God really has called us to a unique path and given us a dynamic mandate, but what do you do when God gives you a mission, role, blueprint, conviction, or message that you haven't heard of before? Reformers are receivers of blueprints that haven't hit the headlines of Earth, yet they are given these blueprints to steward. I hope in this chapter you recognize that you aren't the only one who receives these strange messages and revelation and that you can boldly step into them without fear.

What I have found over the years is that God will use strange and unusual ways to get through to you or to get something to you. Here are just a few of the weird and wacky ways God has spoken to me (not mentioning the normal ways):

- Reoccurring signs over a period of time
- Numbers and number sequences
- Strange prophetic gifts given to me by strangers
- Animals, such as kookaburras, eagles, and butterflies
- Audible voices in my dreams giving me GPS coordinates, names, and instructions
- Strange, physical things happening to me, such as a sudden bloodshot eye before a major assignment (these were indicators of specific types of warfare)
- Complete songs given to me in my sleep that were used for major Kingdom exploits
- Warning dreams giving me names of people to avoid and situations to remove myself from
- Impartation dreams where I had hands laid on me, keys given to me, and healing from generals I have never met and I stepped into significant increase afterward
- Going into trances and opening up every door and cupboard in my house representing revelation being opened

What are some of the strange and unusual ways you have heard God speak to you? Before we really begin this chapter, I want to pray a simple impartation prayer over you because there's no point hearing all my stories; you need some of your own. Put your hands out and receive.

Lord, to the person reading this, I release the wonder of a child over them, where You restore innocence and child-like adventure and receptivity to the Spirit to where it was lost due to religious upbringing and conditioning. Unblock their natural and spiritual senses so they can perceive You in full, high , surround sound, immersive, taste, touch, and smell definition. I release over them the ability to hear You in nature, in the hustle and bustle, and in everything around them. Give them dreams of all kinds, encounters, warnings, and impartation dreams. Let them hear You audibly, see visions, and have the ability to unlock the mysteries of the blueprints You have given them, in Jesus' name!

Okay, now that that's been established, let's move on.

WAKING A DORMANT MESSAGE

In 2011, I received a message from a good friend of mine, Jodie Hughes, another Aussie living in the good old USA. She told me how she had a dream where God boomed loudly, "Nate Johnston has a *global message!*" She was shaken by it and had to tell me right away. When I read it, I was blown away but not excited initially because I was in the deep jungle of my prophetic process after encountering God in a *life-changing* way only a few years before.

For weeks and months later I kept asking God, "What is my global message?" I had no idea. The revelations that God had given me were only getting me in trouble when I shared them. They didn't seem to encourage people or give them insight like I wanted. I think between 2011 and 2014 I deleted my Facebook profile at least twenty times. I would post something that I felt the Holy Spirit upon and then receive 90 percent of posts by pastors and leaders, especially those I looked up to, who disapproved of what I was saying. It was discouraging!

UNLOCKING YOUR BULL'S-EYE

So, it was clear at that stage that my message was young and not ready. I hadn't quite defined it or understood all its facets, but it wasn't until I had a significant encounter that it *unlocked* the bullseye. By bull's-eye, I mean like an arrow is supposed to hit the mark. I needed that one element to fall into place for me to understand what my message was—to define it and then apply it.

One night as I was warming up bottles for my daughter Charlotte, I went into a powerful vision that felt real. I was sitting on a horse on a mountain, dressed in animal hide and metallic armor, I was overlooking a valley where there were tens of thousands of these wild warriors shouting and yelling and waving swords in the air. I simply heard God say, "Nate, who will raise them? Who will lead them?" I felt a shift in my heart from a passionate son or to that of a father, and in that moment, my global message was defined.

What was my global message? It was my story of sonship after having grown up in a broken home to discover the Father. It involved my being misunderstood by the Church and called a heretic and rebel and included my becoming a father who simply called in and raised up the reformers, rebels, and exiles out of the wilderness and into their destiny.

It wrecks my heart to even write these words because I know the journey many take in incubating such stories. Over the years, I have helped many people navigate a reformation calling, and I believe, if we can create more language around those who carry them, we can harness a generation who were never meant to be defined by the current culture or language. We must champion and support them to join the Bride of Christ as effective and powerful voices for the time we live in.

A TABOO TOPIC

When we first started sharing about Christy's breakthrough from depression, we were absolutely blown away by the response from people, as if we had shared something never heard of before. It wasn't that it was a new topic or issue, but people responded to the message because, in many churches and Christian circles, depression wasn't a popular or much discussed topic. Her Instagram following grew overnight as she spoke worth and value into women who had been through all and more of the same things she had been through, and messages were flooding in of breakthroughs and healings erupting all over the world as people read her posts. We were in shock, "I mean really God? Can you use social media this way?" we asked.

At the same time, I was seeing the same thing happening on the Periscope app with the most amazing healings taking place—everything from headaches to deliverance from demonic oppression. I was having the most accurate words of knowledge and seeing people from all religious backgrounds and even atheists come to know Jesus as I simply shared my message online. It was as if we were speaking a new language and people were hungry for more.

ARE PEOPLE REALLY LISTENING?

Before we move on, let's just hold up for a minute. When you have been through a hard life experience and your message or story is born, it can often feel unnatural and even surreal when people suddenly listen and hear what you have to say. I have also been on the other end of the spectrum where people don't listen at all, and that should never be an indicator of the value of your message because the more you own your message and run with it, the more people will begin to listen! Proverbs 18:16 says something interesting, *"A gift opens the way and ushers the giver into the presence of the great."*

The word *gift* here means "gift from God," so in essence this means that we aren't just storytellers who share our experiences, but we are messengers, brokers, or the delivery people to bring Jesus and Heaven's breakthrough power into the lives of those we tell our stories or messages to.

This encouraged us, and it should also encourage you, especially if you face initial kickback or opposition. Let me now share the other side of the story.

LET THE FRUIT SPEAK

Carrying a message may mean carrying it even when it doesn't make sense to people around you. The message John the Baptist carried wasn't popular to everyone. Jesus' message wasn't always popular either. At one point, many even walked away from Jesus because what He said confused and upset them. Carrying a message is not for the faint of heart but for those who are serious about being God's mouthpiece on the earth. Do you have what it takes?

The call of reformation, like pioneering, is putting your money where your mouth is. You often have to be willing to lay it all on the line for many years and face ridicule until what you speak bears fruit. The updates on social media and revelations God gave me were not popular back in 2011–2014, but something shifted in 2015. What was it? Fruit was growing, and even the greatest cynics can't deny fruit; in fact, they normally end up lining up to buy them in the end or saying they grew it themselves.

By their fruit you will recognize them. Do people pick grapes from thornbushes, or figs from thistles?

Likewise, every good tree bears good fruit, but a bad tree bears bad fruit (Matthew 7:16–17).

STRANGE ENCOUNTERS

Reformers are the ones who have the crazy stories people roll their eyes at when they are silly enough to share their latest dream or vision with them. That's exactly what Joseph did, and it landed him in a pit.

When I started having more reoccurring encounters and experiences, I would be so excited to tell people, but it only made me look like I had lost my marbles. Been there? Most of the Old Testament prophets were quirky like Jeremiah who used to passionately speak what God told him but was also known to hide his underwear under rocks. But perhaps the strangest prophet was Ezekiel who had a vision of four-faced creatures and then ate a scroll, went mute, and when he could finally speak, prophesied about mountains. Wow! Reformers have a tough gig!

A NEW LANGUAGE

When the disciples and those who were filled with the spirit in the upper room were heard singing and speaking in tongues, the people in the streets thought they were crazy.

Now, at that time there were Jewish worshipers who had emigrated from many different lands to live in Jerusalem. When the people of the city heard the roaring sound, crowds came running to where it was coming from, stunned over what was happening, because each one could hear the disciples speaking in his or her own language. Bewildered, they said to one another, "Aren't these all Galileans? So how is it that we hear them speaking in our own languages? 9 We are northeastern Iranians, northwestern Iranians, Elamites, and those from Mesopotamia, Judea, east central Turkey, the coastal areas of the Black Sea, Asia, north central Turkey, southern Turkey, Egypt, Libyans who are neighbors of Cyrene, visitors from all over the Roman Empire, both Jews and converts to Judaism, Cretans and Arabs. Yet we hear them speaking of God's mighty wonders in our own dialects!" They all stood there, dumbfounded and astonished, saying to one another, "What is this phenomenon?" But others poked fun at them and said, "They're just drunk on new wine" (Acts 2:5–13 TPT).

Imagine that moment when the Holy Spirit comes upon you so powerfully that you speak in a new language. That would have been wild (pardon the pun). But we need to remember the source of the new ideas and revelation and blueprints comes from Him. The person of the Holy Spirit is what causes us to bubble over.

But you will receive power when the Holy Spirit has come upon you; and you shall be My witnesses both in Jerusalem, and in all Judea and Samaria, and even to the remotest part of the earth. (Acts 1:8)

The word *receive* in this scripture is the Greek word *lambano*, which means to actively lay hold of, to take or receive, with the strong sense of seizing something forcefully compared to two other Greek words *dechomai* and *haireomai*, which mean to passively accept or receive. Reformers are receivers of the divine *now* topics and themes from Heaven, but I believe that not nearly as many who are called to carry these blueprints actually ever pick up their mission card and step into their calling.

Just as the Holy Spirit comes upon us forcefully and powerfully, you need to see this in light of how we receive revelation from the Holy Spirit. What He gives is powerful—like being plugged up to a power source attached to a lightning bolt. It's simply that dramatic and life changing because we become the carriers, the ink wells of Heaven that are used to write the heart of God into humanity!

DIVINE ANSWERS & SOLUTIONS

I always say that a prophetic gift is not meant to speak the problem. That's just telling the news, but reformers are created to carry the solutions and divine answers to every problem in life and every problem that the world is facing. We are the receivers dialed into Heaven to hear the strategies and solutions to every problem we see around us, and God is raising up reformational specialists to go into every sphere of influence to dispense those solutions.

When Jesus was teaching His disciples how to pray, He said for them to pray this:

> Manifest your kingdom realm, and cause your every purpose to be fulfilled on earth, just as it is in heaven (Matthew 6:10 TPT).

That's the mission of the reformer right there: to manifest (to display, make evident, or reveal to the eye) the blueprints of Heaven on the earth! These strategic blueprints are like letters in the mailroom of Heaven ready to be distributed and unpacked.

REFORMATIONAL INDICATORS

There are many ways to unpack your calling, and to make this practical, let's do a little exercise. Firstly, tap into your reformer's radar and think of something that ruffles your feathers and unsettles you or grieves you. It could be one of the following:

- Sex trafficking
- Abortion
- Lying politicians
- Demonic agendas weaved into social justice
- Worldly culture
- Deep darkness in Hollywood
- Values against the family

Whatever thing that grieves or unsettles you is probably an indicator of your mandate in its purest form. Now, what are some of the issues in the Church or the world that you feel you carry a reformational answer or message for? Maybe it's one of these:

- The lack of the Holy Spirit in churches
- Women not being accepted in ministry like men
- Progressive Christianity and woke ideology
- Critical race theory and true healing
- LBGT and gender perversion
- Education reform
- Church reform

What came to mind? Did you just realize what your bullseye is? What did you realize you are called to slap your jacket/mantle at? Let's go further.

REFORMATIONAL MISSION FIELDS

Now, let's look at some of the mission fields and frontlines God is sending His reformers to:

- Governmental positions in both state and federal levels
- Music and the arts
- Hollywood
- Local church leadership and striking the ground in cities
- Business and marketplace ministry
- Education reform
- Medicine and pharmaceutical
- Tech and innovation

What is the mission field you feel called to?

YOU HAVE PERMISSION

Commissioning begins with the encounter, the conception, the reception, and the acceptance of what God gives you. Then what He gives He authorizes you or gives you permission to walk in. The problem, however, is that many times we can be anointed, called, and able but because of religious conditioning, we fail to move into it as we have been taught that, unless it is approved ten times by the clergy or signed off by Father Jenkins, we are being rebellious or violating section 7b of the protocol.

The enemy knows the potency of you being free to dream and walk in freedom to God's will. He knows what you would do if you were unshackled and stepped into the doors in front of you. Summed up in a word, I would say this is the enemy's assignment of *restriction*.

Restriction means to "prevent, confine, or prohibit, or restrain, repress, or hedge in." In the Bible the word *restrict* is described by the Greek word *thlibo*, which means "oppressively afflict, confine, and restrict, and limit." It is often used to describe the affliction of the enemy.

We are hard pressed on every side, but not crushed; perplexed, but not in despair, persecuted, but not abandoned; struck down, but not destroyed (2 Corinthians 4:8–9).

We have known what it feels like to have our hearts squashed, but I believe that, where we are going, we need to *undo* this process and begin to walk in something God has always designed for us. We haven't fully been aware of or known about this. It's called the *permission of God*.

Permission means "the consent and authorization to accomplish something." In essence, it's the freedom for you to be able to do what God has placed inside you without fear of being squashed or undermined along the way. This is a foreign concept for those who have only known religious bondage, but it's crucial we step into it if we are wanting to see our destinies fulfilled.

I love the story of Jonathan in 1 Samuel 14, where he wanted to charge the Philistine camp at night and his armor bearer spoke God's heart to him, *"Do all that is in your heart, I am with you!"*

Wow! Have you ever heard God say those words to you before? This is what God is speaking over the Church now because she has been limited for far too long. How are we expected to see Heaven invade Earth if we don't even know what we have access to or what our inheritance is? Jesus "authorized" His disciples to operate in signs, wonders, and miracles, and we have that same charge. So basically, to fulfill the Great Commission and our reformation calling, we need to walk in the full permission of God, to dream with Him, and to follow Him with *all* restrictions off. No more security checks at the gate. No more sending off your destiny for the approval of the elite, just simply you dreaming with God and walking in the joy of watching God pave the way forward for you.

This is a new day of clarity and permission for you.

PROPHETIC SURVIVAL TIP

Your tool here is permission. Permission unlocks everything else, and you have it. Use it well and don't forget it when people tell you that you are off course. The Father approves you and has given you the mysteries of His heart to steward.

CAMPFIRE PRAYER

Holy Spirit, ignite my message and make it plain and clear. Show me that I'm called and commissioned to be a voice of change and help me walk boldly with courage and with the full permission of Heaven, in Jesus' name.

CHAPTER 28

The Wilderness Commissioning

We've not been assigned to hang out until He returns. We've been given a message and a power that completely revolutionizes life. Why would anyone want to get up in the morning and not shape the course of world history?
—Bill Johnson

I had a dream in 2015 that I couldn't have needed more. In the dream, I was seeing people being knighted for service. Leaders were placing swords on each side of their shoulders and commissioning them for service, but as I sat and watched, I realized I was never going to be validated and commissioned that way. I could sense the same sadness in others watching. Then the Father spoke so clearly to me, "Men didn't appoint you. I did."

At the time, we were out of church and were blacklisted as heretics in our city, and I won't lie. I was constantly wrestling with the desire to have a man call me into full-time ministry and validate the call on my life. I had tried that road, and it never worked. God wouldn't allow it to happen.

YOUR WOMB-LEAPING COMMISSIONING

Now before I say what I am about to say, you need to know that I do believe God uses man to commission, but we have to realize that we have been called and authorized long before man ever notices the call of God on us.

> *He gave us resurrection life and drew us to himself by his holy calling on our lives. And it wasn't because of any good we have done, but by his divine pleasure and marvelous grace that confirmed our union with the anointed Jesus, even before time began!* (2 Timothy 1:9 TPT).

Let me ask you a question to mess up your theology a little, or maybe just correct it a little if this is too hard to swallow. Who ordained John the Baptist? Who gave him his credentials? Who commissioned him into the wilderness to speak about the things that he did?

Okay, let me make it even more clear. Who ordained Jesus? Who said He would walk around healing the sick and forgiving sins? Who? The Father? You are right. So why is it any different when it comes to you? Only because religion has created a system of hurdles to jump over, hierarchal red tape like a filter to make sure that only the most loyal and submissive subjects are given the honor or are commissioned by a denomination or affiliation. Is this God? No, it is not. Luke 4:18–19 says:

> *"The Spirit of the Lord is upon me, and he has anointed me to be hope for the poor, healing for the brokenhearted, and new eyes for the blind, and to preach to prisoners, 'You are set free!' I have come to share the message of Jubilee, for the time of God's great acceptance has begun."*

God's great *acceptance*—this is the heart of the Father to counteract the opposite spirit that religion operates in and commissions by.

John's commissioning was before the world began like yours and mine, but there was a significant moment that I believe was a divine synergy moment and commissioning for him:

> At the moment her aunt heard Mary's voice, the baby within Elizabeth's womb jumped and kicked. And suddenly, Elizabeth was filled to overflowing with the Holy Spirit! With a loud voice she prophesied with power: "Mary! You are a woman given the highest favor and privilege above all others, for your child is destined to bring God great delight. How did I deserve such a remarkable honor to have the mother of my Lord come and visit me? The moment you came in the door and greeted me, my baby danced inside me with joy! (Luke 1:41–44 TPT).

So, was it God that created John and commissioned him into a ministry of repentance, baptism, and preparing the way for Jesus? Yes! Isn't that surprising since his message was heretical in those days? Yes, that's right, but it was God. Reformers, often when God calls you, it looks like heresy at first to the system, but you can't let it disqualify you!

TRADITIONAL COMMISSIONING POINTS

Before I move on, here are a list of commissioning scriptures that are a biblical foundation for us reformers. They point out different functions that we should know:

- Isaiah 6:1–8—call to be a reformational voice
- Jeremiah 1:4–10—call to be a reformational voice

- Nehemiah 1—the burden to rebuild what was broken down.
- 1 Samuel 16:13—David's call to be king/establishing the Davidic line
- Luke 9:1–6—authority over demons and healing and good news
- Matthew 28—discipling of nations
- Luke 24—repentance to the nations
- John 4—commissioning for the harvest
- Mark 16—signs and wonders
- Luke 4:18—Spirit of the Lord upon us
- 1 Corinthians 14—commissioning to operate in the gifts
- Ephesians 4—the fivefold commissioning

A WILD ONES COMMISSIONING

One morning before I was about to go live to teach our online students, the Spirit of God came upon me, and I felt the heart of the Father very strongly. I was about to do a session on new covenant commissioning and fulfilling the Great Commission when God wanted me to go in another direction. He said to me, "I want to commission them today with My acceptance and validation," then I began to write down what flowed from that moment. So, as we end this part of the guide, let the words of commissioning from the Father flood your heart and awaken your spirit. This is the commissioning you should have received instead of the religious holds and chains.

COMMISSIONED IN POWERFUL IDENTITY

- You have been called to a life of wholeness, not bound or chained to the limitations placed over you or the controlling chains others tried to place on you.
- Trauma and deep wounds, torment, depression, oppression, and any other affliction of the enemy are no longer your future.
- You have been called to live with the mind of Christ, knowing your value and identity in Christ, and not live under the labels and words spoken of you by people.
- You have been called to be fully known by God and to know God intimately.
- You are not your parents, family, or family line, and their sins, failures, and dysfunctions no longer apply to you.
- You are called to royalty and not an orphan spirit. The days of taking scraps from under the table are over.
- You are not called to a life of invisibility or isolation. You are set apart, yes, but not called to walk lonely or always be on your own.
- You may have been rejected or cast out, but you are not called to identify as that.
- You are the accepted and the beloved by God.
- You are called to a life of intimacy and purity, where you give your relationship with the Lord first place and there are no idols or lovers except Him.

COMMISSIONED TO UNIQUE MINISTRIES & EXPRESSIONS

- You have been given a unique message and expression, and without it, the world doesn't get to experience a part of the Father's heart only you carry.
- You have been given a powerful niche in the Kingdom, where God wants you to fully occupy and expand.
- You don't have to edit or trim down what you have been given to fit. It's okay if your expression confronts the norm and complacency.
- You have a task only you can carry out, and you have been anointed for it.
- The door is open for you, and the enemy can't close it.
- Have you accepted your assignment, or are you afraid of it? It's time to pick it up.
- You have been given something that will offend the religious but establish the right Kingdom.
- You have been called to something beyond your time. It's the new frontiers.
- You have been called to pull the Church into it.
- You have been called to receive revelation and write blueprints for generations to come.

COMMISSIONED & PERMISSIONED

- You have permission to dream with the Lord.
- You have permission to innovate and create with the Lord.
- You have permission to fill the gap in the Body of Christ that you see.

- You have permission to tear down religious ideals and build God's Kingdom.
- You have permission to explore the vast Kingdom you have been given access to.
- You have permission to pioneer and run with a new message or theme on the Lord's heart.
- You have permission to be the prophet, apostle, evangelist, pastor, or teacher without man approving you.
- You have permission to speak, knowing your voice is valuable and heard.
- You have permission to build what God has given you without fear of others' opinions.
- You have permission to do what hasn't been done yet.
- You have permission to have the right people around you and not the wrong ones.
- You have permission not to be around toxic narcissistic people who rob you of your creativity and steal your pearls.
- You have permission to be fulfilled and happy of soul.
- You have permission to deny control and manipulation and establish boundaries.
- You have permission to stand tall, enjoy favor, and not feel badly for the blessing God brings to you.
- You have permission to sit at the fathers table and belong.
- You have permission to leave the system.

WARRIOR COMMISSIONING
& THE FIERY BAPTISM

- It is time for the warriors to be reinstated.
- We have lots lost our roar and our ferocity, and it's time we get them back.
- Your commissioning is this: Stop holding back. Stop hiding. Step out into the daylight!
- Don't let the fear of man dictate your call.
- You are being commissioned into the fear of the Lord and no longer the fear of man.
- Receive the baptism of fire (see Matt. 3:11).
- Right now, the rags of man's certification are being removed, and you are being revealed.

SOME KEY INGREDIENTS

To finish, there are some key ingredients we can't leave out of the equation that I do want to address:

1. It is God who commissions you, but He can use man to do it. Just because we have seen the abuse of leadership, it shouldn't make us throw the baby out with the bath water and assume God doesn't use man. He does! The picture is unhealthy when we are waiting for or depending on the approval of man, however, before we step into our calling. God leads us all in different ways. Follow His leading!

2. The fruit of true commissioning and calling shouldn't be rebellion. Being out of the box and against the grain is fine, but when someone is making a ministry out of

defying the roles and callings of others, this is a diversion to being truly sent by the Lord and reveals that there are heart issues to deal with.

3. Commissioning that produces entitlement instead of empowerment is birthed out of the need to be seen or recognized, not out of the heart to serve the Father's heart. It's self-seeking, and it's aim is to fill a void of rejection and pain with the praises of man and popularity or being noticed. Commissioning equips and anoints you for your assignment. It's not another highlight for your ministry resumé to flash around.

4. You may be called and gifted and commissioned, but honor will determine the sustainability and longevity of your calling. Honor sees the best in others and looks for ways to serve others, even those you disagree with. Honor recognizes the call of God upon others and doesn't push itself to the front and usurp others to be heard. This is dishonor. This is the case in scenarios where someone rolls onto a church scene and announces they are called by God and they begin to create chaos and strife by usurping the roll of the pastors/leaders there.

5. Submission isn't a dirty word, even to us who have experienced abuse under its imposition. Submission can be one of the most freeing things in its right context and actually multiply and launch you even further. Hebrews 13:17 says to submit to your leaders, and that doesn't mean chaining yourself as a slave to another's will and agenda. It's simply a recognition of God calling you to come into relationship with another to receive the blessing and grace upon their lives and be guided into your calling in a way you couldn't on your own. Where we have gone wrong is we've allowed submission to replace our relationships with God. We have wrongly allowed it to make us forfeit our calling. Submission is coming into a team mentality or family environment and

mission. It should never be abused by leadership to get their way, which has happened often, but I am hopeful this is changing. Submission is surrender, humility, and teachability whereby God wants you to experience more of Him and be added to and enriched by being a student of another's life and calling.

6. And lastly, don't make the same mistakes. This comes back to honor, but it's more a heart thing. When the rejected and outcast step into their calling, is it okay for them to keep identifying as they did in their previous season? No. You need to shift your mindset from victimhood to royalty, or you will only create a mess and hurt others. David was rejected by his family and then attacked repeatedly by Saul, but when his moment to kill Saul came, he didn't take it. Let's not repeat the pain we have been through on our road to pioneering. Let's not reject others or bully others. Let's not live jealously and competitively. When God promotes you, keep your heart in check. Don't use it as an "I told you so" to those who were against you. Just keeping going and live free, and this will ensure that, when the time comes and God sends you sons and daughters who are where you were, they won't get the religious and controlling shakedown but the hand up.

Now *go* into the earth, reformers! I'll see you at the frontlines.

PROPHETIC SURVIVAL TIP

You have everything you need in your hands, and with the authority of Heaven and your mission blueprints in front of you, it's time to move into the legacy God has for you. It's time to stop second-guessing this and just take your first step.

CAMPFIRE PRAYER

Lord, I receive Your commissioning and let Your approval wash away the words that have been spoken over me and the insecurity and rejection I have lived in that which said I could never be used. Today, I begin my odyssey in the Kingdom as a reformer for you, in Jesus' name.

PART 5

The Wilderness Revolution

CHAPTER 29

The Renaissance Begins

The recovery of the warrior is absolutely crucial to the recovery of a man. All else rests on this, for you will have to fight, my brothers, for everything you desire and everything you hold dear in this world. Despite what you feel, or what you may have been told, you have a warrior's heart, because you bear the image of God. And he will train you to become a great warrior, if you'll let him.
—John Eldridge

When writing this portion of the guidebook, I asked the Holy Spirit how He wanted me to end it, and He simply said, "Ignite the revolution!" Though that may sound very strong and forceful, and anti-establishment even, it wasn't until I looked up the meaning of the word *revolution* that I realized what He was really saying.

| /ˌrev.əˈluː.ʃən / noun |

- the overthrow of one government and its replacement with another
- the act of revolving or turning completely round, so as to bring every point of the turning body back to its first position; a complete rotation through 360°
- a total change of circumstances; a complete alteration in character, system, or conditions

- specifically a radical change in social or governmental conditions; the overthrow of an established political system, generally accompanied by far-reaching social changes
- the act of rolling or moving back; a return to a point previously occupied
- the act of revolving or turning to and fro in the mind
- return to a point before occupied, or to a point relatively the same; a rolling back; return

So, in essence, a revolution is the spiritual act of bringing something back to its original design or purpose and the overthrow of anything that has corrupted it. It's the anointing to return the earth to God's original blueprint. That's what reformation is, and we are now in the beginning of the *era of the reformation revolution* where God is raising up reformers as a mighty army to restore the earth and make it look like Heaven.

In the next seven chapters, I feel very strongly that God is going to ignite you, anoint you afresh, and reveal specifics to you about what He has called you to reform in the days to come. I believe you are going to have visitations, encounters, and life-changing moments as the Holy Spirit brands you afresh. Are you ready?

AN ARMY WITH FIRE IN THIER EYES

One of the most significant areas or reformation we are seeing and will continue to see rise in the next few decades is the recommissioning and rising of the army of God. At some point in the last hundred years, the Church stopped being an army and became a country club, and instead of a fiery remnant settled for the boardroom of indifference. The problem is not primarily an inaction problem but a defilement problem.

Religion is quite active and is its own revolution, but it's not the holy, birthed in the throne room kind. Rather, it's the kind of revolution that thrives on putting out the fires of the righteous remnant. Leviticus 6:13 says, *"The fire must be kept burning on the altar continuously; it must not go out."* This is why right now God is re-lighting the furnaces of a generation tempered to the cool glow of religion's apathy instead of burning with the baptism of the Holy Ghost and fire.

> *Those who repent I baptize with water, but there is coming a man after me who is more powerful than I. In fact, I'm not even worthy enough to pick up his sandals. He will submerge you into union with the Spirit of Holiness and with a raging fire!* (Matthew 3:11).

You can't be both neutered by religion and baptized with fire at the same time, so an army with fire in their eyes is going to be a force to be reckoned with and will lead the Church forward out of apathy, mediocrity, and powerlessness.

LIGHT THE TORCHES

Years ago, I had a powerful dream of this very thing. I saw a large multitude of people standing silently in the darkness of a forest. Motionless, empty, there was not a sound. Then I saw it, a person holding a fiery torch running down a huge hill toward them. As he approached, they turned and lifted up their hands, and in one hand they held a timepiece hanging on a chain, and in the other were torches with no fire. One by one the guy with the torch lit every single one until the darkness lit up to reveal an army ready for battle. Then at the command, they ran together through the darkness to their mission.

You are that fiery one holding a torch, and it's time to light up the darkness. Remember Gideon's army that God reduced to 300 after they drank? This is what happened shortly after that:

> Then he divided the 300 men into three companies and gave each of the men a trumpet in one hand and an empty pitcher with a torch inside it in the other (Judges 7:16 NASB1995).

The trumpet similar is to the timepiece I saw in the announcement or the clarion call to rise up and charge, while the torch represents the fire and might of the Spirit and the glory of God which led the Israelites through the wilderness. Verses 19–20 says this:

> Gideon and the hundred men with him reached the edge of the camp at the beginning of the middle watch, just after they had changed the guard. They blew their trumpets and broke the jars that were in their hands. The three companies blew the trumpets and smashed the jars. Grasping the torches in their left hands and holding in their right hands the trumpets they were to blow, they shouted, "A sword for the Lord and for Gideon!"

The smashing of the pots is significant for us because it represents us breaking the limitations or ceilings placed on us by religion. And it represents our being faithful to hold up our torches even when it is unpopular to do so. The torch of the Lord in battle exposes the enemy's face and sends him running back and retreating to where he came from. Look what Samson did:

> So he went out and caught three hundred foxes and tied them tail to tail in pairs. He then fastened a torch to every pair of tails (Judges 15:4).

This reformational army is called to model intimacy/fires lit in their lives so, when they move, it causes the enemy/the foxes to run!

When Gideon's men broke the pots it also prophetically spoke of who we are as God's people. We are a people full of so much that has just been hidden for too long:

We are like common clay jars that carry this glorious treasure within, so that the extraordinary overflow of power will be seen as God's, not ours (2 Corinthians 4:7 TPT).

What if God is breaking our boxes in this season to reveal the treasure hidden in us that has been concealed for far too long?

There is so much Holy Ghost wind on your blind *yes* in this season, and the Lord is saying, "Will you run? Will you run? Will you go? Will you go?" There are people carrying so much precious cargo to be released and exported right now. It's like the rivers are bursting the banks, but will you let it flood out of you, or will you retreat? The dry and weary land you keep seeing in the natural *is not* the spiritual reality! The fields are white and ripe ,and so are you! Army of God, it's time!

I heard Him say, "*Roll call!*"

I heard the Lord speak over this reformational army rising, "It's roll call time!"

The definition of a roll call is:

- the process of calling out a list of names to establish who is present
- checking attendance of students or soldiers for duty
- those who have said *yes* (you vote with your feet)
- present, no longer in the past
- present, not distracted or sidetracked

- present, not listening to the noise or caught in the wrong fight

We are in a roll call moment where the trumpet blast for the revolution has sounded and the Father is waiting to see who will break through the layers of fear and opposition and stand at the frontlines for the sake of shaping history. Can you hear the call?

WE ARE IN THE REDEFINITION OF THE PROPHETIC ARMY

This army is right now being redefined and getting its new marching orders. Part of our redefinition are as follows:

- We are coming out of the bullied, victim mentality we have known and into an era of victorious warfare.
- We can't operate the way we have been—reactionary to the enemy and his opposition. God has mantled us with authority like a general, and generals don't react. They fore-plan, foresee, and look through the smokescreen and preempt what the enemy does.
- We are living in a *holy moment*, a holiness moment. It's an hour of being set apart and consecrated again.
- The Body of Christ and the prophetic movement are in an unusual tension of both ripening and resetting, and they are going hand in hand.
- We are having to let go of many things we have known— ways and methods we have operated in—to pick up what He is giving us to wield.
- We are in an hour of redefinition and refining personally and corporately for the sole purpose of us stepping into this era of greater impact.

- We are being invited into the tuning of our ears to His heart so we will be able to properly receive what He speaks in this new era.
- We can no longer play at the shallow end of the pool. The nations are experiencing injustices that you and I are called to be a voice for. Our mantles aren't for "show and tell" but to raid the gates of hell.
- We are moving out of the fear of man and into the fear of the Lord and into the conviction to speak the heart of God no matter the cost.
- We are moving into an era of power and authority where we will see public displays of the power of God through the lives of people yielded to His voice.
- We as the Church are coming out of the wilderness years of being silenced, without influence or impact, and into our era of being the *roar* of the Lord on Planet Earth!

WHAT THE REFORMATIONAL ARMY OF WILD ONES LOOKS LIKE

Reformers crave definition, not in a legalistic way, but part of their modus operandi is language. Something I have loved over the years is asking the Lord about specific things and then Him giving me specific details and definition.

One night, I asked the Lord to define some more characteristics of this reformational army, and that night, all night, I heard the song I grew up singing in Sunday school: *"Blow the trumpet in Zion, sound the alarm on the holy mountain!"*

This song is from Joel 2, which is a chapter that prophesies a coming army. Read Joel 2, then come back and read the traits of this army I discovered:

- They will sound the alarm from the secret place/intimacy of the time we are in.
- They will be a mighty army. This is *the* army.
- They will be a devouring fire.
- While the earth seems to be in darkness, they will make the earth like Eden and behind them a wasteland.
- They will be like wild horses that look like an army (wild ones).
- They will carry a noise like chariots (they won't sound dignified or be politically correct and sweet).
- They will leap over mountain tops, scale walls, and charge like warriors. There will be *no* obstacle too great for them.
- They will plunge through defenses and be unseen, go under the radar of the enemy's plans.
- They will be focused and fixed, unwavering, not diverted from the course, with Jesus in their sight.
- They will champion each other and not fight each other
- They will be an army that obeys *the Lord*, not culture, not media or anyone else.
- The Lord will thunder over them! He will let them be known by mighty exploits.
- The Lord will *give voice* for them.

THE SEASON OF GLOBAL TURNAROUND/TURN BACK

- They are an army here to reset/recalibrate the heart of the Church and usher in an era of global turnaround. Repentance means to turn around, change direction, altar your course (see Joel 2:12–13).

- They are the rescue team, not the rebels. They are here with a hammer, but they aren't against the Church, but agents sent to *aid* the Church.
- They are new season specialists.
- Right now, they are coming out of the woodwork/out of the wilderness, coming out of hiding or obscurity (to suddenly start publicly doing something or saying something, when previously you did nothing or kept quiet)
- They are appearing or materializing suddenly and unexpectedly.
- They are coming into formation.
- An army comes into formation/it's taking your position.
- They are an army, so they are coming together, taking shape, growing, taking structure, into arrangement, configuration, and development.
- They are finding family and tribe (healing phase).
- Acceptance has begun (see Luke 4:18).
- Hearts are being refreshed right now, and they will have a glow about them.
- They will not be bitter or nor have unforgiveness in their hearts.

REACTIVATE HERE

The Lord wants to reactive the warrior, the fighter, the war-hammer, and revolutionary in you. I hear Him asking, "Who said you didn't have permission? Who silenced you?" You are about to feel a second wind come upon you and feel a roar where you lost it. You will take back your authority where you dropped your keys. Creativity and ideas will come flooding back where there was a blockage, and clarity will come where you are under a cloud of confusion. You will find new orders in your pocket, the weapons back in your hands that you dropped, and the boldness to step up to the plate.

THE RENAISSANCE AT THE FRONT

I heard the Lord say that this reformational army will bring about a creative renaissance in the Body of Christ. This renaissance is an eruption of unusual and unconventional creative expressions and language that will show more facets of the nature of God and His heart for the saved and the lost. This surge is going to cause the world to recognize the weight the Church carries in being on the forefront of creativity and in releasing strategies and ideas as answers for problems in the earth.

The Renaissance period between the fourteenth and seventeenth centuries was an Age of Enlightenment, where creativity was the catalyst that burst the banks of expected influence and completely reformed the rest of society and even religion. Today, God is calling out His renaissance revolutionaries to allow Him to birth His ideas and creative expression through them. This will alter history itself and extend the Kingdom of God.

Something is dramatically shifting and changing, and there is a sound being released from the creative reformers that will dethrone principalities over regions and cities and usher in a revival that doesn't just refresh the Church but awakens the world to the beauty of Jesus!

There are songs that are yet to be sung, innovations that are yet to be discovered, ideas, strategies, language, and themes from Heaven that are just waiting to be pulled upon by these revolutionaries who are hungry enough to withdraw from their inheritance.

I feel such a weight on this word and a responsibility upon us as sons and daughters to dream with God and bring it forward into this season. Reformational authors dust off your pens, singers loosen up your tongues, songwriters stir up your hearts, and dancers enter the throne room for this is a time of an epic, creative surge and a renaissance revolution!

PROPHETIC SURVIVAL TIP

Say *yes* to whatever He says for you to do. It may be strange or crazy, but regardless, say *yes*. Long to wield your hammer. Go, go, go!

CAMPFIRE PRAYER

Lord, I give You my future. I give You all my days on this earth and into eternity. I love to make Your name famous in the earth, to tell the world about you, and to tear down the kingdom of darkness in my wake. This is the moment of my second yes, to go where You send me and to do what You ask me to do in Jesus' name.

CHAPTER 30

Setting the Table

And you did not receive the "spirit of religious duty,"
leading you back into the fear of never being good
enough. But you have received the "Spirit of full
acceptance," enfolding you into the family of God. And
you will never feel orphaned, for as he rises up within
us, our spirits join him in saying the words of tender
affection, "Beloved Father!" —Romans 8:15 TPT

Prophets need family. Reformers need family. Pioneers need family. Emerging voices need family. The wild ones need family. It's not a choice or an option. If you are wanting to see the full potential of the call of God upon your life and run on all cylinders, then you will need a family, a tribe, a people who get you.

Family is healing. It's belonging. It's acceptance. It's the kiss from the Father that builds, raises, and launches us into our God-given destinies. That's why the enemy has warred against family since day 1. That's why he has created dysfunctional family traits, patterns, and cycles, and normalized them. Society has taken the bait, and the result is the degradation, devaluation, and deconstruction of the home, weaving of its poison into every part of the way the world lives and functions. What is it? It's the father-less worldview that breeds every kind of evil, destroys life in the womb, has brother fight against brother, race against race, and sees women as objects. Religion has been a major contributor to breeding this in the Church and creating the empires of orphan-ages instead of eagles nests.

GOD'S PROMISE OF
THE REVOLUTION OF FAMILY

During our season out of the Church, I spent some time processing with the Lord over this, and the Lord told me that beyond any other aspect of this new wineskin transition, at the very core was the reformation of the Church from an institution to a family. People don't want membership; they want to belong. In the last ten years, there has been a dissatisfaction starting to rise in a people created for more, and they simply are tapping into what God is moving us into.

I heard the Father speak to me, "There are so many out there who don't want information or even the most profound revelation. They just want family." Suddenly, my spirit began to burn as I felt His heart for those who spend all their waking moments looking, searching, and craving for people who will accept them. So many of us spend hours a day scrolling through social media with that God-given desire for true connection, but often we leave with a few cheap quotes and a virtual high-five. We need more, and we need to be more.

THE DYSFUNCTION & THE PURE DESIGN

One morning I sat with God, and He asked me to write a list of what I felt were counterfeits to the true Kingdom family we had experienced, and this is what I wrote:

- **Mission relationships:** You are only in relationship while the mission lasts. If you leave a role, capacity, or place, the relationship ends with it.
- **Beneficial relationships:** You are only in relationship while the other person is receiving something from you that they need.
- **Empire building relationships:** You are seen by leaders or others as someone who will fill a gap in their system, fill a role, or be a brick in the empire they are building.
- **Compliance relationships:** You do something the way others want you to do it so you earn a seat at their table.
- **Comradery relationships:** You are only in relationship because of similarity of passion, convictions, a common enemy, same political persuasion, race, or commonality.

I sat grieved and asked, "Lord, what is your version of family?"

He led me to Acts 2:42, where it speaks about the early church and how believers simply came together, ate together, prayed and prophesied together, and were linked in heart, not just in mission or belief. This was what we were longing for but were missing from the Church.

If I'm honest, we didn't experience this for ourselves right away; in fact, when we were called back to be part of a church, we faced the same institutional mentality we had always known, faced the same orphan-minded jealousy of being a newcomer to the club, and dealt with the same hierarchical positioning and elitism as well. But we decided that, while others around us were choosing to do Kingdom relationships that way, we would be unapologetic about pioneering something authentic. We put boundaries in place that honored others in that old system but were not pressured to buy into that inferior and counterfeit version of community.

About a year later, we were travelling to the States when a friend of mine texted me and connected me with his other friend and said, "You guys need to connect," so we did. The friend of my friend invited us over for dinner one night in LA. We didn't know him and his people at all but felt like we needed to go.

As we arrived, another family arrived as well, and they invited us in and to our surprise didn't talk church, ministry, stats and figures, ego talk, or how we would benefit them. It was just three families hanging out together. The kids were laughing and playing, the men barbecued, and the women talked about creative things. Something so simple felt like a dream, but it wasn't until after dinner that I was undone. Our new friend just naturally in conversation started prophesying over us, then another person did the same and yet another, and these were the purest prophetic words we have ever received. They didn't know our past or what we did in the Kingdom. They had no motivation except connection.

We spent the next hour praying and prophesying over each other around the kitchen table, and I could barely keep myself together. This was the vision God had given me. This was the revolution of family he had been showing us! It was so simple yet so rare. It was the original purpose and design that the Church had lost, and yet God is restoring His Church back to this place again. From that place, we are going to see the Church become the effective, loving family she was always called to be. It starts with us.

THE EMPTY TABLE

Years ago, I was invited to my first prophetic round table in Australia after years of being in isolation, navigating my calling. As I sat around the table hearing many recognized voices share their hearts, I felt excited, grateful, but also sad. They had created a space for prophets to process, and that in itself was a feat in Australia, where the prophetic office and gift has been on rocky ground in the Church. In that moment, I remember thinking, *Where are all the others like me?* I couldn't help but think of so many other outcasts and misunderstood ones who hadn't been invited to a table or given a space to be healed, heard, and championed. But that wasn't their job. I knew it at that moment because it was mine.

Prophets weren't created for the Lone Ranger life. It was never God's design but the enemy's goal to keep us from experiencing the fullness that true family brings. In the years to come ,I just want to set a table for prophetic people to come, belong, feel safe, process, and grow in their calling. It's that simple.

WE OWE THE WORLD AN ENCOUNTER WITH THE FATHER

I grew up knowing the fatherless life, and during my entire life, I was just a kid looking for his daddy everywhere and anywhere I could. I was seventeen when I was kicked out of home. I recently had graduated from year twelve, and suddenly my life drastically changed.

I was living on a property in a caravan. I have never felt more alone that that season and more castoff and rejected. I was a very troubled and messed up kid because I didn't know the Father at all. I hung around the wrong crowd, was consumed by heavy metal music, and would see and sense demons around me regularly. This was my path because I didn't experience a good father but the godfather. The Church knows God as the godfather, too. He is their boss and protector at a high price.

My point is this: Unless we encounter the Father and find family deep down, we will feel orphaned and never live up to the full potential upon our lives. Unless we model it to the world, they will never know it even exists and will keep being led astray by orphaned teaching that leads people to orphanage warden, fake Jesus, not son and daughter, Champion Father who wants us to feel fully known.

Bill Johnson says, "We owe the world an encounter," and I agree. What if we owed the world an encounter with the Father as our bare minimum? We are used to pushing Christian literature at people with Heaven and hell statements, but have we given people the encounter with the Father that they are really needing?

When I started writing this book, I was aware of this one thing. This was going to be less of a book of teaching reformation as much as a Father's permission to be the reformation, and there is a difference. I knew this would be the book I didn't have in my wilderness that I wanted to make sure others did. I knew it was going to be the wet sloppy kiss from the Father that the religious church omitted not to offend. I understood it would be the baptism of love of being fully known and endorsed by the King that the clergy can never ever give you. It needs to come from Him.

I owe you that. We owe the world that. In fact, stop for a minute. More than anything else I have shared in the pages of this book, I just want you to finish reading this book feeling encountered by the Father. *"Father, show them who You are. Let them feel fully known by You. Heal the abandoned hearts and those who haven't known You. Father, we need You."*

LET'S PAUSE... & GO BACK

Before we go any further, I feel convicted and compelled to say this. I may not be right on theologically, but I want to share my personal opinion here. If reformation is about being restored to our original design, then what if the whole goal of reformation was to bring us to the Father who "formed" us in the first place?

Before I formed you in the womb I knew you, before you were born I set you apart; I appointed you as a prophet to the nations (Jeremiah 1:5).

I believe the very core of our calling is for us to bring people into relationship, right standing, and intimacy with the Father. He wants us to help make the same connection that was lost. We may be called to overthrow demonic systems and create Kingdom infrastructure and all those amazing and wonderful things, but there is no deeper mission than reuniting and reconciling lost sons and daughters to the Father.

And God has made all things new, and reconciled us to himself, and given us the ministry of reconciling others to God (2 Corinthians 5:18 TPT).

SETTING A NEW COVENANT PRECEDENT

Malachi 4:5–6 reads:

Behold, I will send you Elijah the prophet before the great and awesome day of the Lord comes. And he will turn the hearts of fathers to their children and the hearts of children to their fathers, lest I come and strike the land with a decree of utter destruction (ESV).

These are the last two verses of the Old Testament, and what you need to know is why. These two verses are the bridge between the Old and New Testaments and the old and new covenants because the Elijah this verse refers to is John the Baptist who prepared the way for Jesus by "turning hearts" back to the Father.

The word *turn* here is Hebrew word *shoob*, which means "return to original conditions, restore, or reform." It is saying that unless we see the reformation of the people of God, His people reconciled back to Him and to the garden before the fall, the land will be cursed. Look around you today and look at any city or place where the war is taking place against the womb, identity, marriage, and godly family, and you will see an obvious curse or stain.

Our role as reformers is to flip that back around and heal the land. Where does it start? Turning the hearts of sons to fathers and fathers to sons. It's restoring the earth back into relationship with the Father. This is the spirit of adoption. It's casting your jacket over the orphan and calling them home.

The 99 or the 1?

> *Suppose one of you has a hundred sheep and loses one of them. Doesn't he leave the ninety-nine in the open country and go after the lost sheep until he finds it?* (Luke 15:4).

When Jesus spoke about leaving the 99 to rescue the one, He may have been speaking about the heart of the father to leave those who were found so he could go after the one stray sheep, but there is also something else in there that I have always seen. It speaks volumes to me about the way God thinks, that His eyes are always on those who are away from Him, those who are lost and in trouble. In human standards, it doesn't make sense. We wouldn't go after the one because we would conclude that it's better odds just to leave the one and settle our losses with the 99 that are left, right? But God does things differently, and the ministry of Jesus reflected that.

Did Jesus go and spend His days in the temple trying to convert the Pharisees? No, he left the 99, even though in this case they were just as lost, so He could save the one. The thieves, the tax collectors, the murderers, and prostitutes. That was the "one" to Jesus, and He modeled that well and simultaneously revealed the pioneer heart of God. Yet again, that breaks away from the modus operandi to go after the one who really needed Him most.

SETTING THE TABLE

"Who will set the feast?" I heard the Lord say to me. "Who will call them to the table?" As a dad of two very lively girls, our kitchen table has been the scene of many messy spills over the years, but it's also been the place of much laughter and connection. Some of my own favorite God-moments have happened around the table, where we have had raw and painful conversations about life with friends but also glorious times of love and encouragement, prophesying over each other until midnight.

Setting the table is messy, but it is where revival happens in its purest form. It's where revival begins. God is increasing our awareness today of that which we have built—that it will not truly sustain a move of the family of God. God is simply asking us to set the table. It's where we look beyond religious bounds and simply love the people in front of us.

There are also many Lone Ranger prophets, apostles, and evangelists whom God is calling out of isolation and into true connection right now. Years ago, God told me that my full potential would only be revealed in the context of community because isolation may help me learn to fight bears and lions like David did, but it's only when I have family around me that it draws out who I really am and leads me to impossible victories and exploits.

ISOLATION IS BREAKING AS REVIVAL IS BIRTHED THROUGH FAMILY

I believe God is breaking cycles of isolation in the Body of Christ, where it has felt like connection to God is accessible but connection to people seems difficult, and finding a tribe is rare. We can become so mission focused that we gather around the boardroom table more than the kitchen table and network for opportunities instead of breaking bread with no agenda. God is reinstating the true heart of family back to the Church and detoxing us from the past.

In the days to come, I see the greatest healings, miracles, signs, and wonders breaking out in lounge-rooms, where the encore of the Holy Spirit comes when the service is over and people gather for fellowship. I see broken families standing to their feet after years of dysfunction, marriages healed, kids encountering God, and livelihoods restored as the home becomes the focus for revival again. I see those who have been rejected and excluded from cliques and exclusive tables spreading their own table, without restriction, bias, or sales pitch, and the hopeless and heart sick being resurrected.

God is healing our roots right now. He is invading homes with His presence and reminding us of what matters the most to Him, and in turn we will see an overflow. The lonely will find families, the disconnected and invisible will be seen, Kingdom family values will be held high again, men and women will fight for the home again, we will see all evils and injustices against the womb and life abolished, identity will be restored where it has been twisted, and the Father heart of God will be revealed to the earth in a way we haven't seen before. Yes, your isolation is ending, and the era of family has begun.

REVIVAL FAMILIES ASSEMBLE!

A few years ago, I was with my friend Seth Dahl, talking about Kingdom families, which is a topic we both love as both of us are pioneering new frontiers in ministry and family, when He jokingly likened us to the *Avengers*. Later that day, I was on the flight home when I kept hearing what he had said resounding in my spirit. Then I heard, "Avengers, *assemble*!" just like in the movie.

The word *avenger* means "to exact punishment or harm for an injury or wrong," and *assemble* means "to fit or come together for a common purpose." Instantly, it hit me. What if God is raising up families who through their synergy will unleash Heaven upon injustices and see revival touch the four corners of the earth?

I feel that God is using these revival families to bring alignment to acceptable dysfunctions and bring order to places of chaos. They will reveal God's heart for the season to come and break the mold into new undiscovered territory for Jesus!

> *To the fatherless he is a father. To the widow he is a champion friend. To the lonely he makes them part of a family. To the prisoners he leads into prosperity until they sing for joy* (Psalm 68:5 TPT).

I hear the Lord saying to you, "Dear wild one, right now I am healing every wound that the institution inflicted upon you and revealing my purpose for the Church to be the family I have always wanted her to be. In place of the pain and rejection, I am placing the spirit of adoption upon you and the desire to set the table for those who have been left out in the dark."

PROPHETIC SURVIVAL TIP

Let the love of the Father be your everything. Let it be your sustenance and your only motivation. Now set a table and watch Him bring the lost home.

CAMPFIRE PRAYER

Father, use me to bring the world back to You and the Church who have forgotten you. Anoint me with the spirit of adoption and the love of the Father that cuts through to the heart and rescues the most broken and destitute. Help me live my life emptying orphanages and leading people into Your acceptance in Jesus' name!

CHAPTER 31

The Path Home

Humility will take you far, being teachable will give you longevity, and remaining a novice will cause you to live with wonder. Just like fruit you have to stay green because if you ripen you'll rot. —Terry Walker

Seasons of growth and advancement feel ironic because they are always coupled with refining and re-schooling. It's like being handed a new toy, and instead of picking it up and hoping to figure out how to use it along the way and possibly damaging it, the Lord reveals the manual for the season, the divine blueprint. He gives instruction and removes what is unnecessary. We see this often in the function of the reformer that they hold both the torch to light and launch you and the scalpel and oil to heal and deliver you. This is happening as we step into this glorious era of the awakened Bride.

I want to share three dreams I had recently that have gripped me deeply and have convicted and ignited me for the days ahead. I pray they do the same for you.

DREAM 1: CLASSROOM IS IN SESSION

In the first dream, I was in a classroom about to teach but didn't have a message prepared. As I looked around the room, I saw faces of people in bondage to different demonic agendas, and they were staring back at me. Instantly, I sensed that the Lord wanted to bring deliverance to them. A young generation Z guy stood out to me in the second row, and I walked over to Him, and when I put my hand on his head, he shook and began to get delivered. Suddenly, he spoke, "I am progressive Christianity, and we are taking over!" I continued to pray and speak truth over him till it left.

After that, I looked around the room and could see God moving and delivering others. As I walked toward one girl, she blurted out, "I am worldly love and tolerance," and then she was delivered.

Another person yelled out, "I am compliance and conformity to culture!" and another said, "I am perversion!" and then another said, "I am the fear of man!" All the people in the room were being delivered, and I could feel the pure love of God flooding the room.

Then I walked back to the young man I first prayed for, bent down, and said to him, "The Lord says it's time to encounter His face and be lost in His gaze once again," and suddenly he and the rest of the room fell to the floor in repentance and worship. The dream ended.

Let me share what I feel the Lord was saying through this dream:

- The classroom of students is the Church today, and God is declaring that the classroom is back in session.
- God is bringing exposure, deliverance, and healing to where we have fallen for the lies and counterfeits of the enemy.
- God is revealing where we have made idols out of social justice movements that didn't originate from Him.
- God is bringing deliverance to the Church where we have partnered with mixture and started preaching a different gospel, a culture-friendly gospel.

- God is delivering the Church from the fear of man, and He is loosing us from the false love that tolerates evil and calls it good.
- God is bringing the Church back to her first love, back to encounter, and back to His face, where we cannot be perverted or taken off course.
- Right now, there is a move of deep repentance taking place where many are beginning to have their veils removed and see what they couldn't see before.
- Catching the wave that is coming depends on us being novices and teachable again. We don't want to be so experienced that we miss the wave that is in front of us.
- We don't want to be the critic or the expert but the surrendered.
- We need to get our gaze and wonder back because a church without intimacy becomes a humanistic, intellectually-driven church that isn't led by the Spirit.
- When we aren't Spirit-led, we catch the wrong wave.
- The world needs revival and a church that is revived and not deceived.

Let's represent Him well.

DREAM 2: THE THRESHING ROOM FLOOR

In the second dream, I was witnessing what I could only describe as a threshing room floor process, but instead of grain, there were tens of thousands of people lying down on the floor. I watched as they endured the crushing, and then the fire over and over. Then I heard the Lord say, "Now for the wind!" A hurricane-force wind entered the room, and people began to stand to their feet. Then the Lord spoke again, "The true Church is emerging!"

This is what I feel the Lord is saying in this dream:

- The Church has been in the threshing room floor process where God is separating what is good and what isn't, what is Him and what isn't.
- It's a "tares and wheat" season, and God has sent people into the threshing floor for processing.
- We have all been experiencing this process, and it's been difficult and painful as God has been removing what has been keeping us in bondage.
- The people on the threshing room floor are us, the Church, and God has been bringing us through the refiner's fire, not to harm us or shame us, but to *free* us and *ready* us for what is to come.
- The Church has been through the fire and endured the crushing, but we are about to experience the wind of the Spirit! It's the winnowing that leaves the dead and old behind and reveals the new.
- The true Church is emerging, and we are going to experience a second wind!
- The Church is about to experience a fresh baptism of the Holy Ghost and fire!

Those who repent I baptize with water, but there is coming a man after me who is more powerful than I. In fact, I'm not even worthy enough to pick up his sandals. He will submerge you into union with the Spirit of Holiness and with a raging fire! He comes with a winnowing fork in his hands and comes to his threshing floor to sift what is worthless from what is pure. And he is ready to sweep out his threshing floor and gather his wheat into his granary, but the straw

he will burn up with a fire that can't be extinguished!
(Matthew 3:11–12 TPT).

THE CRY OF THE BURNT-OUT EMPTY BRIDE

Recently, I have been stirred and convicted. In seasons of movement, God will often take you back to go forward, or remind you of where you have been to bring extra closure and launch you into the new.

When Elisha was mantled by Elijah, it says that he went back to his parents to say goodbye and then slayed the oxen and burned his tools. Sometimes, moments of looking back are to remember God's faithfulness and close the door. Think of a bow being pulled back then released. The pullback enables the arrow to launch farther. In the same way, I have felt the stirring in me to revisit the wells I dug in the Spirit at the beginning. I have been reminded of the times in my teens where I would go to youth services around Australia and experience God in powerful ways, and the tent revivals where I would encounter the glory of God and be out in the Spirit for hours as the Lord ministered to me. I miss the straw in my hair and messy crying as the Lord branded me deeply. This craving is always the prelude to a new season of visitation and encounter, and many are now feeling that stir.

There is a cry resounding in the earth right now of a bride who has lost her way, ran out of oil, and dropped her torch, exclaiming, "Bring me back! Bring me back to my first love! Bring me back to the encounters, bring me back to being on my face in the glory!"

Writing this book for me has been the "going back" journey. I can't even tell you how many days I have been a blubbering mess as I looked back and could only see the faithfulness of the Father. I didn't have this guide in my journey, but knowing it's going to help you and others like me is the greatest gift and honor. I am very grateful.

THE GREAT RESET & THE BLANK SLATE

I believe God is bringing us back in many areas because the enemy's plan over the years has been to *add* things to our lives that *subtract* from us. It's like living with so much overhead that you can't function in the day-to-day effectively, and that needs to change, so don't fear His great emancipation of your life. It will bring you back to the beginning. Back to joy. Back to wonder. And back to the adventure. It will feel like a blank slate, but that's a great place to be! He will free you from:

- pressure and expectations
- fears and foreboding
- the wrong assignments or projects
- the wrong people and alignments
- soul clutter and fogginess of vision
- bad experiences and painful memories
- bad theology and mindsets
- hardness of heart
- busyness and wasted energy

BRINGING US BACK TO OUR ROOTS

Earlier in the book, I mentioned that God is bringing us back to the garden of intimacy and that is the heart of reformation—to restore what was lost and reset us back to our factory conditions and settings. But looking globally and corporately, what else is God bringing us as the Church back to?

Here are a few that are burning in my heart right now:

- We are coming back to face-to-face encounters with Jesus.
- We are forsaking the intellectual experience for the glory.
- We are coming back to the Bible again as our foundation. We need a revolution of the Word of God!
- We are coming back to our mandate for souls and preaching less to the choir.
- We are rattling the pews and mobilizing the Church.
- We are kicking out the weak gospel and coming back to the powerful gospel again.
- We are repenting where we have sold out for acceptance and favor with man and the world.
- We are losing our brands, idols, and prostitution of the gospel for business and profit.

A ZIKLAG MOMENT

One of my favorite Bible stories that speaks prophetically of reformation is the story of David and his men who after returning to Ziklag find their camp had been raided.

> David and his men reached Ziklag on the third day. Now the Amalekites had raided the Negev and Ziklag. They had attacked Ziklag and burned it, and had taken captive the women and everyone else in it, both young and old. They killed none of them, but carried them off as they went on their way. When David and his men reached Ziklag, they found it destroyed

by fire and their wives and sons and daughters taken captive. So David and his men wept aloud until they had no strength left to weep. David's two wives had been captured—Ahinoam of Jezreel and Abigail, the widow of Nabal of Carmel. David was greatly distressed because the men were talking of stoning him; each one was bitter in spirit because of his sons and daughters. But David found strength in the Lord his God. Then David said to Abiathar the priest, the son of Ahimelek, "Bring me the ephod." Abiathar brought it to him, and David inquired of the Lord, "Shall I pursue this raiding party? Will I overtake them?" "Pursue them," he answered. "You will certainly overtake them and succeed in the rescue" (1 Samuel 30:1–8).

This story always stirs my spirit in the call of reformation because it's the "rescue" of what was lost, stolen, or forgotten. David's men were heartsick with grief, and David knew that the only way it was going to turn around was if he sought the Lord.

The meaning of the name Amalek, who are the oppressors in this story, is "to twist, to wring," and in a spiritual sense this represents the demonic assignments and influences that twist us into submission and steal what God has given us. Truth, purity, power, identity, and anointing—the adversary wants all of these stripped from us, but God has armed us with an anointing to *go back* and *take back* what is rightfully ours.

We are in another Ziklag moment of history. The enemy has taken our kids, our families, and nation, and God is saying to the Church to get off our pews and go pursue and recover all. We can't wait until the clergy approve it, or the evangelistic committee arranges it. We must decide what is most important to us— our comfort and hiding from confrontation or our freedoms. It's time to be a voice for something and be willing to be teachable and moldable under the Holy Spirit on the way.

PICK UP WHAT YOU DROPPED

I had another dream recently where I sat at a piano and felt the rush of disappointment hit me, the fears, and pain of a past season where I dropped my worship. I didn't know what to play, and then I felt Jesus come up behind me and put His arms on my arms and hands on my hands. He and I began to play together.

As I continued to play, suddenly a song erupted from me, and I began to sing what sounded like a new sound and a soundtrack of revival. When I woke up, I heard the Lord say, "Pick it up!" but I knew this was something the Lord was doing in the Church right now. Many have dropped their tools, their confidence, their ferocity, and fight. Many have dropped their passion and fire, promises and purpose, but let this be the moment that you clear the slate and *start again*. It's time to pick up what you dropped in your season of warfare, opposition, and wilderness.

- It's time to pick up your hope and joy.
- It's time to pick up your authority.
- It's time to pick up your unfulfilled promises.
- It's time to pick up your boldness and fire.
- It's time to pick up your tools and weapons of warfare.
- It's time to pick up your new mantle and let go of the grave clothes.

It's time to pick your instrument, your pen, your assignment, and *don't ever look back again*!

As wild ones, the mandate in this is simple. We are those called by Heaven to reinstate what was removed or demolished and to remind the Church what she dropped. We expose the things we have tolerated and allowed to taint us and lead the way forward. Wild ones, it's back to school time!

PROPHETIC SURVIVAL TIP

Always be teachable and moldable by the Holy Spirit. Stay a novice and never feel like you have seen it all or arrived. Live your life at His feet, and you'll never stumble.

CAMPFIRE PRAYER

Holy Spirit, take me back to the feet of Jesus and let me live my life camped there, fixed on You. Remove from me what isn't You and reinstate what I dropped or was cheated from by the enemy, in Jesus' name.

CHAPTER 32

Holiness & the Rise of Counterculture Reformers

An idol is something you have to check with before you say yes to God. —Jack Taylor

Warning: Polarizing content ahead. Proceed with offendable heart switched to off position.

Reformation doesn't feel fun all the time; in fact, I sometimes feel like the party pooper at times where others just seem to be able to settle into mediocrity, complacency, and avoid the bumps in the road that reformers are called to address. This was highlighted to me a few years ago when God revealed a major area of compromise in our church leadership. I didn't hear about it; God showed me in a dream, and then God told Christy the same thing the next day! I really struggled to bring it forward, but when I did, I thought they would appreciate my heart in how I did it. That was not the case at all, however. We were told we were judgmental and critical for bringing what we saw forward.

What you need to know right here is that you will not always be popular for being reformational. It seems to work backwards. The people you expect to stand with you while you are address-ing an issue and swinging your hammer are the ones who seem to oppose you or tell you to get out your rubber mallet instead. But they are always the ones who come back around years later, wanting to eat the fruit of your obedience. So, no, it's not a popular profession, but since when has this been about popularity?

The call of the reformer is a set-apart life of holiness and purity. It sounds like I'm saying you can't be human, but that's not what I'm saying. I'm saying that it's simply a life living with a strong conviction to ensure that you are burning brightly for Jesus and nothing and no one else.

> *Those who repent I baptize with water, but there is coming a man after me who is more powerful than I am. In fact, I'm not even worthy enough to pick up his sandals. He will submerge you into union with the Spirit of Holiness and with a raging fire!* (Matthew 3:11 TPT).

The word *holiness* means "set apart," and that is exactly who reformers are. They are set apart for a purpose. They are the new wine that is kept for last because they will be needed to usher the Church out of compromise and into being fiery hot lovers again! Think about John the Baptist for a minute. His message was simple and powerful, but he wasn't popular for it. No.

POLARITY OR POPULARITY?

There was no one more polarizing than Jesus. You could take almost anything He said and see the loud invitation in blazing neon, "*Choose!*" People had become used to being oppressed by Rome, distant from God, and paying huge religious penance just to stay under the atonement. Their lives were a constant list of people to appease and hurdles to jump over. Enter Jesus.

Jesus upset the apple cart quickly because He was suddenly giving the Israelites a second option other than traditions and sacrifices. He healed the sick so they didn't have to wait by the pool, set the demon-possessed free, and forgave sins. They no longer had to bow down to the only option they were born into. They had a choice, the ability to choose God or man, freedom or religion. Think of even these well-known words of Jesus:

> *The thief comes only to steal and kill and destroy; I have come that they may have life, and have it to the full* (John 10:10).
>
> *Jesus answered, "I am the way and the truth and the life. No one comes to the Father except through me"* (John 14:6).

In these two statements, Jesus paints the picture very clearly: "Choose Me. The other way isn't good for you." If Jesus were walking on the earth today, He would have been called an insensitive, polarizing preacher when all He did was try give people the ticket to a better way.

The word *polarize* means to cause something, especially something that contains different people or opinions, to divide into two completely opposing groups.

When you elevate the things of the world over the things of God, then yes, you are left with two polar opposites, and right now we are at this crossroad.

GOLDEN CALVES OR GOLD CROWNS

We have the choice to either go along with the flow of culture or to be representatives of Heaven's culture. This is the decision every single person on the planet must make every day in small and large decisions. In one of Jesus' most polarizing statements. He said this:

No one can serve two masters. Either you will hate the one and love the other, or you will be devoted to the one and despise the other. You cannot serve both God and money (Matthew 6:24).

At its core, the deception of modern culture is not just double-mindedness but idolization. It's choosing the golden calf instead of the glory, the public image and sparkling reputation instead of seeking to represent and reveal Jesus. And the decision of the hour for the Church is yet again, who will we serve?

I know that it may be easier to take the road of least resistance, but can you live with yourself like that? I want crowns to throw at the feet of Jesus, not earthly accolades. No thanks.

"But if serving the Lord seems undesirable to you, then choose for yourselves this day whom you will serve, whether the gods your ancestors served beyond the Euphrates, or the gods of the Amorites, in whose land you are living. But as for me and my household, we will serve the Lord" (Joshua 24:15).

HOLD THE CAKE

There was a time when Jesus was approached by a rich young ruler who wanted to know how to have eternal life.

Then a young man approached Jesus and bowed before him, saying, "Wonderful teacher—is there a good work I have to do to obtain eternal life?" Jesus answered, "Why would you call me wonderful? God alone is wonderful. And why would you ask what good work you need to do? Keep the commandments

*and you'll enter into the life of God." "Which ones?"
he asked. Jesus said, "Don't murder, don't commit adultery, don't steal, don't lie, honor your father
and mother, and love those around you as you love
yourself." "But I've always obeyed every one of them
without fail," the young man replied. "What else do I
lack?" Jesus said to him, "If you really want to be perfect, go now and sell everything you own. Give your
money to the poor and your treasure will be trans-
ferred into heaven. Then come back and follow me
for the rest of your life." When the young man heard
these words, he walked away sad, for he had great
wealth* (Matthew 19:16–22 TPT).

The way Jesus dealt with this was brilliant because He used the situation to reveal the state of this young ruler's heart. Let's break down the conversation.

The young man was after eternal life, not the Life-giver. Modern culture wants all the rewards without the commitments

Jesus challenged him on his works mentality. The ruler wanted to know what he had to do for Jesus and what Jesus would do for him. He was after a product and wanted to know how he could buy it.

Jesus' answer was for him to keep the commandments, which He knew a performance-based person like this young man would have done, but Jesus said it as a setup to reveal the real decision the young man needed to make that wasn't about a trade.

"Sell all your own and give it away" was referring to giving all the man had for Jesus. Giving this life away for an eternal one disappointed this man because he thought he could have his cake and eat it, too. He thought he could have a life on earth his way as well as eternal life.

The Kingdom is an all-or-nothing Kingdom because, the moment you start compromising the pure thing you have, it cheapens it, waters it down, and diminishes it. The result?

- A watered-down gospel
- No transformation
- No healings
- No signs, wonders, and miracles
- Fewer salvations

THE GOSPEL OF MIXTURE

In essence, a *mixture* that is deceiving so many is a culture of mixed values. It wants the benefits of the Kingdom with the acceptance of man, the praises of man, and the popularity of the world. It's where we take a truth of the Kingdom and mix it together with an earthly value that sounds holy but isn't. Add anything to the Word, and you have a compromise. Add anything to what Jesus said, and you have polluted the truth cake, and the whole batter needs to be thrown out.

In the heat of the myriad of different tensions throughout 2020 and the Covid year, I had never felt more at a crossroad in my life and calling. It was in a good way. It seemed that any gray that was previously there was suddenly gone, and people had to choose where they were going to stand. I'm not meaning politically; I mean that everyone had to either choose between standing with good or evil. They had to decide whether they were going to be a voice for the right thing or a voice for what looks like the right thing but isn't.

Mixture can also be defined in this way:

- Almost good

- Almost right
- Almost pure
- Almost truth
- Almost restoration

A few degrees off the axis of God's best is where we have to use our discernment most to distinguish mixture.

> *But solid food is for the mature, for those who have their powers of discernment trained by constant practice to distinguish good from evil* (Hebrews 5:14).

NO COMPROMISE!

Recently when praying for the new year, I had a dream. I was at a Christian carnival and was invited to be with the "in" crowd, which included some A-list Christian names, but I felt strongly not to join them. Next, I saw a friend who also turned down this group, and he said to me, "Nate, where we are going, we cannot compromise!" I woke up shaking in the fear of the Lord.

The word *compromise* means a stance in between two different things, to find or follow a way between extremes, or in other words to sit on the fence, take the easy path, the road of least resistance, and not make a stand in one place or conviction. In this time in history, we can no longer be lukewarm or call the middle ground the higher ground, as if it were some kind of spiritually enlightened place. Let's call it for what it is: being neither hot nor cold, not standing for truth or for the lies, and avoiding confrontation so you are appeasing everyone around you. This doesn't last long, and eventually the sand beneath begins to shake, and you must stand somewhere.

In this time in history, we cannot be the kings of mixture, holding both the ropes of culture and the ropes of the Kingdom. It's a tug of war we can't win. We must take a stand for righteousness!

In this time in history, God is wanting us to be in fruitful relationships and alignments, not convenient ones for the sake of networking or being in the who's who. God is jealously leading you out of unequally-yoked relationships and connections that are not sustainable. He doesn't want you opening yourself up to immature people who lack the character to go the distance or the desire to follow the Lord where you are. But watch as God brings you people who are lovers of Himself and not lovers of themselves or some other temporary, fleeting affection.

In this time in history, we need to be a people of no compromise, knowing our convictions.

We need to learn to protect the anointing and not let flies in the ointment.

We need to learn how to *discern* better and not cast our pearls.

We need to learn how to establish better boundaries and expectations in relationships and learn how to honor better than we have.

In this time in history, it may feel like your inner circle gets smaller, but your tribe will get bigger.

CHRISTIAN CELEBRITY CULTURE IS LOSING ITS INFLUENCE

A standout point of my dream was the fact that many were following Christian celebrity culture and, in doing so, had lost their discernment and way.

In this time in history, God is purging leadership, redefining motives, and removing worldly influence from the high places of the Church. We can't operate with high charisma and little character. The fruit of this is damage and pain and communities that never experience transformation.

I believe that celebrity culture in the Church will begin to show its cracks and inability to hide its motives and salesmanship.

Those in prominent positions given by men who have no true desire to build the kingdom will be uprooted.

Celebrity culture doesn't raise soldiers but cheerleaders who have no clue how to swing a sword, and where we are going, it will not be green rooms that will be the training ground for the best warriors but the hard-knock seasons of wilderness.

There is a famous Australian military training camp called "puckapunyal" or "valley of winds" in the indigenous language, which has been known for raising the best soldiers. This year, we need the wind of the Spirit upon us and through us, not the wind and hot air of ego and self-righteousness.

God is burning the golden calves that have been holding the Church back from being effective, from where we have chosen to elevate and worship anything else other than King Jesus.

Ministry and status have been an idol, and they must be thrown in the fire.

In this time in history, we must have one affection and motivation: to know Jesus and to make Him known on the earth.

"Yet I hold this against you: You have forsaken the love you had at first" (Revelation 2:4).

THE RULING SWORD & THE RENDING SWORD

Three years ago, I was in worship in my room when I went into a vision and saw myself holding a sword out as is done in battle. Instantly, I thought, *Wow! This is the reigning sword for the nations!* and I felt the power and authority in it. This was the ruling sword God was placing in the hands of the Church to bring nations into alignment and see injustices fall. But then I watched as in the vision the sword began to turn counterclockwise toward me until the point was pressed up against my heart. Suddenly, I felt like the fire of Heaven was hot on me, and God began speaking, "Will this generation be a lover of themselves, or will they be a people set apart unto Me? Who will be My holy ones, My separated ones? Who will defy the culture of today and stand apart? Who will choose My mountain over the mountain of man's achievements? Who will be My holy ones?"

After this night, I truly haven't been the same. This deep cry of the Lord's desire for this generation was revealed as plain as day. God wants to use this generation for great governmental and cultural change, for walking in power and miracles, signs, and wonders, but first He is looking for a people who will say *yes* to the *rending* sword of holiness. Who will choose to make themselves low so He will be made great?

> "*Rend your heart and not your garments and return to the Lord . . .*" (Joel 2:13).

So let the cry of this hour be, "God, rend our hearts! Have Your way in us!"

OUT OF THE CRACKS

We have never lived in a time where it is more crucial to live holy lives. In the days to come, it will begin to be harder to distinguish good from evil because the enemy is casting his veil over the nations and calling evil good, but the gift that the wild ones bring to this era is that they have already been set apart by God for a long time, so they are able to see the things that others don't.

The Church has been waking. Sure, it's messy right now and chaotic. Opinions are flying left and right, but I see something amid it all. It's a church that is discovering her voice after appeasing culture for so long. I'm seeing a church that doesn't want to be silent anymore and wants a role in the writing of history. I see a church that has been stifled and ostracized, tamed, and distracted away from her purpose suddenly leave the sidelines and put her hand up for the sake of the gospel.

So, where we go from here is up to us. Will we push into the discomfort of having to grow in critical areas? Put on our battle armor and raise our swords against darkness and lower our daggers against others in the Body? Will we start to be part of the worldwide reformation and rebuilding God has initiated, or will we be sheep in this hour? Will we play humanistic games and jockey for self righteous ideals and thrones, or will we be filled with the Spirit and follow Him into the unknown?

No, we aren't going underground, into hibernation, round the mountain again, or into another season of captivity and inactivity. We are rising and shining, and we have only just begun, Church.

PROPHETIC SURVIVAL TIPS

Choose the road of purity. No mixture. No defilement. Don't get mixed up in the world's seductive narratives that look good but is far from holy. Stay hot for Jesus, and you'll see the difference.

CAMPFIRE PRAYER

Lord, keep me set apart unto You. Increase my discernment so I can see the difference between You and the sly ways of the world. Keep me on fire and never let me get far from Your presence, in Jesus' name.

CHAPTER 33

The Rise of the Media Army & the Silence of the Prophets of Baal

I heard my voice begin to rise up from my cave of defeat.
It sounded like a Lion cub looking for its roar, then the
Spirit came upon me, and I was never the same again.
How could I ever go back to silence again?
—Nate Johnston

There is a reformation coming to the high places of the world, the high places of man's achievement and ability. The high places are currently being used by the enemy to enforce his agenda. The enemy uses the high places to taint and intimidate the Church like kindergarten bully tactics, in essence yelling, "I'm the king of the castle!" The reality is that he is an imposter fulfilling a role that wasn't his to take. It never was his in the first place.

THE VACUUM & THE COUNTERFEIT

But in the vacuum of the lack of solid prophetic voices rising up and taking the media mountain, Jezebel has hired her false prophets to be the spokesmen for her fear and lies campaign that has spread a veil of confusion and manipulation upon the whole earth. The true prophets have been in hiding out of fear just like the story in 1 Kings 18:4.

While Jezebel was killing off the Lord's prophets, Obadiah had taken a hundred prophets and hidden them in two caves, fifty in each, and had supplied them with food and water.

In the meantime, the prophets of Baal have been taking the microphone and dictating their demonic agenda, and in the absence of truth, the world has been lapping it up.

FROM THE GROUND UP

The difference between the voices of God and the voices of Baal is simple. True prophetic voices speak from Heaven to Earth. Truth is from the Father. It's not manipulated or contrived. It's pure. The false prophets of Baal speak from the ground up. It's soulish and worldly at best, and straight up demonic, manipulative, and super-spreader lie at its worst.

Genesis 11 speaks about a people who wanted to get closer to Heaven outside of seeking God:

Now the whole world had one language and a common speech. As people moved eastward, they found a plain in Shinar and settled there. They said to each other, "Come, let's make bricks and bake them thoroughly." They used brick instead of stone, and tar for mortar. Then they said, "Come, let us build ourselves a city, with a tower that reaches to the heavens, so that we may make a name for ourselves; otherwise we will be scattered over the face of the whole earth" (vv. 1–4).

In the rest of the story, we see God bringing confusion upon them, and they begin speaking other languages and then disperse into the nations. My point? The false media prophets of the world are using lies as bricks to make a name for themselves for the sake of power and achieving Godlike status. Who does this remind you of? Lucifer had this same heart.

But we are now in the middle of what I believe is a reformational shift of power in the mountain of media.

THE DREAM OF THE SECOND HEAVEN BATTLE

Last year, during the beginning of the pandemic, I had a dream where I was witnessing a second Heaven battle that was horrific. It was a battle, not of two sides, but involving many different armies that were all colliding in a bloodied battle of ideals, opinions, and beliefs. What shocked me was that I could distinguish that some of these armies were believers who had become caught up in the wrong fight and were battling in the same way that the world was.

As I was watching this scene, I could sense that this was the fruit of the mainstream media and the demonic principality behind it: mass hysteria and onslaught. The battle was causing a flood of witchcraft to permeate the airwaves and release a global cloud of confusion and haziness that was blocking the Heavens in a sense. When I woke up, I felt a deep travail for the Church and began to prophesy, "The witchcraft needs to stop now in Jesus' name!" and then I logged into my social media accounts and started prophesying this over every platform and over the world news stations.

MEDIA WARFARE, THE SHIFT OF POWER, & THE RISING MEDIA ARMY

As I continued to prophesy, I saw that a shift was coming to the media mountain. I saw the eyes of the Lord staring at the media of the world, and His eyes burned with a holy justice. I knew it was a reckoning day for the media of the world that has lied, twisted, and skewed the truth for far too long. In the absence of the prophetic office taking up their place and influence in governing the airwaves, the counterfeit prophetic has been occupying it. The leviathan, twisting spirit and Jezebel have been lording it over the earth and releasing deception, lies, and demonic propaganda to champion the enemy's causes. It has blinded generations and people groups for far too long, but right now God is raising up a prophetic remnant who will take back their birthright.

The line that keeps bubbling forth from my spirit has been, "We must be the new media!" which is timely since we are in what I call "the roaring epoch" for the Church and the beginning of a new prophetic revolution. There is a Davidic people who are stepping up now. They sound differently than what we have been hearing. They are not party prophets but *Kingdom voices*. They will be the radical and confronting *voice of truth* in an age of smoke and mirrors to restore the Word of the Lord to the land that has been dry and cracked from the lack of oil and revival rain. They won't bow down to the cultural kings and gods to appease people so as not to be alienated or attacked, and they won't use the arrows of the enemy to fight their fights either. They will be the revolution of clear Kingdom voices that *expose* deception and point the Church and world back to Jesus.

THE THIRD HEAVEN STRATEGY
& THE CLEARING OF THE AIRWAVES

As I continued to prophesy, I heard a line from the old 90s song by Bittersweet Symphony: "But the airwaves are clean, and there's nobody singing to me now." I knew that the Lord was speaking that the airwaves needed to be cleared and cleaned by the sound and song of the David generation, the worshipers, intercessors, and watchmen who would dare to rise up of the second Heaven warfare and into the place of speaking into what God was doing.

The media of the world literally operates in the same spiritual realm as the place where angels and demons war, the second Heavens. The word *media* comes from the word *medium*, which means "middle layer" or "middle place." This is the second Heavens, but we as the Body of Christ cannot operate from the same realm. Instead, we must come up higher and release the word of the Lord from our jurisdiction and position *"in heavenly places."* This is the place where God is calling us to as the Church, and we must ascend right now if we are going to see the shift we have been wanting to see.

> *He raised us up with Christ the exalted One, and we ascended with him into the glorious perfection and authority of the heavenly realm, for we are now co-seated as one with Christ!* (Ephesians 2:6 TPT).

Our strategy is simple. We can't keep wrestling flesh and blood, but we must get out of the distraction and counterfeit fights and come up higher and worship, prophesy, and pray in the heart of God into the earth. It is only when we come up higher that we will see what God is doing and not just the chaos the enemy is wreaking on the earth. We must hear and release the solutions of Heaven! Let the pure voices arise, clear the air, and reveal the heart of our King in this chaotic time.

After this I looked, and there before me was a door standing open in heaven. And the voice I had first heard speaking to me like a trumpet said, "Come up here, and I will show you what must take place after this" (Revelation 4:1).

It's time for you to be the voice you were called to be, to clear the airwaves and speak *unbridled truth* from the Heavens and lead the Church out of the opinion-fueled, bloody battle of the second Heavens, where the media of the world operates. Set the record straight from the Lord's heart. The waters are murky right now and the prophets are being bashed, but watch the ones God anoints and mantles to take down the Goliaths who have been casting a veil over the earth. This is a clashing of kingdoms and the take back of the airwaves, a removal of imposters from usurped places of influence and authority, and the beginning of the emerging of Davids sent into the broadcast hub of the earth.

Make no mistake, this is not a skip-through-the-tulips religious excursion. It's a hostile takeover of darkness where the reigns have been held for far too long by those who deceive and use witchcraft to blind the nations and muzzle the ones who confront it. Media movements arise. Media prophets arise. Watchmen, let's go higher and let's clear the air!

We are the new media, and we don't operate the same way the world does. We don't employ gossip and chatter as a weapon for our purposes, and we don't dishonor to prove ourselves right. We don't judge others' opinions as if we know their process, and we don't assume people's hearts based from a soundbite or post. That's what worldly media does. At the same time, this doesn't mean we settle and go along with the herd. We don't bow down to the cultural gods to appease people or back out of truth because we fear being alienated or attacked, but it means that we don't use the arrows that came at us to establish our case or stand firm at our post. There is a way to be boldly unashamed of what we stand for and what we believe without being another biting and hurtful voice on the airwaves. We are the Kingdom. We live higher than that.

We have this burning conviction, and we must sound different to the world, to the media, to the wisest and most knowledgeable earthly voices alive. We must sound like the Father. We must carry His tone, His timbre, and His thunderous roar. It is those who will set themselves apart in the days to come that will find their mouths being filled with the language of Heaven and the newscast from the throne. They are the ones the world is longing to hear because the world is craving the sound of truth as the sound of the counterfeit has been turned up to eleven in the last year. Let's be that sound.

Let's prophesy to the airwaves! Let's hold strong to our post without wrestling flesh and blood. Let the pure voices arise, clear the air, and reveal the heart of our King in this chaotic time.

The culture war doesn't end here. This is where we need to stand our ground and make our voices known.

We will be the new media!

We will be the new sound!

We will crash the airwaves with truth!

CRASHING THE ENEMY'S TOWERS

I shared earlier how in 2018 we went to Washington, DC, on a prayer mission, and as we were taking an Uber, the driver said something interesting. He said that, when the women's march took place in January of 2017 in protest of Trump's inauguration, there were 500,000 who turned up for the event. Because of that, something happened no one expected. With 500,000 women all on their phones, texting, calling, and Face Timing, it crashed the towers, and no one was able to communicate until it was fixed.

This statement made me think, *What if God's people crashed the enemy's towers? What if we were to take back the airwaves for God?* And herein lies our challenge. Will we run to the cave, or will we be a voice for the times?

A NEW LANGUAGE & THE BREAKING OF BABEL

The Lord has been speaking to me about a new language that is going to unlock new dimensions of God. It's a vocabulary and heart that we haven't heard or understood. These are new expressions on the Lord's heart that are about to manifest through His sons and daughters.

Do you know the tower of Babel was built to access the Heavens without intimacy? It was an illegitimate access, so it was denied. It created confusion and disunity. Babel actually means "a confused noise made by a number of voices," but the Lord spoke to me and said, "It is time for the one sound. It is time for the sound of unity." There has been many streams, but there has been no rivers. It is time for the rivers. It is time for the rivers. "No more Babel," says the Lord.

There will be utterances of the Spirit of God that are going to burst forth from inside you. Get ready for the Lord to speak to you in fresh ways. Many are about to have dreams and visions like they have never known before. Many are about to step into different areas of revelation, and the Lord is speaking and declaring things to them and showing them things that they have never heard anywhere before. The Lord says, "Get ready. Get out your pen. Get out your pen, bring forth what I show you is to come. Bring forth. Write down, declare it, and speak it," because we are in a season of a fresh infilling of God where new rivers are flowing.

THIS IS YOUR CHARGE

- Don't hide.
- Be bold.
- Lift your voice.
- Speak truth no matter the cost.
- Stand up for righteousness.
- Be God's mouthpiece no matter what the enemy says.
- Recognize there is healing in your words as well as truth.
- Don't apologize for confronting lies.
- Be the new media!
- Don't be afraid of the censoring spirit.

Wild ones, this is your charge: Be the new media!

PROPHETIC SURVIVAL TIPS

Leave the cave. Shut the door. Never go back. Stand up for justice and don't let religion shut down your righteous roar in this hour. Set the standard high and let others meet you there.

CAMPFIRE PRAYER

Lord, show me how to be a voice for this hour that speaks from Your heart and clears the airwaves from all the noise. I will be Your mouthpiece and Your messenger. Fill me with Your words, in Jesus' name!

CHAPTER 34

The Prophetic 2.0 Emerging & the Bare Teeth Bride

*The wicked flee though no one pursues, but the righteous
are as bold as a lion.* —Proverbs 28:1

I couldn't shake the visions I would see over and over of church
buildings emptying and people leaving the safe shores of ministering to the Body only to step into their odyssey of apostolic
sending into the nations and governmental influence. Ever since
I had the encounter in December 2009 in Redding, I was a wreck.
I came from an outreach-focused church, so I knew what church
out of the walls looked like, but it wasn't like this. What I was
seeing was a mass exodus of some kind or a shift of focus or an
awakening?

More recently, I walked the halls of Bethel Church. I felt that
I needed to come there and remember what God did that Friday night in 2009, but I asked new questions this time: What are
You doing, Lord? What is coming? Where will the Church be in
another twelve years? I know this much. Reformation is needed.
We have needed the entire Church to stand up, not just the few,
and we have desperately needed an awakening of the Bride like
in the days of John the Baptist.

*From the moment John stepped onto the scene until
now, the realm of heaven's kingdom is bursting forth,*

and passionate people have taken hold of its power
(Matthew 11:12 TPT).

I believe almost twelve years later that what I saw is right now upon us. We have seen the old wineskin burst, and this max exodus from the prison of stale and powerless Christianity, and the beginning of the rising of a remnant once exiled who are moving into position as the navigators and voices of this great move.

THE DEATH, BURIAL, & NEW BIRTH

In 2016, the Lord said to me that a death to an era was coming. I wondered why He didn't say end rather than death. I believe it was because where we are going won't be a transition into a new time with the same paradigm. No, it will be so far removed from what we have known that it will feel like the old move and old ways and old methods died. Just like at the wedding of Cana that I have mentioned many times, the old wine had to run out before the new could come. This is what we call transition.

> *Let me make this clear: A single grain of wheat will never be more than a single grain of wheat unless it drops into the ground and dies. Because then it sprouts and produces a great harvest of wheat—all because one grain died* (John 12:24).

I believe we have all been witnessing that death. Things are not working how they used to, and those who have attached themselves to moves and structures and not Jesus will have to adjust to move with the Spirit. But what is this era we are moving into? It's the era of the voice of the Bride. I believe it's the Church discovering she has something to say and has a major role in shifting the course of history and shaking the nations.

Who can teach the Church, guide the Church, and lead the Church forward in being an influence in a chaotic time? That's right, the wild ones. They are the John the Baptists who step in as the prelude to the main event that is coming. They are now stepping up and instructing the Church, "Rise up, stand up, and speak, or someone will speak for you! Champion truth, or truth will be defined for you! Write the laws, or morality and values will be defined for you! You got this, Church!"

SPEAKING TO THE BONES OF
A "ONCE WAS" ARMY

The following scripture spoke to me recently.

Some time later, when he went back to marry her, he turned aside to look at the lion's carcass, and in it he saw a swarm of bees and some honey (Judges 14:8).

Why would something sweet be in something dead? Then it hit me! This is our calling. We see beyond the storm, and we see the honey in the middle of the dead carcass. Wild ones have a strange knack and purpose that in a death-season they call forth the new life and new beginning that others don't see. They are the ones at the tomb calling forth Lazarus, even when Lazarus feels done and doesn't want to come. This is your role to the Church. You are a reformer, yes, but you are a cheerleader, champion, and coach as well. Our priority is this: We only have one thing in our sights, the *ecclesia* being raised up, roaring, bold, and shining bright in the earth.

We are in an Ezekiel 37 moment where the dead, dormant, and decommissioned need to be called back to life. This is what we are about to see:

- We are about to see the dry bones army. The sleeping Church will become some of the most radical warriors we have ever seen because the pandemic woke them up.
- We will see the Church throw out the pointless tools and weapons and messages and get back to the simple gospel again.
- We will see those who were decommissioned get back their fire and those who were stuck in a rut and on the sidelines get back their passion and purpose.
- We are going to see a soul-winning army arise. It will be an army whose anointing is to go after souls, and they will go hand in hand with revivalists who are called to uncap wells in the nations.
- We are going to see the next level of awakening around the earth, and it's our job to prophesy them awake.

So I prophesied as he commanded me, and breath entered them; they came to life and stood up on their feet—a vast army (Ezekiel 37:10).

THIS PLACE IS TOO SMALL!

I believe we are in a parallel time in history to 2 Kings 6 where the company of prophets said to Elisha:

"Look, the place where we meet with you is too small for us. Let us go to the Jordan, where each of us can get a pole; and let us build a place there for us to meet." And he said, "Go." . . . As one of them was cutting down a tree, the iron axhead fell into the water. "Oh no, my lord!" he cried out. "It was borrowed!" The man of God asked, "Where did it fall?" When he

showed him the place, Elisha cut a stick and threw it there, and made the iron float. Lift it out," he said. Then the man reached out his hand and took it" (2 Kings 6:1–2, 5–7).

How is that time like our time now? The company of the prophets recognized they were limited. There was a ceiling, and they needed to break through. It's the realization of the time of the 1.0 being over and needing an upgrade into something new.

They knew they had to build. This is a time of the building of the voices of God.

The lost axe head and the miracle retrieval represent the power of the Spirit and how this upgrade cannot happen by man's hands but only be birthed by the Spirit.

It's the removal of man's tainted ways over the prophetic.

It's building something lasting that is pure.

Elisha performing the miracle represents the double-portion anointing.

VISION OF THE BARED TEETH BRIDE

In September of 2020 in Rosh Hashanah, I had a vision of a lion that was roaring, and then it opened its mouth even wider to reveal all its teeth. The Lord then spoke to me and said, "This will be the year that the Church goes from beginning to roar to baring its teeth!" I believe we are going to see the Church rise up as the bold Bride she was always called to be, not tolerating and passively allowing robbery or being bullied. It's time we rise up as the lions we were called to be, not the ones preyed upon by lions. This is who we are!

IT'S TIME FOR THE PROPHETIC 2.0

In February 2016, I was in worship when the Lord said with heavy grief on His heart, "Where are the Kim Clements of the earth?" I felt it. It was the grief that not many have taken up the prophetic office the way that Kim Clement had, with full abandon, with full worship like Kim had—with the heart of a David who knew how to blast the prophetic trumpet from deep within. It was an all-or-nothing thing for Kim. He was all in. You can't be someone in that governmental authority in the office of the prophet but still operate in the fear of man or go after the praises of man. You can't do both, and the Lord is doing something right now in the prophetic camp.

There is a deep marking and a burning for prophets to step into office at all costs. It requires a laying down, a surrender, and a commissioning of fire on the prophets. I heard the Lord say, "Will you speak what I give you? Will you say what I tell you to say? Will you not edit what I give you? Will you step into the weightiness of the calling upon your life? Will you be a heavyweight voice for Me? It will cost you everything. You will be misunderstood and live before your time, but you will live in the fulfilment of the call upon your life."

Again, at the beginning of 2021, I heard the Lord say something similar to what He said to me in 2016. He said, "Where are the prophets? Where are the heavyweights? Where did they go? It's time for Issachar to rise up! It's time for Issachar to rise up! There is specific revelation I want to give and strategies I want to hand them to build. I have insight for nations and cities that will evict principalities and break down walls of darkness. There are keys that I want to give them. It's time for Issachar to arise and lead the charge!"

When I woke up, I felt the fear of the Lord envelope me, and I realized there were areas were I had been taming my voice. I felt the conviction of Heaven on me and a new boldness and purpose rise up in me. This is what I felt like the Lord was speaking;

- Firstly, when the Lord said, "Where are the prophets?" I knew it was in reference to the many prophets who went into hiding prior to or after the US election in January. The assault on the prophetic movement was so severe that it took many out. I believe God is healing and reviving those who felt like they fell in the battlefield and have been stuck since.

- When I heard, "Where are the prophets?" my spirit heard, "Where have my weighty glory prophets gone?" The enemy has targeted the weighty, unedited Word of the Lord by hurling the fear of man and fear of reputation at the prophets, and many have changed their message, but the Lord is removing the fear that caused them to change what they were called to say.

- God has been refining the house of the prophets and from the ashes has forged and commissioned a new breed of prophets who like Gideon's men will not be sold out to culture or to the praises of man. This 2.0 is the result of the refiner's fire and the threshing floor that are producing an army of warriors that will stand and persist and set their faces like flint.

- They will restore the office of a prophet to its former glory, and we will see a wave of prophetic heavyweights rise up.

- So, who are the sons of Issachar? Genesis 49:14 says that *"Issachar is a strong donkey, lying down between the sheepfolds."* The two places it is speaking about is Manasseh ("withdrawal, debt, hope evaporated") and Zebulun (the wished-for dwelling place, promise).

- I believe Issachar is the prophetic anointing to take people and nations from lack and debt and into the promise. They stand in the gap and speak and prophesy, leading the way into the new day.

- First Chronicles 12:32 says, *"From Issachar, men who understood the times and knew what Israel should do."* This means they had the anointing and responsibility of knowing the times and seasons, knowing what God was doing and receiving the blueprints and practical knowledge of how to walk them out.

- The name Issachar means "there is recompense," and as the name suggests, these ones can see the promise arising from the ashes of the wilderness and speak restoration in the middle of calamity.

- The Issachar prophets are critical in these times because they can sense the changes and shifts in specific epoch cycles. They help give a roadmap and clarity to both the macro- and micro-processes. They know how to speak governmentally and personally to those walking through blind or unknown periods. They connect the dots for those feeling lost and hopeless.

- These prophets know that government is not a dirty word and that it's actually a major component of the call. Remove that, and you have lost your major sphere of impact.

- This dream revealed to me God's heart for the prophetic church. We are so quick to throw the baby out with the bathwater, but without the prophets, we are sitting ducks.

- I believe God is stirring up the hearts of those who have dropped their zeal and voice, and He is asking them to pick up their zeal and raise their voice again.

- He is commissioning a new army and a new sound of prophets who will lead the charge into this glorious new season. Will you pick up the baton?

This is what I believe we will see moving into the 2.0:

- We will see the prophetic movement face a crossroads of either baring their teeth or being silent and inactive. The days of passive prophecy without power are over, and God is refining the prophetic, pulling prophets up higher into their weightier calling, and extending an invitation to step into the mantle of real prophecy.

- Sugar-coated words are not going to take us anywhere in 2021; in fact, the conviction of the Holy Spirit is going to fall upon those using prophecy as a marketing ploy, and they will either lose the show and shape up, or go back to prophet character school.

- We are going to be so surprised who God raises up and surprised at who God restores and brings back from the brink of hell. We will be shocked by whom God mantles with prophetic wisdom and insight for the hour.

- The houses without real prophets are going to be stumbling in the dark, constantly thrown back and forth in the dichotomy of culture, while those who embrace the pure prophets will stand the tests that come, have deep roots, and be on the cutting edge of what God is doing.

- God is raising up a prophetic company that will stand true to what He has said no matter what shakes and no matter what comes against the Church. They are the ones that against all odds, opposition, and ridicule have not moved from their post and they will continue to point the church to true north in turbulent times.

I believe we have just stepped into the era of the prophetic 2.0 where God has commissioned the Church not to be silent anymore but be a mighty influence in the earth. This is the hour that the prophets are needed to arise and step into a place of responsibility to decree what Heaven is saying governmentally and see it shift nations. But *all* of us as believers are a prophetic people, and we carry the *words* of the Father that shift things around us.

STEP INTO YOUR OFFICE!

So I prophesy, "Prophets arise!" There are many out there who have been operating as prophetic encouragers, but they are actually mantled as prophets. I heard God say, "Step into the weight of your jacket, step into the weight of your mantle, step into your office!" It's time to step out of that place where you're just sitting on the fence waiting and hoping that someone is going to validate you. It's never going to come! You're going to need to dig a little deeper. You're going to have to let the Father's embrace commission you because it's not going to happen by man.

If you're waiting for that moment, it's not going to come. Prophets, it's time! We're stepping out of the schoolyard and into the deep rivers again. Prophets are not just going to be mouth-pieces bringing the Word of the Lord to the four corners of the earth. We are going to see their words come to pass. We're going to be people that activate and raise up this generation in the voice of the Lord.

A NEW VOICE, A NEW SOUND, & A NEW LANGUAGE

"I'm giving you a new voice and new unction, and you will operate from your office, not from the fear of man, not trying to say what is acceptable or even okay by the cultural norms or politically correct terms and language and verbiage, no! But you will speak forth from the Spirit. You will speak forth from the throne what I give you," says the Lord, because culture needs to be shifted and your voice carries power.

The trumpet blast needs to be sounded. Gates and doors need to be opened for governmental insights and strategy that are going to come. You are going to step into new realms. God is going to open your eyes, and you are going to see.

"Prophetic worshipers, arise! Prophetic worshipers, arise. It's time to demonstrate what it means to rule and legislate from Heaven," says the Lord.

The prophetic company is changing.

Kim Clements are rising.

The seers are rising.

The caves are emptying.

The bold ones are rising.

The wild ones are picking up their torch and running because it's time.

PROPHETIC SURVIVAL TIPS

Step into your jacket. Grab your calling with both your hands and occupy that space. Be the heavyweight you were called to be and be it unapologetically.

CAMPFIRE PRAYER

Lord, increase me! Expand me and grow me into all You have called me to be! I step into the 2.0 of this call upon my life, in Jesus' name!

CHAPTER 35

The Governmental Era, Wild Movements, & the Call to the Frontlines

There is some good in this world, and it's worth fighting for. —J. R. R. Tolkien

"God gave me a dream!" Christy said one morning in February 2020.

"What was it?" I asked.

"In the dream, I saw a calendar, and all the dates were crossed off except March 10. We need to fly to the USA on that date and no later," she said emphatically.

It didn't make sense, but we were obedient and left on that date like God instructed us in the dream.

On the flight, I was agitated, and I didn't know why. I felt like I was spiritually feeling a tearing or a massive closure but that made no sense at the time either. Three hours before landing, I was asleep when I was shaken awake by a demonic presence that was screaming at me, "You cannot come here! Stay away!" and for three hours I prayed and fought this relentless spirit that was clearly trying to scare me and keep me from coming. I recognized it was a demonic torment because we had experienced this flying into other nations and cities before, but never into San Francisco. I didn't understand it.

By the time we arrived, I was slowly getting back my peace yet was still a little rattled. This demon said we wouldn't be able to get in, that we weren't welcome, and that we had to go home. Was that true? As I stood in the customs line I began to worry and think, *What am I doing here? Maybe we should have stayed in Australia? What difference can I make anyways?*

No sooner had I had those thoughts when the soothing voice of the Father said to me, "Watch very carefully. I want you to learn something." Suddenly, two angels appeared right next to me as if they were standing in line with Christy, myself, and the girls. They were about nine feet tall, and down each of their sides they had the scripture Isaiah 45 written clearly enough for me to remember. I only saw them for a few seconds but instantly felt peace knowing God was with us and He was.

ISAIAH 45 GOVERNMENTAL MANDATE

As soon as we got to our destination, I opened my Bible to read Isaiah 45:1–3, which says:

> *"This is what Yahweh says to his anointed one, Cyrus, whose right hand I have grasped as my servant to conquer nations and dethrone their kings. For I will open doors before him and no fortified gate will remain closed. 'I will march out in front of you and level every obstacle. I will shatter to pieces bronze doors and slice through iron bars. I will give you hidden treasures from dark, concealed places and wealth waiting in secret sites so that you recognize me, for it is I, Yahweh, the God of Israel, who calls you by your name!'"* (TPT).

In that moment I realized two things: (1) the demonic presence I warred with on the plane was a demonic principality that was afraid of us coming, and (2) the two angels sent on assignment to us were governmental angels sent to break open the way for us and clear the path!

This is the governmental Isaiah 45 mandate of those called to occupy specific regions, areas, and spheres of influence, but this year they have been opposed and blocked from moving forward. Why? Because the enemy knows what havoc you are going to wreak on his plans in the years to come as you swing your reformational hammer. The principalities are shaking in their boots and are working overtime to stop you from moving into position.

Isaiah 45:1–3 is a governmental blueprint for reformers, stating we have authority and an anointing to:

- conquer nations and dethrone kings (remove the wrong influences, principalities, and spiritual overlords affecting these locations).
- open up all gates and doors with no access issues.
- level every obstacle, shatter doors, and cut through bars.
- discover and uncover the gold that has been hidden until we arrive on the scene!

What an incredible governmental reformational blueprint!

THE EVICTION NOTICES HAVE BEEN SENT

Recently, as I was prophesying over some friends who have a call to Hollywood, I went into a vision and saw a mass eviction taking place, where evil had been hidden and weaved throughout the industry. It was like a disease that had wrapped itself around something good, and it looked impossible to remove, but then I saw the root plucked out, and suddenly the rest began to dry up and die. Its source had been removed, and the eviction was in effect.

Then I began to prophesy, "The Lord says that there is a level playing field coming to the industry because the old titans of industry are losing their grip, and I am sending in kings in their place." I remembered Isaiah 45:1 after I prophesied this—*"to conquer nations and dethrone their kings."* What if the eviction was only the beginning? What if God was sending Kingdom kings into places where earthly kings once occupied seats of power?

INJUSTICES & VACANCIES
DRAW OUT THE DAVIDS

God is breaking our boxes of what ministry looks like because God has called the anointed, gifted, and fivefold offices, not just to the Church, but also to bring salt and light into the world. There are empty spaces and seats that are being filled that *no one* has ever occupied, and it's time we started to ask the question in this time of recalibration and relocation, "Where am I meant to be?"

In a vision, I saw a military strategy boardroom where there was a map showing people were being moved into new positions and vacancies that were not currently filled. These were strategic counterculture positions being filled so we would see the shifting of major strongholds in the nations and the takedown of giants that have been dominating and enforcing culture.

This year, God is raising up a reformational army for both the Church and an army sent into the heights of the secular. It already began in 2020, but we will start to see the rudder turning in specific areas in 2021.

God has Daniels, Josephs, and Esthers already planted in influential roles with the kings of the earth, but watch in the next few years as they emerge and God gives them a voice.

I believe that Goliath's taunts pulled upon the destiny of David and brought him to settle the score. The injustice in Esther's day pulled her into the favor and wisdom she needed to save her people. In the same way right now, the current issues of the earth are causing the sons and daughters of God, the wild reformers, to step up and put a target on the back of giants that have been holding regions and cities under their usurped dominion and enforcing demonic values.

In 2010, I woke up to hearing a groaning sound and saw Christy encountering the Holy Spirit in a way I hadn't before, and with tears running down her face, she cried, "I *must* save the babies! I must see Roe v. Wade fall and see the adoption reforms and the sanctify of life valued and protected again!" We have been pursuing this call ever since.

WRITE THE NEW SCRIPT

The irony is that God would use misfits. Those who have never felt validated or fully used by Him and have broken seasons and stories. He will use them to be the writers of the new script. They are the ones who are taking the messed up narratives, broken histories, and dysfunctional futures cast by a society that doesn't know the Father and are rewriting the script. How? God is sending wild ones into every sphere of the earth and using them as rebuilders and reformers for His plans and His designs. That is the era that is upon us.

The prophetic architects are here to establish the Kingdom of God, and they will *not* leave one stone unturned or ignore even one injustice.

He told them still another parable: "The kingdom of heaven is like yeast that a woman took and mixed into about sixty pounds of flour until it worked all through the dough" (Matthew 13:33).

RADICAL MOVEMENTS FROM RADICAL RIGHTEOUSNESS MOMENTS

The fruit of your *yes* after coming through the wilderness and navigating this unique calling is greater than you know. It doesn't stop here. God turns your message into a movement that results in reformation in the area you are called to speak into. A movement is more than just you; it's the mobilization of countless others into the very heart of God for that niche they have been created to pioneer with Heaven. It's the many movements that start because countless others receive their breakthrough through your movement. The key is being faithful with the wild radical pull on inside you even when others don't understand it.

When we launched our grow school in 2017, we were flagged by some religious watchdogs because our way of teaching and equipping was unconventional, but we knew God equipped people in His way. They said we were raising people up to be radical and undignified, and I said, "Yes, that's a byproduct of knowing God's heart. You do it with full abandon," but they didn't approve. To them, it was attacking what they had built because what they had built was built around a mainframe of religion and philosophy void of the Spirit. The fruit now is that we have raised and released many voices into the earth, and many movements have come from our school in its short four years. The key? We said *yes* when God said *go*. We were over religion stealing amazing voices and over those on the fringe feeling like outcasts. We were over seeing people and churches deal with the Jezebel spirit and not know what to do. So, we walked alongside people and saw ridiculous breakthroughs because of it.

We were on the Golden Gate Bridge for Sean Feucht's first #letusworship event, and we could tell it was the beginning of something great. As we were worshiping, we looked over and saw a policeman on a bike standing there with tears running down his face as we worshiped. He was the officer responsible for preventing suicide attempts and had prevented 200 so far in 2020 alone. We got to pray and bless this amazing brother and see the beginning of something that God breathed begin.

Unfortunately, leaders and even people close to Sean said he was being brash and arrogant, but he saw a violation, a potential vacancy in the spirit, and he chose to go after it. Talk about wild!

Movements are mobilizers. It may have started by one or two people and the Holy Spirit, but the purpose of a movement is for it to *move*! It becomes a raging wildfire that can't be contained, awakening and mobilizing people who then create their own movements. Movements evict and replace, like an exorcism: out with the demon and in with the Father's love and purpose. Then the second phase of a movement is to establish and occupy.

WILDFIRES & MICRO-MOVEMENTS

"Movements are beginning, and voices are rising," God said to me. Then I heard a peculiar phrase in my spirit, "micro-movements." What are they? What does that even mean? Then I saw the same vision I saw in 2009 and many times since of millions of fires lighting up the globe.

> micro (mī'krō) means "very small, microscopic, or small scale"

"What are you trying to say, Lord?" I asked.

He said, "I have given blueprints of millions of movements to my people that are needed for this time, but many are holding back because they look small and insignificant. But they need to know that they may look small in size or in comparison to other movements of the past, but they carry the same might, power, and backing of Heaven. They are wildfire movements that will be catalysts for revival around the earth and become the infrastructure for stewarding the greatest harvest the earth has yet seen!"

"So, what does this look like?" I asked. And again, I saw the parks with people gathering together and worshiping, fields with people praising the name of Jesus, coffee shops with people talking about Jesus and praying together, and homes where people were coming together and prophesying over each other. In my spirit, I knew this wasn't confined to the physical either, but people would begin movements online, in chats, social media groups, and fiery gatherings to mobilize believers around the world. The scripture that came to mind was Mathew 18:20, *"For where two or three gather in my name, there am I with them."*

ORGANIC MOVEMENTS & GARAGE BAND STARTUPS

The Lord then took me into a vision where I saw a worship band playing in a garage, and they were raw, unpolished, and yet carried so much anointing. In fact, in the vision I began to long for the sound of worship I haven't heard in a long time. The focus was less on the perfection and back onto the Presence.

Firstly, this spoke to me about God's heart in this season is not about the polished look and sound of the movement, but it's about His heart being revealed. He is after those who would simply reveal His heart instead of trying to look shiny and polished.

Secondly, it reminded me of the bands I grew up listening to that began in their garages and soon came into international demand. They didn't know that the sound that began in a garage would soon become anthems sung in stadiums, and in that same way, God is pouring out His Spirit upon that which looks foolish or rough around the edges.

Revival doesn't begin because we have the best building, band, or usher team, but because people decided they are going to come together and pray and invite Jesus into their city and state, and that is the very purpose of these rising movements. It's the convergence of two commissions:

> *"If my people, who are called by my name, will humble themselves and pray and seek my face and turn from their wicked ways, then I will hear from heaven, and I will forgive their sin and will heal their land"* (2 Chronicles 7:14).

> *"The Spirit of the Lord is upon me, and he has anointed me to be hope for the poor, freedom for the brokenhearted, and new eyes for the blind, and to preach to prisoners, 'You are set free!' I have come to share the message of Jubilee, for the time of God's great acceptance has begun"* (Luke 4:18 TPT).

These movements are rising as an answer to the problems in our nations, evil that has been hidden for far too long, and principalities that have long bullied our regions. These movements are beginning to release the Spirit of God into places He has not been invited into so that healing can come, freedom can come, eyes can be opened, hearts can be awakened, captives can be set free, the message of the gospel can go into the earth, and people who do not know God can encounter Him!

MICRO MOVEMENTS WITH MEGA INFLUENCE!

What I saw next was sobering and convicting. I saw these micro-movements being moved and positioned into key positions, regions, and spheres where they were needed most. God was not just raising up movements in the Church but in all mountains of influence: government, family, economy, and the arts and more. As the wild ones were positioned, they were releasing a turnaround anointing that was bringing Kingdom *alignment* to those areas they were in. God then said, "But will they cross over the line? Will they dare to break away from the religious and political spirit that moves against the flow of My Spirit?"

Then the scripture came to mind from Luke 4:8, *"Jesus answered, 'It is written: Worship the Lord your God and serve him only.'"*

I felt that God was saying, "Will you launch with only Me in mind? Will you lay down your reputation and image for Me? Will you jump out and live for Me alone?"

WHAT MOVEMENT IS IN YOU?

So, let me ask you, what micro movement is in you? What looks small but carries huge potential and anointing? Just like the word *microscope*, your movement may look small, but when God takes a hold of it, He *magnifies* it!

Here are a few keys for those wanting to launch in this season:

- Change your perspective on what a God has given you. Look through His eyes. "Do not despise these small beginnings, for the Lord rejoices to see the work begin, to see the plumb line in Zerubbabel's hand" (Zech. 4:10).

- Realize that God has chosen and anointed you for this hour and for they mission. Cast off the grasshopper mentality. "We seemed like grasshoppers in our own eyes, and we looked the same to them" (Num. 13:33).
- Refuse to cater to the fear of man. Even the most well-meaning person who is more motivated by fear and caution will give you the worst advice.
- Move in faith. Do something to move forward, and God will keep meeting you at every step.
- Lay down your reputation. In a time where people are trying to maintain their territory and image, God is calling to lay it down for the Kingdom. If you are trying to keep everyone liking you and agreeing with you, you will likely not move out in faith.
- Let the Holy Spirit guide and lead you, not the news, cultural opinions, or man-made agendas.
- Stop looking for approval from the old wineskin and be the new wineskin!

PERSONAL REVIVAL & RE-BRANDING

God is pouring out His spirit upon *you* in an unusual way right now. Let me ask you, do you feel the internal shaking and deep heart-work right now? God is preparing you to be a move of God. This is your personal revival. It's the awakening and recalibration of the Church back to the feet of Jesus and the commissioning of harvesters for the harvest. It will disrupt your life because it is meant to. You can't sit on the couch and watch this one on God-tv. God is removing your ability to sit when you are called to stand, and there is an invitation to you to be on the frontlines again.

Let me pray for you.

"Baptism of fire, come and shake every person reading this to their bones. Ruin them for the ordinary and give them a distaste for the mediocre and apathetic. Put a rumble in their bellies they didn't have before and a fire that can't be extinguished, in Jesus' name!"

ITS TIME FOR HARVEST!

True reformation is unto harvest. Through these movements, we are about to see the greatest days of soul winning we have ever seen.

In past moves, revival has been in specific locations that people have flocked to, and I still believe we will see more of that, but like a river spreads and breaks off into smaller rivers, then into creeks and streams, so this rushing river is going to spread and manifest in the earth. The reason I keep say "moves" instead of "move" is because this outpouring of the Spirit of God contains many, many moves of God. It includes many, many revivals, expressions, and flavors of the Kingdom of Heaven that we are about to see. These moves of God are about to show up in the most unlikely places and in the most unusual ways. There are cities that are ripe and ready but have been overlooked or not stewarded well, but God has been repositioning and relocating people to move into Kingdom governmental roles to better steward these moves in their region.

These will be unlikely moves because the places God moves will be in places many in the Body of Christ have overlooked or underestimated. They have said, "That place is a place of sin," and yet God had not forsaken it. They have said, "God could never move there or change and transform that," yet this is the hour He is shining His light even brighter in the darkness.

This is a multidenominational, multi-stream move of the Spirit of God; in fact, there are denominations and streams that are about to experience a move of God so powerful and profound that initially people will be skeptical because of their theological beliefs, and yet the expression will be very real. This is the Joel 2:28 outpouring that comes for all and reveals itself in unique and unusual ways. Was the upper room "usual" and "normal"?

I hear the Lord saying, "Oh, it is time! It is time for those carrying *reformational*, radical, out-of-the-box movements to *bring them into the earth*! Do not hold back. Do not retreat right now. As you birth, it will start a chain reaction that will cause many others to birth. That's right. It will usher in an anointing that will *lift the lids off* those who have been stuck, caged, and contained. You can't keep looking around you and trying to measure and compare what your baby is because *you will not find anything like it*! But I have given it to you for a reason! Man will never approve it. Religion will not validate it, but *I do*, and I have given you permission to *open the door* and author it into this time of history. It will be a catalyst for revival and a container for harvest!" I prophesy, "*It is time*," over those carrying unusual and out-of-the-box movements!

Wild ones, welcome to the frontlines!

PROPHETIC SURVIVAL TIP

Step out with your movement and watch God multiply it. Let your gift take you before kings and your anointing before giants that need to be slayed.

CAMPFIRE PRAYER

Set me on fire, Lord, and let me burn for You all the days of my life, in Jesus' name!

About Nate Johnston

Nate Johnston is a prophetic voice and worshiper who has a heart to see sons and daughters unleashed into passionate friendship with God and an effective supernatural lifestyle. Through his ministry school "Everyday Revivalists," he leads people from the basics of the gospel to being sent and released into their mission field, as well as championing and raising up emerging prophetic voices around the world. His burning cry and desire is to see the body of Christ become a beacon for the lost by raising up a generation that walk in the love and power of God, representing Him well. Nate and his wife Christy have three daughters, Charlotte, Sophie, and Ava, and live in Redding, California.